PIETIST AND WESLEYAN STUDIES
Editors: David Bundy and J. Steven O'Malley

This monograph series will publish volumes in two areas of scholarly research: Pietism and Methodism (broadly understood). The focus will be Pietism, its history and development, and the influence of this socio-religious tradition in modern culture, especially within the Wesleyan religious traditions.

Consideration will be given to scholarly works on classical and neo-Pietism, on English and American Methodism, as well as on the social and ecclesiastical institutions shaped by Pietism (e.g., Evangelicals, United Brethren, and the Pietist traditions among the Lutherans, Reformed, and Anabaptists). Works focusing on leaders within the Pietist and Wesleyan traditions will also be included in the series, as well as occasional translations and/or editions of Pietist texts. It is anticipated that the monographs will emphasize theological developments, but with close attention to the interaction of Pietism with other cultural forces and to the sociocultural identity of the Pietist and Wesleyan movements.

16. Floyd T. Cunningham, *Holiness Abroad: Nazarene Missions in Asia.* 2003.

THE PRESENCE OF GOD IN THE CHRISTIAN LIFE:

John Wesley and the Means of Grace

by

Henry H. Knight III

Pietist and Wesleyan Studies, No. 3

The Scarecrow Press, Inc.
Lanham, Maryland • Toronto • Oxford

This book is based on the author's Ph.D. dissertation, "The Presence of God in the Christian Life: A Contemporary Understanding of John Wesley's Means of Grace," Emory University, 1987.

SCARECROW PRESS, INC.

Published in the United States of America
by Scarecrow Press, Inc.
A wholly owned subsidiary of
The Rowman & Littlefield Publishing Group, Inc.
4501 Forbes Boulevard, Suite 200, Lanham, Maryland 20706
www.scarecrowpress.com

PO Box 317
Oxford
OX2 9RU, UK

British Library Cataloguing-in-Publication data available

Library of Congress Cataloging-in-Publication Data

Knight, Henry H., 1948–
    The presence of God in the Christian life : John
Wesley and the means of grace / by Henry H. Knight
III : introduction by Don E. Saliers.
        p.   cm. — (Pietist and Wesleyan studies ; no. 3)
    Revision of thesis (Ph.D.)—Emory University,
Atlanta, 1987.
    Includes bibliographical references and index.
    ISBN 0-8108-2589-9 (alk. paper)
    1. Grace (Theology).   2. Grace (Theology)—
History of doctrines—18th century.   3. Wesley,
John, 1703—1791.   I. Title.   II. Series.
BT761.2.K58   1992
234'.092—dc20   92-33900

To Eloise

Contents

Editors' Foreword

John Wesley has been a mentor for thousands of clergy and scholars. However, scholarly analysis of Wesley as a theologian has lagged, partly because his thought escaped and superseded the traditional easy categories of theological reflection. For that reason, Wesley could be accused in his own time of holding two mutually exclusive "heresies" of "enthusiasm" and "formalism." In this volume, Henry (Hal) Hawthorn Knight III demonstrates that Wesley refused to be limited by "oppositional" thinking and worked to synthesize presumed opposites. The means of grace—keeping the commandments, prayer, the eucharist, fasting, fellowship, rules of holy living, visiting the sick, and so forth—have generally been treated as isolated phenomena by scholars of Wesley's thought. This examination of the means of grace studies for the first time the function of each of the individual graces in the larger context of the Christian life, the life of love, demonstrating their interconnectedness.

It is a goal of the Pietist and Wesleyan Studies series to contribute to the project of revision of traditional modes of reading Wesley by exploring the relations between Wesley and Wesleyan spirituality and the theological and ministerial structures of the Wesleyan tradition. *The Presence of God in the Christian Life: John Wesley and the Means of Grace* will help shape that discussion.

Following undergraduate studies at Emory University (B.A. 1970), Knight served as a First Lieutenant in the U.S. Air Force (1971–1975). He returned to the Candler School of Theology at Emory University, where he received the M.Div. (1977). The M.Div. thesis compared the hermeneu-

tics of Wolfhart Pannenberg and Hans W. Frei. During and
after his seminary education, Knight pastored three United
Methodist Churches (1975–1981). He returned again to
Emory University, where he enrolled in the Graduate School.
This volume is a significantly revised form of the dissertation
presented for the Ph.D. degree (1987). Knight, the author of
numerous scholarly articles and reviews, is now adjunct
lecturer at Candler School of Theology in Wesleyan theology.

We are pleased to publish his study as the third volume of
Pietist and Wesleyan Studies.

David Bundy
Associate Professor of
  Church History
Librarian
Christian Theological
  Seminary
Indianapolis, IN

J. Steven O'Malley
Professor of Church
  History and Historical
  Theology
Asbury Theological
  Seminary
Wilmore, KY

Preface

My serious study of John Wesley began after I graduated from seminary, while serving as the pastor of a local church. It was there I first realized Wesley—although clearly a man of the eighteenth century—spoke directly to issues which face the church today. The problems addressed in this study are no exception: formalism and enthusiasm, despair and presumption are all very much with us, and continue to foster competing spiritualities. Certain means of grace are still championed at the expense of others. As in Wesley's day, the Christian life suffers accordingly.

What was so attractive about Wesley was his refusal to engage in oppositional thinking. He could make theological distinctions and was not hesitant to take a stand on those issues he deemed important. But where others saw only mutually exclusive options, Wesley found mutual interdependence. Reason and experience, catholic and evangelical, word and sacrament, personal and communal, evangelism and social action, faith and works—all were seen by Wesley as intrinsically related in becoming and living as a Christian. He did not, as some might think, simply assert a unity of opposites; rather, he characteristically questioned the presuppositions upon which their supposed conflict was based and offered an alternative account of their necessary interrelation in the Christian life.

This book is a result of that interest in Wesley. Although in it I analyze Wesley's thought and practice in terms of his own context, I also seek to present a contemporary understanding of the means of grace. Certainly Wesley himself never directly described the interdependence of the means of grace as I do. Yet this pattern of interrelationship is not only consistent with all that Wesley does say, it makes intelligible the inner logic of the practices he advocated for the people called Methodists.

This book is a revision of my Ph.D. dissertation submitted to the Department of Theological Studies of Emory University. It has been said that writing a dissertation is a lonely process. But at the end, I have come to realize how many people have given their assistance. I am grateful for the many conversations concerning my dissertation I have had with my student colleagues in the graduate program. These include Craig Gallaway, Bob Cornelison, Steve Rhodes, Chuck Twombly, and most especially, Curt Lindquist, who helped me so much in clarifying my approach to the topic.

I am immensely grateful for my teachers at Emory and for their generous assistance. Richard Bondi read early drafts of several chapters and offered helpful suggestions. Roberta C. Bondi, who read the final draft, helped me to reflect on the relation of grace and discipline in the Christian life. Walt Lowe not only read the manuscript, but prepared the way by directing my M.Div. thesis. Through his guidance over the years, I have grown in my skills of theological reflection, analysis, and argumentation. Rex Matthews and Ted Runyon carefully made their way through two drafts of the dissertation. Their many suggestions enabled me to strengthen its argument considerably. Don Saliers directed the dissertation with patience and grace. His own work on the religious affections, liturgy, and religious language have had a significant impact on this reading of Wesley. In our many discussions he has always been concerned to assist me in presenting my own position, and he has consistently mixed helpful advice with kindness and encouragement.

It was Rex Matthews who first encouraged me to think of the dissertation as a potential book, and I am grateful for his editorial advice. Series editors David Bundy and Steven O'Malley read the manuscript with care and offered many helpful suggestions; they also answered my many questions concerning the publishing process with patience and kindness.

I thank Abingdon Press for permission to quote from the new critical edition of *The Works of John Wesley* (Frank Baker, General Editor). Portions of chapter six were previously published in *Worship* and are gratefully used with permission. Finally, I am thankful beyond measure for the love and support of my wife, Eloise. She not only typed the manuscript, but has without hesitation made whatever sacrifices necessary for me to attend graduate school. Her encouragement has been constant throughout. It is to her I dedicate this book.

Henry H. Knight III

Introduction

John Wesley continues to be a lively yet elusive figure on the theological scene today. There can be little doubt that his life and work, along with that of his brother, Charles, is enjoying a renaissance. The question continues to be asked: what is John Wesley's contribution to contemporary theology? This book by Hal Knight provides an answer—one which illuminates the shape of Wesley's thought and is remarkably relevant to a range of questions facing those who yearn to hold catholicity and evangelical faith together.

Everyone knows that the Wesleys were accused of two opposite "heresies" in the context of eighteenth-century Anglicanism: they were called *enthusiasts* and *formalists*. Ironically, as Knight helps us see, these were in fact two of the very central problems John Wesley sets out to address. Wesley is immensely attractive to our present religious situation precisely because he refused to engage in "oppositional thinking." That is, Wesley did not wish to engage in a polemic of mutually exclusive theological oppositions. He was, as readers of this volume will note, capable of a range of subtle doctrinal and practical distinctions. But such theological reasoning supported a mutual reciprocity and interdependence between such seemingly polar categories as catholic and evangelical, experience and reason, personal and social holiness, faith and works of mercy. Above all, as Knight's work reveals, Wesley saw the necessity of understanding the deeper assumptions and presuppositions underlying the apparent conflicts between the forms and disciplines of the Christian life and the vitality of Christian experience.

By carefully tracing Wesley's characteristic way of reading

such oppositions in Christian life and thought, Knight enables us to see a powerful pattern of interdependence of the means of grace, whether instituted by Christ or as prudential means. Wesley's various ways of construing such means of grace turn out to be exceedingly important strategies aimed against the misunderstandings of the Gospel. He did not shy away from the tensions inherent in living the Christian life in community; but, in fact, uses these permanent tensions in order to show how integrity of life and authenticity of faith is made possible. He is, therefore, not a systematic theologian, but a "systemic" theologian. By this we know that he thinks consistently and coherently about the issues, both systemic and constitutive, of the Christian life itself. Thus Knight elucidates the "logic" of Wesley by virtue of learning to think with him *about* challenges and misunderstandings arising from the practice of Christianity. He emerges not as one who must systematize in propositions the truth of God's grace in Christ Jesus, but as one who is our guide to the intelligibility and mystery of grace at the intersection of life and thought.

More concretely, however, this book sheds light on the depth of Wesley's own sacramental theology—again, not as a systematized whole, but as a coherent vision of the grace of God which reflects both the identity and the modes of presence of God. In showing how the Christian life itself is a dynamic and processive movement in and through the forms and the disciplines of the means of grace, a doctrine of God emerges. By interpreting how the means of grace actually function in the real life of the Christian and the community of faith, Knight claims that Wesley's distinctively relational view of God and humanity is made accessible to future theological reflection. The means of grace are neither subjective nor metaphysically objective, but relational, remaining both the source and the true object of the religious affections. The same means of grace thus nurture faith by countering human sins of immediacy, but at the same time, they nurture faith through focusing attention on God. In and through the formed affections we learn who God is and come to receive the grace of God's presence. In this way Knight contributes at one and the same time to Wesleyan studies and to the current theological work on the relationships between doctrines and experience, and between the divine life and human praxis.

Don E. Saliers
Emory University

Chapter I

The Means of Grace

1. THE CHRISTIAN LIFE IN CONTEXT

Unquestionably, John Wesley's central concern was the Christian life. The story of Wesley's own life is to a great extent the story of his own frustrations and joys in seeking to live a Christian life. His evangelistic ministry was a passionate affirmation that this new life was offered to all; his pastoral ministry involved the patient nurture and direction of those who sought to grow in this life. Certainly no treatment of Wesley's theology can long avoid an examination of the soteriology which lies at its heart.

This acknowledged concern of Wesley has in our day received mixed reviews. The contemporary awareness that human lives are much the products of their social context makes Wesley seem too individualistic. The modern sensitivity to the social and psychological roots of human suffering makes Wesley seem superficial. And our present appreciation of the role of unconscious motives in our lives makes Wesley's talk of Christian perfection seem hopelessly naive, if not dangerously presumptuous.

These are real concerns. As a person and a Christian, Wesley himself can be defended from such criticisms, especially in their extreme form. But what of his theology and praxis? Can a soteriology which makes Christian perfection the goal be said to have taken these concerns seriously? Does Wesley offer something for our day, or have major elements of his theology been superseded by more recent developments?

We cannot properly evaluate Wesley's understanding of the Christian life—and his call to Christian perfection—if we examine it outside the liturgical, communal, and devotional contexts within which Wesley himself understood it. The common tendency to describe Wesley's "order of salvation" for the individual in abstraction from these contexts is fundamentally misleading, for it does not show concretely how Wesley believed growth in the Christian life actually occurred. Wesley was not offering a vision of the Christian life which could be reasonably sought in any church and under any conditions, but one which could be sought within the structures and discipline of the Methodist movement in the Church of England.

The term for these contexts is the means of grace. By "means of grace" Wesley meant much more than the two Protestant sacraments. As we shall see, the means of grace include a wide range of activities associated with public worship, personal devotion, and Christian community and discipleship. I shall argue that the means of grace form an interrelated context within which the Christian life is lived and through which relationships with God and one's neighbor are maintained.

These relationships constitute the Christian life for Wesley, and it is God's grace which enables and invites our participation in them. Means of grace are means through which persons experience and respond to the loving presence of God.

2. THE MEANS OF GRACE: WESLEY'S TYPOLOGIES

To understand more fully those occasions or practices considered by Wesley to be means of grace, we begin by examining the three typologies he uses to organize them. While each makes important distinctions, none shows the interrelationship of the means of grace in terms of their function in furthering growth in the Christian life. One of the goals of this study is to offer a functional typology of the means of grace, a typology which is broadly described in the section to follow.

The first of Wesley's typologies distinguishes between "general" and "particular" means of grace. The general means denote certain attitudes and practices which pervade the Christian life: keeping the commandments, self-denial, and taking up our cross daily. The particular means are more specific acts of worship and discipline: prayer, fasting, the Lord's Supper, searching the scriptures.[1]

The second typology distinguishes between instituted (or ordinary) and prudential means of grace. The instituted are those which are appointed by God as means of grace, and include those listed as particular means of grace above. The instituted means belong to the universal church in all eras of history and in all cultures. In contrast, the prudential means of grace vary from age to age, culture to culture, and person to person; they reflect God's ability to use any means in addition to those instituted in accordance with different times and circumstances. The prudential means of grace include a number of specific occasions and practices not mentioned in the first typology, such as classes, bands, and love feasts; they also include those practices listed as general means of grace.[2]

A complete list of Wesley's means of grace will conclude this section. Following Borgen,[3] I have combined the two typologies into a single typology with three categories: general (as in the first typology), instituted or particular, and prudential (as in the second typology, but omitting those included under the general means of grace).

In addition to these first two typologies, Wesley makes a third distinction based on the object of the human activity in the means of grace. The first category are works of piety, which are directed to God; these are the "ordinances of Christ" and are thus identical to the instituted means of grace. The second category, works of mercy, occur when "we are called to relieve the distress of our neighbor, whether in body or soul,"[4] and are related to certain prudential means of grace. Yet works of mercy are more than *means* of grace; they are acts of love, which is the *end* of religion. Therefore, "when they interfere with each other," Wesley prefers "acts of mercy before matters of positive institution; yea, before all ceremonial institutions whatever," as the means must be suspended if they clash with love as their end.[5]

One should not conclude from this that Wesley valued love of neighbor more than love for God. For him, we cannot love our neighbor unless we first love God, and we can only love God when we have been transformed by God's love for us. Acts of piety serve as means to express our love for God even as they are means through which God's love changes our lives.

Wesley's concern is to prohibit pious activities from becoming means of avoiding love when they should be means through which God enables and evokes love. His argument parallels that of the prophets, who warned against resting in ritual while people were suffering from injustice. For Wesley, to fail to love one's neighbor indicates a deficiency in our love for God, and therefore that we have not been recreated by God's love for us.

To view our love for God as in competition with our love for our neighbor is to misunderstand God's love for us. The intent of God's love is the transformation of the world into the image of God, so that all its relationships are characterized by love. Acts of mercy are both means to and signs of that transformation.

This illustrates a pervasive feature of Wesley's thought: love must be *active;* it is something which is done. There can be no "inward" love without a corresponding change in one's active relationship with God and neighbor.

All means of grace have as their end the life of love, the Christian life. The diversity of those occasions and practices seen by Wesley as furthering the Christian life is shown by the following list:

I. GENERAL MEANS OF GRACE[6]
  1. Universal obedience.
  2. Keeping all the commandments.
  3. Watching.
  4. Denying ourselves.
  5. Taking up our cross daily.
  6. Exercise of the presence of God.

II. INSTITUTED (PARTICULAR) MEANS OF GRACE[7]
  1. Prayer: private, family, public; consisting of deprecation, petition, intercession, and thanksgiving; extemporaneous and written.[8]
  2. Searching the scriptures by reading, meditating, hearing; attending the ministry of the word, either read or expounded.
  3. The Lord's Supper.
  4. Fasting, or abstinence.
  5. Christian conference, which includes both the fellowship of believers and rightly ordered conversations which minister grace to hearers.

III. PRUDENTIAL MEANS OF GRACE[9]
  1. Particular rules or acts of holy living.
  2. Class and band meetings.
  3. Prayer meetings, covenant services, watch night services, love feasts.
  4. Visiting the sick.
  5. Doing all the good one can, doing no harm.
  6. Reading devotional classics and all edifying literature.

3. THE STRUCTURE AND METHOD OF THIS STUDY

John Wesley sought to describe the content of and means to the Christian life. He never intended anything other than a recovery and restatement of the Christian life according to scripture and tradition: the "character of a Methodist" was nothing more nor less than the character of a Christian.[10] His goal was to uncover and give contemporary expression to those disciplines and practices which provide a context for the Christian life to begin and grow.

The task of this study is to discover the inner logic of Wesley's pattern of means of grace. Theologically, this logic is best seen by examining beliefs and practices which Wesley rejects—those that in some way endanger growth in the Christian life. More positively, this inner logic is reflected in the practices and discipline which Wesley advocates, that is, in the means of grace themselves.

The chapters are organized accordingly. Chapters II and III examine Wesley's understanding of grace and means of grace in light of his conflict with alternative positions. This is followed in Chapters IV through VI by a study of the means of grace themselves in order to see their mutual interdependence in forming the Christian life over time.

This order can be misleading. Wesley did not develop a theology which he then applied; *he participated in a range of practices which became both the source and object of his theological reflection.* It is because of this that his theology offers clues to the inner logic of practice: that which occasioned reflection was that which endangered the Christian life through deficient practice. At the same time, his own positive understanding of the means of grace developed through reflection upon the practice of Christians. Those practices which were beneficial to Christian growth he retained; those which were not he dropped or opposed. He thus defends and explicates what he took to be essential in belief and practice against those beliefs and practices which undermine the Christian life.

Unless this style of theological reflection is recognized, interpretations of Wesley can themselves reflect misunderstandings which Wesley wished to avoid. Dealing with problems one at a time, Wesley usually responded to an opponent by asserting only those theological and practical aspects of the inner logic which that opponent was ignoring. The unfortunate tendency of both Wesley's contemporaries and later interpreters has been to focus on some debates while giving less attention to others, thereby failing to take a comprehensive view of Wesley's position.

I shall attempt to avoid one-sidedness by arranging the discussion around pairs of misunderstandings. Chapter II places Wesley between the Scylla of formalism and the Charybdis of enthusiasm; Chapter III shows him navigating between the dangers of antinomianism and perfectionism. In opposing each of these misunderstandings, Wesley was forced to break with persons or institutions for which he had respect and affection. These disputes were painful for Wesley, yet necessitated by his overriding concern for the Christian life.

In each of these two chapters, the first section not only introduces Wesley's understanding of either new birth or perfect love, it also begins a discussion of one of the misunderstandings which is carried forward into the second section. The third section then considers the opposite misunderstanding. This structure within these chapters does not reflect a disproportionate concern on Wesley's part to oppose one danger more strongly than another. Rather it results in part from the first section containing material which can be assumed by the third, and in part by the historical circumstances and longevity of particular disputes. The first two sections of each chapter deal with an initial position which Wesley rejects; the third with those who drew extreme and incorrect inferences from this initial rejection.

This way of organizing the content of the chapters actually gives special significance to the third sections. Here we find Wesley not simply attempting to find a middle way between two extremes, but critically examining the common assumptions which underlie both positions. Wesley's own position is thus not a compromise but a fresh conceptual approach.

This study, then, is divided into two parts: Chapters II through III and IV through VI. Chapter II examines the *means* to the Christian life, contrasting Wesley's understanding of grace and the means of grace with formalism and enthusiasm. Chapter III is concerned with the *end* toward which the

Christian life is moving, comparing Wesley's position with
antinomianism and perfectionism.

Because Chapter II is concerned with the means to the
Christian life, the dangers of formalism and enthusiasm
discussed in that chapter form the basis for both a functional
typology and the organization of Chapters IV and V. Chapter
IV discusses those means of grace which counteract formalism; Chapter V those which avoid enthusiasm. The means of
grace described in both chapters each also work against the
second pair of misunderstandings (antinomianism and
perfectionism), though in different ways.

Put positively, Chapter IV is concerned with means of
grace which open us to the *presence* of God, and Chapter V
with those which enable us to experience the *identity* of God.
Together, the means of grace form a pattern which invites us
to relate to a God who is both descriptively distinct and a
living presence. At the same time, each of these chapters
describes how the means of grace encourage both an optimism of grace and a realistic recognition of sin, both an
assurance of salvation and a holy discontent with our lives as
they are.

Chapter VI concludes with a consideration of the Christian
life as lived over time in the context of the means of grace. It
shows how this reading of Wesley can assist our understanding of his seemingly confusing view of baptism. More importantly, it offers criteria to evaluate the role of means of grace
in assisting growth in the Christian life in our contemporary
situation.

4. THE PRESENCE AND IDENTITY OF GOD

It will be helpful at the outset to preview the argument of
this study. It consists of two interrelated claims. The first is
that grace, for Wesley, is *relational:* grace both enables and
invites us to participate in an ongoing personal relationship
with God. The second is that there is a *pattern* of means of

grace which is essential to the maintenance and growth of that relationship.[11]

To describe grace as relational is already to place Wesley over against certain other conceptions of grace. Because a relationship involves the presence of an other, this view of grace resists locating the saving activity of God merely in some "objective" or abstract past or future event. Certainly the past activity of God (e.g. the death and resurrection of Jesus) and future activity (e.g. the coming kingdom) may be foundational to the relationship, and certainly the present relationship is in continuity with past and future divine activity. Wesley insists, however, that salvation is a present experience, a new way of life which is lived in an ongoing relationship with the living God. It is not simply a formal action of God for us in the past, but is most centrally a present action of God in us and with us.

Grace for Wesley is most essentially God's triune act of love which has as its goal the renewal of human lives. The foundational act of grace is the atonement of the Son for us; present acts of grace are the work of the Holy Spirit in us. The content of grace is the love of God, which was manifested in Jesus Christ, is presently exhibited through word and sacrament, and is presently applied by the Spirit to each human life.

Wesley saw grace not as irresistible but as involving free mutual response. It is true that Wesley also has a "causal" view of grace, a recognition of the transforming power of God at work in new birth, in Christian perfection, and (preveniently) in conscience. But these instances of God's transforming power are always placed within the larger context of an ongoing personal relationship with God in community. The grace of God *enables* and *invites*, but does not force; for the goal of grace *is* the relationship and the transformation of human life within the relationship. The transforming power of God acts preveniently on all persons, so that a relationship is possible, and then later in new birth and Christian perfection, to those who within that relationship are seeking these changes and are gradually being changed in the process of seeking.

Wesley's opposition to irresistible grace rests on his different vision of the Christian life. For him the Christian life is constituted by a relationship with God; hence grace is not only the means to that life, but the Christian life is itself *essentially graced.* This is because the heart of the Christian life is our love for God and our neighbor in response to God's love for us. God's grace in Jesus Christ is the supreme expression of God's love for us, enabling and inviting a loving response.

Put differently, our love, which constitutes the Christian life, is not a possession apart from God but a temper or affection which is intrinsically relational. We cannot be loving apart from an ongoing relationship with God, and we cannot grow in love apart from a deepening of that relationship over time. We cannot have a Christian life apart from grace and the means of grace, apart from God and the community of faith.

This relational understanding of grace enabled Wesley to transcend the common grace versus works controversies of his day. The formalists in the Anglican church, recognizing the need for human responsibility, stressed human "religious" activity. In the process they lost a sense of God's own initiative and activity through locating grace in church and sacrament. Enthusiasts, such as the Moravians at Fetter Lane, wanted to maintain a lively sense of the activity of God, but sought to do so by encouraging human passivity. In both cases a perceived conflict between human and divine activity diminished the ability to talk of a mutual, ongoing relationship.

Wesley envisioned a free and dynamic relationship with God in which divine activity enabled and invited human activity, and human participation was essential if the relationship was to grow and deepen. God was faithful yet free, in that God bestowed certain promised blessings (such as the new birth) in God's own time. The human was free to be faithful, able to truly respond in love because the response was not forced.

A relationship necessarily involves the *presence* of an other who has a distinctive *identity*. I shall argue that it is the necessity of experiencing the presence and identity of God in a relationship with God that implicitly underlies Wesley's insistence on the patterning of the means of grace.

The presence of an other is not sufficient in itself for there to be a relationship, for the other must be perceived, sensed, or experienced as present. Our lack of perception cannot alter the presence of an other, but it can prevent a mutual relationship between us and the other.

This is the problem of the Anglican formalist. The God who is present becomes identified with the means of grace and the institutional church. Although grace is described as mediated through the church, this mediation implies an indirect relationship with a distant God. Grace is received somewhat mechanically and automatically, and our relationship is not with God but with the institution entrusted by God to mediate grace. The idea of experiencing the presence of God is threatening to the formalist because, given the formalist understanding of mediation, it implies a direct relationship with God that bypasses the church and opens the door to religious fanaticism.

To Wesley the formalist was "dissipated": so attentive to and divided by the things of this world that he or she was unable to sense the presence of God. He agreed that grace was mediated, but for Wesley this meant presence or nearness, not absence or distance. Potentially, the means of grace were means to a relationship with God. The problem raised by his controversy with formalism was how to maintain a living faith, an ongoing sense of God's presence in the midst of a life that tempts us to "forget" God.

The experience of presence is not enough, however; a relationship requires that we know *who* it is that is present. In a relationship not just anyone is present, but a distinctive person who has a distinctive character and history. It is not enough to be attentive to God; we must come to know the identity of the God who is present.

Moravian enthusiasm—which took the form of quietism—
missed this essential point. Concerned with confusing human
activity with the divine, some Moravians substituted a passive
waiting on God for active participation in the means of grace.
Fearing the formalist error of substituting the means of grace
for the presence of God, they in turn confused God's activity
with having certain experiences or feelings. Specific instances
of felt experience, seen as signs of God's presence, became
substitutes for an encounter with God who has a distinctive
character and who remains distinct from our own experience.

Wesley insisted on active use of the means of grace, not
because he could not conceive of unmediated presence, but
because such an experience was neither normative nor recog-
nizable apart from the experience of mediated presence in the
means of grace. The problem raised by his controversy with
enthusiasm was how to experience the particular character and
history of God which enables us to know God as God is.

Neither the Anglican formalist nor the Moravian enthusiast
could provide a means to the Christian life as envisioned by
Wesley, because both had minimal expectations for the
Christian life. The formalist provided certain institutional
assurances that one would go to heaven, while the enthusiast
sought experiential assurances. Neither saw the Christian life
as involving change over time within an ongoing relationship
with God, or as a continual growth in love. Like them, Wesley
was concerned with assurance—but as a means to this larger
vision of the Christian life, not as an end in itself.

Wesley approached the issue of presence and identity
through his understanding of the means of grace. The
presence of God can only be perceived by faith, and faith is
both received and maintained in a community whose participants were encouraged and enabled to see themselves and the
world before God. The identity of God can only be known by
faith through participation in those means of grace which
convey identity, such as scripture and the eucharist. In the
process Wesley offers fresh insight into the mutual interrelat-
edness of the presence and identity of God.

While the means of grace cannot be categorized exclusively in terms of presence and identity, a functional typology can be made according to which element in the relationship particular means emphasize. Because of their differing emphases, the means of grace are mutually interdependent, and together form a necessary pattern of activity for the Christian life. An impoverished participation in this pattern of means of grace risks the separation of presence and identity, and thus diminishes the relationship with God.

The means of grace which encourage openness to the presence of God include Christian community, works of mercy, extemporaneous prayer, fasting, and the general means of grace. These involve practices which enable and encourage us to be attentive to God's presence.

Some practices increase our sensitivity to God's presence through the experience and practice of love in the Christian community and in service to the world. These practices counteract despair or complacency in the Christian life by moving us outward from ourselves and placing us in loving relationships with God, other Christians, and the world.

Other practices work against barriers to God's presence. Fasting, repentance, and mutual sharing of perspectives counteract self-deceptive and presumptive attitudes toward God. They move us critically inward, and enable us to love with humility.

In encouraging attentiveness to the presence of God, these means of grace provide a context for the recognition of the identity of God. The practice of love enables us to know the identity of the God who is love. The practice of mutual sharing and confession provides a critical evaluation of our preconceived notions of who God is.

The means of grace which encourage the experience of the identity of God include scripture, preaching, the eucharist, and the prayers of the tradition. These describe the character and activity of God. They give content to our experience of God and thereby make such experiences distinctive; they provide descriptions of the God who is the object of our affections.

They counteract a presumptive knowledge of God by enabling us to *remember* (experience anew) what God has done, and therefore who God is. This in turn gives us insight into our own condition before God, who we are in light of divine salvific activity.

They counteract despair and complacency in the Christian life by presenting us anew with God's *promise* of new creation, what God will do and therefore who God is. This in turn shows us who we are to be in light of the divine promise.

The interaction of remembrance and promise in these means of grace provides a context for the experience of the presence of God. The present activity of God and the life of the Christian community is placed within the larger perspective of God's past and future activity. It is this which enables the community to be both realistic and hopeful at the same time. This larger context provides the stories and descriptive imagery which evoke and form our affections, and which give us patterns to imitate in the practices of the community.

To "experience the identity of God" may itself sound presumptive unless it is remembered that to know God truly is not to know God exhaustively. The use of this expression points on the one hand to the necessity to "know" (experience) God through faith and not just "know" (cognitively) information about God. On the other hand it underscores Wesley's reliance on the trustworthiness of scripture and the eucharist in their depiction of the character and activity of God. Thus while we grow in the knowledge and love of God, we nonetheless remain confident that the character of the God we increasingly come to know is the same one revealed to us in Jesus Christ.

Those who share Wesley's vision of the Christian life need at the same time to insist on a complete pattern of means of grace. To use the means of grace which encourage the experience of God's identity without those which encourage attentiveness to God's presence invites formalism; to do the reverse invites enthusiasm. To use only the negative, critical practices or to remember only God's past activity can lead to despair or complacency in the Christian life; to use only the positive practices or to remember only God's promises can lead to presumption and self-deception. The Wesleyan pattern of means of grace is essential because it avoids the tendencies toward malformation of the Christian life found in a partial pattern.

Because the Christian life is constituted by a relationship with God, there is never a point in the Christian life when the means of grace are no longer necessary. The Christian grows in love through a continuing and deepening of the relationship. Christian affections cannot remain Christian apart from God as their object; the Christian life cannot reach a point of perfection where further growth is impossible. The means of grace provide the context within which an ongoing relationship with God is sustained over time, and the Christian life is correspondingly enabled to grow in love.

Chapter II

The Means to the Christian Life

1. THE RELIGION OF THE HEART

It could well be argued that John Wesley's final break with the Anglican establishment occurred on August 24, 1744, upon his preaching the sermon "Scriptural Christianity" to the University community of Oxford. In the explosive "plain practical application" with which he concludes the sermon, Wesley asks

> Where, I pray, do the Christians live? Which is the country, the inhabitants whereof are "all (thus) filled with the Holy Ghost"? . . . Who one and all have the love of God filling their hearts, and constraining them to love their neighbor as themselves? . . . Why, then, let us confess we have never yet seen a Christian country upon the earth.[1]

Wesley goes on to deny that Oxford is a Christian city,[2] and to claim that the "general character" of the faculty was not described by the "fruits of the Spirit," but all too often by pride, haughtiness, impatience, sloth, and other vices.[3] The students were "a generation of triflers; triflers with God, with one another, and with" their "own souls."[4] Of the life Wesley describes as truly scriptural, he tells the faculty, "Let it not be said that I speak here as if all under your care were intended to be clergymen. Not so; I only speak as if they were all intended to be Christians."[5] It was probably a surprise to no one, least of all to Wesley, that the Vice-Chancellor sent for his sermon

16

notes, and that it was arranged in the future for other clergy to preach to the University when Wesley's turn came around.[6] As we shall see, Wesley later qualified the starkness of his distinction between true and false Christians. But even so, his radical concern for true religion over against a nominal Christianity remained the focus of his controversy with the Anglican leadership, and the primary motive for his rebellion against the authority of the institutional church. Wesley insisted on a vision of the Christian life which sharply conflicted with that picture of a good Christian held by most Anglican leaders in the eighteenth century. These different descriptions of the Christian life necessarily involved different understandings of what was necessary for one to become and remain a Christian.

In this section I will first examine, primarily from Wesley's point of view, this disagreement over the content of the Christian life. Then, I will contrast the understandings of faith which serve as the foundation of these two pictures of Christianity. Here some of Wesley's distinctive emphases will become apparent. In section two, I will examine what is necessary for the means of grace to be means of transformation in human lives.

Wesley offered his own description of what was commonly considered to be the characteristics of a religious person:

> . . . by a religious man is commonly meant, one that is honest, just and fair in his dealings; that is constantly at church and sacrament; and that gives much alms, or (as it is usually termed) does much good.[7]

Indeed, to many being a Christian consisted in having faith, defined as an assent to certain propositions concerning Christ, plus repentance, which was obedience to the teachings of Jesus. This minimal belief and minimal morality were enhanced by the performance of certain religious duties, which were assumed to provide the believer with the grace of God, and thus were means of grace.

Wesley accepted neither this description of the Christian life nor the corresponding assumption concerning the means of grace. Religion, he argued, "does not consist . . . in any ritual observances; nor, indeed, in any outward thing whatever;" "neither does religion consist in orthodoxy, or right opinions" which belong to the understanding.[8] Even when such a person had in addition to the above qualities "a real design to serve God, a hearty desire to do his will . . . a sincere view of pleasing God in all things," that person is nonetheless an "almost Christian" rather than an "altogether Christian,"[9] that is, one who has "the form of godliness, but not the power."[10]

Wesley is "grieved at the sight" of "on every side, either men of no religion at all, or men of a lifeless, formal religion."[11] He would "greatly rejoice" in convincing some

> that there is a better religion to be attained, a religion worthy of God that gave it. And this we conceived to be no other than love: the love of God and of all mankind; the loving of God with all our heart and soul and strength, as having first loved *us,* as the fountain of all the good we have received, and of all we ever hope to enjoy; and the loving every soul which God hath made, every man on earth, as our own soul.[12]

"Wherever this is," Wesley continues, "virtue and happiness" go "hand in hand." There is found "humbleness of mind, gentleness, long-suffering, the whole image of God," along with peace and joy. This religion has "its seat, in the heart, in the inmost soul" but ever shows itself "by its fruits, continually springing forth," not only in doing no harm but in "spreading virtue and happiness all around."[13]

Several features of this picture of true religion should be noted. First, the Christian life is most fundamentally lived as a response to God's love for us. To know God truly is to experience that love.

Second, our love for God and our neighbor are core affections, emotions, or tempers which govern the Christian life. True religion consists in having certain affections which are both capacities (enabling us to love) and dispositions (inclining us to love). This is what Wesley means in saying Christianity is "inward" rather than "outward," and of the "heart" rather than the "understanding." He rejects the description of Christians as remaining sinners, though forgiven and reconciled, and as doing good works out of obedience in spite of the sinful hearts which remain. Rather, Wesley saw the Christian life as the result of a transformation of the heart, wherein these affections grow over time and sin correspondingly declines.

Third, these affections are relational, in that they constitute relationships with God and our neighbors, and are themselves maintained, formed, and shaped by these objects. Wesley never talks of love in general, but always of love of God, of neighbor and, in both appropriate and inappropriate forms, of the love of self and the world. This means the religion of the heart is not "inward" in the sense of being unrelated, but is only found in and maintained by ongoing relationships of love to those outside the self. Christian affections are either social or nonexistent.

Fourth, Wesley equates this love, along with its attendant affections, with holiness. To be a loving person is to be holy as God is holy. And, Wesley consistently links holiness with happiness, described as peace and joy in the Holy Spirit. Indeed, he interprets each of the Biblical phrases "Kingdom of God" and "Kingdom of heaven" as describing holiness and happiness jointly, for holiness and happiness are the present experience of the rule of God in the heart and the life of heaven "(in a degree) . . . opened in the soul."[14] Holiness always implies happiness because to have this love is to recover our humanity as God created it to be.

Wesley thus sees salvation and the Christian life as a present realization and anticipation of eschatological promise.

> By salvation I mean, not barely (according to the vulgar notion) deliverance from hell, or going to heaven; but a

present deliverance from sin, a restoration of the soul to its primitive health, its original purity; a recovery of the divine nature; the renewal of our souls after the image of God, in righteousness and true holiness, in justice, mercy, and truth. This implies all holy and heavenly tempers. . . .[15]

If this is true Christianity, then how does one attain it? It is clear from the foregoing that human religious activity is insufficient. Wesley argues that salvation is by faith, and that faith is a free "gift of God."

No man is able to work it in himself. . . It requires no less power thus to quicken a dead soul, than to raise a body that lies in the grave. It is a new creation; and none can create a soul anew, but he who at first created the heavens and the earth.[16]

Faith enables the Christian life to begin because it enables the true knowledge of God upon which that life rests and to which it is a response.

Without faith we cannot be thus saved; For we can't rightly serve God unless we love him. And we can't love him unless we know him; neither can we know God unless by faith. Therefore salvation by faith is only . . . the love of God by the knowledge of God, or the recovery of the image of God, by a true spiritual acquaintance with him.[17]

Faith likewise enables true self-knowledge, where one knows oneself to be "foolish, vicious, miserable," and longs to be "truly wise, virtuous, and happy." This it enables through "restoring the due relations between God and man."[18]

The nature of this knowledge is made clearer by contrasting it with other ways of knowing. Wesley is not primarily concerned with the question of God's existence.

The whole creation speaks that there is a God. But that is not the point in question. I know there is a God. Thus far is clear. But who will show me what that God is?[19]

Wesley thus distinguishes between knowing that there is a God and knowing the nature or character of God. To acknowledge God's being is not to be acquainted with God, no more than to know there is a Chinese Emperor is to know the Emperor.[20]
But Wesley makes a further distinction. Faith is more than a rational assent to certain doctrines or propositions, and to define faith as this alone is to make a serious error. Even the devils know information about God, even they believe the scriptures and the creeds in this sense. Faith includes an assent to divine revelation but goes far beyond it.[21]
The knowledge of God enabled by faith is the experiencing of God as one who loves and forgives. This is the core of faith for Wesley, and he has several ways of expressing it. Faith is "a divine evidence or conviction" that God was in Christ, reconciling the world, and, in particular

> the Son of God hath loved me, and given himself for me; and that I, even I, am now reconciled to God by the blood of the cross.[22]

"It is by this faith," Wesley says, "that we 'receive Christ' . . . in all his office as our Prophet, Priest, and King." And, based on this divine evidence and conviction, faith is also a sure trust and confidence in Christ, a reliance on Christ.[23]
Wesley underlines the distinction between faith as pure assent and faith as conviction and trust by pointing out its dispositional and relational nature.

> . . . it is faith in Christ—Christ, and God through Christ, are the proper object of it. . . . it is not barely a speculative, rational thing, a cold, lifeless assent, a train of ideas in the head; but also a disposition of the heart.[24]

Like love, faith is relational; to have faith is to be in a living, interacting relationship with God. This living faith is sharply distinguished from a "cold, lifeless" rational assent apart from the religion of the heart.

Alongside these descriptions of faith Wesley uses another, faith as "the evidence of things not seen" (Hebrews 11:1), and as a "spiritual sense."[25] The latter is a metaphor for faith analogous to the natural senses in eighteenth century Lockean empiricist epistemology. Contrary to theories of innate ideas, this empiricism held that reality was immediately accessible to us through our senses. Reality was thus experienced prior to being an object of rational consideration. This means experience for Wesley was not purely "subjective" but that which connected us to objective reality. (Wesley's lack of a strong subject/object dualism has been noted earlier in our discussion of affections as "inward" dispositions constituted in large measure by their "outward" objects.)

As there is a visible, physical world accessible to us through our natural senses, so too is there an "invisible world" which is nonetheless real though consisting of "things not seen." Faith is the gift by God of a spiritual sense whereby the things of God can be discerned and experienced.

Extending the metaphor, Wesley describes faith as the "eye of the new born soul" through which the invisible God is seen, the "ear of the soul" which hears the voice of Christ, the "palate of the soul" which tastes the powers of the world to come, and the "feeling of the soul" which perceives the presence of God and most especially feels "the love of God shed abroad" in the heart.[26] Faith enables God's love to be more than something read or heard; through faith God's love is experienced as a present reality. Faith as a spiritual sense thus cooperates with the five senses in such a way that the reality of God is experienced when scripture is read, the word proclaimed, and the eucharist celebrated.

The reason, then, so many are not "altogether Christians" was that they lacked this faith through which they could experience that reality for which their natural senses were by themselves inadequate. Their relationship was with doctrines or forms, not with the living God.

In contrast with Wesley, many of his Anglican opponents made a sharp distinction between reason and experience, or emotion. Reasonable religion was calm and dispassionate; emotional religion was prone to excess, self-deception, or fanaticism. Against the background of the religious turmoil of the 16th and 17th centuries, they feared an increase of emotionalism which would undermine the authority of the church and invite individualism and sectarianism among the uneducated classes. The term "enthusiasm," popularized by John Locke, had become a commonly and loosely used designation for any person or movement that seemed "emotional." The centrality of religious experience for Wesley, combined with his refusal to abide by parish prohibitions against his preaching, his preaching in the open air, and his use of irregular, unordained preachers, made him an ideal candidate for the enthusiast label.[27]

But Wesley had a great respect for reason, and was, as his opponents soon learned, a skilled logician. He never intended to supplant the traditional Anglican authorities of scripture, tradition and reason, but only to add experience as a fourth source of authority. Nevertheless, with respect to reason, Wesley did give experience a certain priority. Assuming experience does place us in contact with objective reality, he argued it is only through experience that one has data for reason to analyze, for "your *reasoning justly* . . . presupposes *true judgements* already formed whereupon to ground your argumentation."[28] That is, one's experience involves judgement concerning reality in advance of rational arguments.

If Wesley is right, then it would seem we cannot avoid enthusiasm. But Wesley denied the commonly assumed connection between experience, emotions, and enthusiasm. Wesley defines enthusiasm as "a sort of religious madness" whereby a person has "a *false imagination* of being inspired by God."[29] or imputes to God or expects from God those things which ought not be imputed or expected.[30] By this definition Wesley not only includes those who claim extraordinary gifts or experiences, but also those who imagine themselves to be Christians while lacking the requisite faith and love, i.e., his Anglican opponents.[31] For Wesley, an enthusiast is not

someone who has religious emotions, but rather one who
lacks certain emotions or tempers appropriate to the Christian
life while possessing inappropriate emotions. This issue is not
emotions versus reason, but which emotions are providing the
basis for rational argumentation.

When accused of enthusiasm, Wesley characteristically
defends himself in terms of the kind of emotions he is
advocating. To the distinction of the Rev. Mr. Church
between doing what God commands and obeying "sensible
impulses, or feelings" Wesley contends that by rejecting
"inward feelings *toto genere*" Church rejects the love of God
and neighbor, joy, peace, and all other fruit of the Spirit.
Since the point of salvation is to have a new life characterized
by such fruit, Church has rejected "the whole gospel of Jesus
Christ" and accused Wesley "with enthusiasm for asserting
the power as well as the form of godliness."[32]

In another essay Wesley clarifies his definition of "inward
feelings." The phrase means "being inwardly conscious of"
the graces which the Holy Spirit operates in oneself, that is, of
the fruit of the Spirit; it does not mean being conscious of the
manner by which the Spirit operates.[33]

And in writing to Quakers, Wesley denies that the Spirit
leads "by *blind impulse* only," by "*moving* you to do it, you
know not why." Rather the Spirit "*shows* us the way wherein
we should go, as well as *incites* us to walk therein." If one is
hungry, the Spirit convinces us that it is God's will to relieve
the hunger, and fills us with love toward the one who
hungers.[34] The Spirit thus leads by conviction and love.

In his controversy with formalism, then, Wesley insists on
the present activity of the Holy Spirit and the centrality of
emotions as the fruit of the Spirit. At the same time as he
rejects an anti-emotional rationalism, he also opposes a
reliance on individualistic impulses or transient feeling states.

We have yet to consider the conditions for receiving this
gift of faith and why the means of grace were so often means
of self-deception. However, we must first consider Wesley's
modification of this sharp dichotomy between "almost" and

"altogether" Christians. This discussion will set the stage for an examination of the other issues.

The modification occurs by way of a distinction between "the faith of a servant" and "the faith of a child."[35] Lying behind this distinction is Wesley's important theology of prevenient grace. This we shall examine first, for it is the larger context within which justification and new birth occur, and will clarify Wesley's descriptions of faith.

As is well known, Wesley held to a Reformation doctrine of original sin (which was strongly supported by his observation of human nature)[36], but rejected the predestinarian tendencies which usually accompanied it. Wesley's stark view of the consequences of the Fall was more than balanced by his belief in God's present power to overcome sin. More particularly, he defined the sin that could be overcome as intentional actions and thoughts, while acknowledging the ongoing problem of involuntary transgressions which violated the will of God and needed forgiveness.[37]

Wesley's alternative to predestination was universal prevenient grace. Seen from this perspective, salvation begins not with new birth but with prevenient (or preventing) grace,

> including the first wish to please God, the first dawn of light concerning his will, and the first slight transient conviction of having sinned against him. All these imply some tendency toward life; some degree of salvation, the beginning of a deliverance from a blind, unfeeling heart, quite insensible of God and the things of God.[38]

Prevenient grace is not given only to an "elect" portion of humanity, or even only to those who hear the gospel. Rather, it is a gift of God to all persons, making it possible for all to seek God in spite of the effects of original sin.

Prevenient grace is manifested in human life in the form of conscience.

> No man living is entirely destitute of what is vulgarly called 'natural conscience'. But this is not natural; it is

> more properly termed 'preventing grace'. . . . *Every one*
> has sooner or later good desires, although the generality
> of men stifle them before they can strike deep root or
> produce any considerable fruit. . . . So that no man sins
> because he has not grace, but because he does not use
> the grace which he hath.[39]

No person, then, is in a "state of mere nature, . . . wholly void
of the grace of God."[40] And to obey one's conscience, to yield
to the desire for God and the good, invites an increase of
grace.[41] Thus the person who acts on the inclination of
conscience is already in a relationship with God. Within
limits, that person can increase in the knowledge of God (in
the sense of God's will as right and wrong) and in self-
knowledge (in the sense that one falls short of the expectations of one's conscience).

It would seem that the movement from the "first slight
transient conviction" to the new birth would be a gradual one,
a synergism in which grace is both prior and enabling. And
indeed, this is the case, except that this teleology culminates
in an "instantaneous" experience of new birth. The faith we
have described which begins the Christian life remains for
Wesley a transformation of the heart, both a culmination of a
process and a qualitative change. He leaves no doubt that a
sharp distinction remains when he describes a person prior to
the new birth:

> . . . he is not *sensible* of God. He does not *feel,* he has no
> inward consciousness of His presence. . . . Nor is he
> sensible of any of the things of God; they make no
> impression on his soul. . . . It is true he may have some
> faint dawnings of life, some small beginning of spiritual
> motion; but as yet he has not spiritual senses capable of
> discerning spiritual objects. . . .[42]

Thus these are not "anonymous Christians" (Karl Rahner), for
without faith they cannot truly know God and live the
Christian life. Yet they are not wholly without God or God's
grace.

This combination of teleology and "crisis" language is a highly significant feature of Wesley's theology, which makes it appealing and problematic at the same time. We have already seen how Wesley (admittedly pre-Kantian, but certainly post-Cartesian) lacks a subject/object dualism in his understanding of experience and affections. Now we can see in the interplay of "crisis" language an attempt to avoid an exclusivistic supernatural/natural dualism while nonetheless retaining the distinction in the face of the reductionism explicit in deism and implicit in formalism and rationalism. Wesley is opposed to those who would *de facto* collapse the supernatural into creation, reason, or the means of grace; he is equally opposed (to anticipate section 3) to those who place the natural and supernatural in *de facto* opposition.

Of course, this has been the struggle of the entire Christian tradition: immanence without reductionism or pantheism, transcendence without Docetism or Deism. For our purposes, the focus is on God's presence and activity in the Christian life through means of grace, and whether Wesley offers a distinctive and helpful approach to the problem.

In discussing new birth, Wesley locates the problem not in a sharp distinction between natural and supernatural realities, but in the lack of faith due to the Fall.

> Hence he has scarce any knowledge of the invisible world, as he has scarce any intercourse with it. Not that it is afar off. No; he is in the midst of it: it encompasses him round about. . . . It is above, and beneath, and on every side. Only the natural man discerneth it not; partly, because he has no spiritual senses, whereby alone we can discern the things of God; partly, because so thick a veil is interposed as he knows not how to penetrate.[43]

And, we might add, God's presence is manifested inwardly, in what many have called "natural" conscience.

Prevenient grace is the clue to the whole, for there Wesley clearly sees the supernatural mediated through the natural.

Yet he does so without losing the sense of God's agency, and of our intercourse or relationship with a living God. That intercourse remains hidden in prevenient grace, in the form of obeying the moral direction of conscience; after faith and new birth, it is open as a response to the God who loves us. In all this, there is for Wesley one reality which includes God, heaven and creation; it is only the effects of the Fall which makes the natural seem so real and the supernatural so unreal and distant. At the same time, all three are distinct, and the free agency of both God and humanity are preserved. Faith restores the conscious relationship between God and humanity within this reality.

We began this investigation of prevenient grace with the distinction between the "faith of a servant" and the "faith of a child." If the difference between prevenient grace and new birth is a conscious relationship with God, then the "faith of a servant" represents a position between the two. It is more than belief in those truths which God has revealed, although it presupposes this. The faith of a servant "is such a divine conviction of God, and the things of God, as, even its infant state, enables every one that possesses it to 'fear God and work righteousness' "; such persons are, "at that very moment, in a state of acceptance" by God. Yet they lack the "faith of a child" through which God's love, forgiveness, and acceptance is experienced, such that they are born anew and live a new life of love. That is, they have not yet begun to love God and their neighbor with their heart, but are acting out of fear and duty. They are not truly holy or happy, but they do have a form of faith acceptable to God.[44]

These are, in fact, indistinguishable from the "almost Christians" Wesley earlier described, provided that the "almost Christians" have a true sense of repentance (self-knowledge) before God, from which good works come as fruit. In his later, mature thought, the "almost Christians" are not as far from the kingdom as they seemed when Wesley preached at Oxford; nor was Wesley as far from it prior to 1738 as he had once supposed. The transformation indicated by the language of "new birth" and a "new order of senses" remains, but it is placed securely within a gradual process of God's gracious activity and humanity's faithful response.

2. AGAINST FORMALISM: THE FAITH THAT WORKS BY LOVE

It would seem from the foregoing that Wesley, by emphasizing the religion of the heart, would correspondingly de-emphasize the means of grace. Indeed, some of his opponents accused him of that, contrasting the "sudden agonies, roarings, screamings," etc. on the part of some hearers of Wesley's sermons (especially in the early years of the revival) with "a due and regular attendance on the public offices of religion, paid by good men in a serious and composed way," wondering if the latter "does not better answer the true ends of devotion, and is not a better evidence of the co-operation of the Holy Spirit. . . ."[1]

Here again, in another form, is the presumed conflict between reason and experience, composure and emotion. And again, Wesley challenges the premises. He first argues that the "roarings" and "screamings" were taken out of their several contexts and strung together, giving not only a false picture of the tenor of his preaching but completely ignoring that to which they were a response.[2] The question is not whether such responses occurred, but whether they were appropriate to their object (such as sudden self-knowledge that one stands as a sinner before God).

Wesley insists extreme feeling-states or behavior (which are not the kind of dispositional emotions he means by fruit of the Spirit) cannot be used as evidence either for or against a particular response being a work of the Holy Spirit.[3] To set composure against excessive emotion was to entirely miss the point.

Then, Wesley goes on to deny that a "regular attendance on the public offices of religion," which include holy communion, necessarily serves "the true ends of devotion," or the love of God and humanity. Wesley notes that he had faithfully attended them for many years while having "no more of the love of God than a stone." While public worship sometimes enables growth in love, "sometimes it does not."[4]

Nor is this an evidence of the co-operation of the Holy Spirit. Many are under the delusion that "this *opus operatum* would bring them to heaven" because "they confounded the means with the end."[5] "Nine times in ten" says Wesley, when he asks a dishonest tradesman if he is a Christian, the tradesman replies "As good a Christian as yourself! Go to heaven? Yes, sure! *For I keep my church* as well as any man."[6]

What is true of the eucharist is true of other central means of grace. Thus, Wesley asks, isn't prayer, whether public or private, often performed as "a thing of course, running round and round in the same dull track, without either the knowledge or love of God? Without one heavenly temper, either attained or improved?"[7] Likewise scripture: without faith, the oracles of God "are a mere dead letter."[8] And as for baptism,

> Lean no more on the staff of that broken reed, that ye *were* born again in baptism. Who denies that ye were then made 'children of God, and heirs of the kingdom of heaven'? But notwithstanding this, ye are now children of the devil; therefore ye must be born again.[9]

In this debate we see two fundamentally different understandings of grace and means of grace. Formalism presupposes an institution created by God to provide forgiveness for sins and dispense divine favor. Grace is conceived mechanistically; the activity of the Holy Spirit is automatic, inextricably tied to the means of grace.

Wesley understands the Holy Spirit to act in gracious freedom, drawing persons into an ongoing, recreative relationship with God and neighbor. Grace is relational and personal, not mechanistic and institutional; means of grace do not in effect possess the Holy Spirit, but are means used by the Spirit. This freedom of the Spirit is not arbitrary; it is directed to the fulfilling of the divine promise of new life. And new life cannot be received or maintained apart from a relationship with the God who gives it. We will miss the point of Wesley's polemic against formalism if we only look at the means of grace. The assumption that the "serious and composed" use of the means of grace would in and of itself result in a Christian life was so prevalent and invited such self-deception that it was certainly a central issue. But we can better understand Wesley's concern through his examination of formalism among the Quakers, who had themselves rejected the means of grace as too formal.

Wesley begins by observing how the Quakers had disavowed "formal worship" for that which "springs from God in the heart," and that persons thus led by the Spirit use plainness of speech and plainness of dress. However, he finds that the Quakers have confused plainness of speech with *"one particular* way of speaking"; the point is not to say thou or thee, but to speak the truth.[10] In another context Wesley complains about the superficiality and repetitive style of those who are supposedly free of prayer books: "I myself find more life in the Church Prayers, than in any formal extemporary prayers of Dissenters."[11]

Among the Quakers Wesley also finds inconsistencies concerning dress. While avoiding gay and gaudy apparel, the younger generation of Quakers buy the most expensive plain apparel they can find.[12] The "sinfulness of *fine apparel* lies chiefly in the *expensiveness,"* says Wesley,

> . . . it is robbing God and the poor: it is defrauding the fatherless and the widow; it is wasting the food of the hungry, and withholding his raiment from the naked to consume it on our own lusts.[13]

What is at issue in both speech and dress is a way of life involving relationships with God and our neighbor. Formalism loses this relational quality; or rather assists in our

self-deception concerning the true nature of our relationships. The doing or the refraining from doing certain things
displaces the religion of love, and the means become mistaken
for the end itself.

Wesley seeks to make clear to the Quakers the difference
between worshipping God "in a formal way" and worshipping
"in spirit and in truth":

> The seeing and feeling and loving him is spiritual *life*.
> And whatever is said or done in the sight or love of God,
> that is full of spirit and life. All beside this is *form,* mere
> *dead form;* whether it be in our public addresses to God,
> or in our private; or in our worldly business, or in our
> daily conversation.[14]

Thus "formality in *common life*" can "have no place in anything
we say or do, but so far as we forget God."[15]

Relationships of love with God and our neighbor depend
on our experience of God's presence, our living and walking
in eternity. If the means of grace are used without that sense
they are dead formality, for they are not the means through
which we have a living relationship with God. We cannot
forget God and receive grace, for we cannot respond unless
we perceive that which elicits our response.

Forgetting God is discussed by Wesley under the name of
dissipation. The term was commonly used to describe a
person "violently attached to women, gaming, drinking; to
dances, balls, races" and to fox hunting. But Wesley uses the
term more broadly, in include "the serious fool who forgets
God by a close attention to any worldly employment";
indeed, "whoever is habitually inattentive to the presence and
will of his Creator, he is a 'dissipated' man."[16] It is "the art of
forgetting God."[17]

Wesley sees us as "encompassed on all sides with persons
and things that tend to draw us from our centre." Only those
who are "created anew in Christ Jesus" through "faith alone"
are "restored to the image of God" such that they can attend

to God.[18] Those prior to new birth, though subject to dissipation, can nonetheless respond to God in terms of conscience and with the "faith of a servant." Even those who have experienced new birth find in the self "the remains of that 'carnal mind', that natural tendency to rest in created good" which can draw one away from "simplicity towards Christ."[19] Insofar as "any one yields to this temptation" one is dissipated, although with the believer God's grace is sufficient to resist such temptations. But whatever occasions the dissipation, its content is the same: our thoughts, desires, and passions (emotions, tempers, affections) become "unhinged from God, their proper centre, and scattered to and fro among the poor, perishing, unsatisfying things of the world."[20]

Wesley equates dissipation with ungodliness,[21] that is, living as if there were no God. To live a dissipated life and trust in the means of grace is to have the illusion of salvation; it is at best to go through the motions of being a Christian while in reality remaining without God. A minimal piety and common moral respectability cannot stand up to the radical claims of the living God revealed in Jesus Christ.

The "radical cure of all dissipation" is the faith that works by love. Christians should continue in the faith they have received, setting God before them always, and live their lives in response to God's love.[22] Presumably, in accordance with Wesley's views on prevenient grace, one can abate dissipation by responding with whatever faith one has. But the "radical cure"—contrary to the opinion of that otherwise "excellent writer" William Law—is available only to those who "begin with repentance, the knowledge of themselves; of their sinfulness, guilt, and helplessness," and who then "seek peace with God, through our Lord Jesus Christ."[23]

This is why Wesley could deny the charge that he placed his preaching ahead of the "offices of the Church" or "set the one in opposition to the other." Rather, he insists that attending church did not answer the "true ends of devotion" for his hearers until they attended "the preaching of remission of sins through Jesus Christ," which is always "accompanied with the co-operation of the Holy Spirit." Because the preaching enabled the hearers to be more attentive to God, while at the same time to be aware of their own sin, guilt, and need for grace, they began to attend the offices of the church more often than before.[24] While Wesley believed that preaching and conversation are normally the means used by God to awaken persons to their need for forgiveness and new life,[25] he insisted other means may be used as well. Even the Lord's Supper could be a "converting ordinance."[26]

However this faith occurs, it is essential to overcome dissipation. Drawing upon Thomas à Kempis and Jeremy Taylor, Wesley gives further definition to the faith which works by love, equating it with simplicity in intention and purity in affection. Simplicity is to "always see God," purity is to love God.[27] This is the "exercise of the presence of God" recommended by "so many wise and good men";[28] it is also to be simple ("setting the Lord always before me") and recollected ("gathering in my scattered thoughts").[29]

The avoidance of formalism requires an attentiveness to God, a faithful response, and a sense of one's need for the grace which God offers. Formal religion involves forgetting God or inattention to God, a taking for granted the means of grace, or a satisfaction with oneself. What Wesley says concerning prayer applies to all the means of grace:

> It is not on this circumstance,—the being at set times or not, that the acceptableness of our prayers depends; but on the intention and tempers with which we pray. He that prays in faith, at whatsoever time, is heard.[30]

The faith which works by love, which is the religion of the heart, turns formal religion into living faith. The means of grace, instead of being substitutes for God, become means to encounter the living God, means through which a relationship with God is maintained and growth in the Christian life is nurtured. Wesley insists that the outward ordinances of God then profit much, when they advance inward holiness, but when they advance it not are unprofitable and void, are lighter than vanity; yea, that when they are used as it were *in the place* of this, they are an utter abomination to the Lord.[31]

Faith, whether of the servant or child, is a gift of God which enables us to sense God's presence and respond to God's initiatives. Without our continued response, the faith we have may be lost. The avoidance of formal religion depends not only upon our receiving faith, but upon its nurture.

It was here that the traditional means of grace of the Church of England were most vulnerable: people could come to them again and again without experiencing the presence of God. What was needed were other means of grace which would nurture faith through encouraging a receptive and expectant openness to God, and a faithful and loving response.

These Wesley provided within the Methodist movement. The small groups, with their attendant discipline, became centers for nurturing faith, enabling persons to experience the presence of God in the means of grace of the church. The intent of the movement was not to replace the church but to open persons to reality of God in the church.

That, at least, was Wesley's intent; not everyone agreed. Some reasoned this way: Granted that faith prevents the means of grace of the church from degenerating into formalism, can not the life of faith be realized apart from means of grace? In fact, do not the means of grace invite formalism by diverting persons from grace to their own actions, or from God to earthly forms?

Wesley's answer has been anticipated at some points. Formalism is in fact a much broader problem than simply a misunderstanding of the means of grace. There also is a danger in turning the necessary distinction between nature and supernature into a chasm. But given this, what do the means of grace of the church *contribute* to the Christian life that makes them so necessary? I will begin to answer this question in section 3.

3. AGAINST ENTHUSIASM: THE TRADITIONAL MEANS OF GRACE

Wesley's encounter with the Moravian Brethren, beginning on board a ship bound for the colony of Georgia and culminating in the remarkable year 1738, was the turning point in his life and ministry. It was in 1738, the year which included his Aldersgate experience, that salvation by faith as a gift of grace became the foundation upon which his theology of sanctification could rest. Given the significance of the Moravian influence, Wesley eagerly sought to continue his relationship with them. He traveled to Germany to visit the Moravian community at Herrnhut, as well as other centers of pietism, and in London joined with German and English Moravians to form the Fetter Lane Society.

It was not long, however, before Wesley's excitement with the living faith of the Moravians was tempered with disillusionment. They did not share Wesley's optimism of grace in the face of original sin, and they rejected sanctification understood as a process of growth. Thus, they were unconcerned with that which Wesley believed was the whole point of salvation. This issue I will examine in the following chapter.

Here I will look at the Moravian doctrine of "stillness" or quietism which was directly opposed to Wesley's active waiting on God's grace by way of using the means of grace. The controversy over the means of grace became so severe, and the stakes for the Christian life so high, that Wesley felt compelled to leave Fetter Lane and form a new society at the Foundery.

My inquiry will begin by delineating the different understandings of nature and grace and the Christian life which underlie this controversy. Then, a brief description will be given of the varieties of enthusiasm which Wesley attributes to the Moravians. Finally, I will ask what the means of grace themselves contribute to the Christian life which makes them so essential.

Wesley himself gives a clear outline of the issues separating him and the "stillness" faction at Fetter Lane, led by Phillip Henry Molther. Though lengthy, the following quote from Wesley's journal, originally written to Molther, nicely lays out the two positions:

> As to the way to faith, you believe,
> That the way to attain it is, to wait for Christ, and be still; that is
> Not to use (what we term) the means of grace;
> Not to go to church;
> Not to communicate;
> Not to fast;
> Not to use so much private prayer;
> Not read the Scripture;
> (Because you believe, these are not means of grace; that is, do not ordinarily convey God's grace to unbelievers; and
> That it is impossible for a man to use them without trusting in them;)
> Not to do temporal good;
> Nor to attempt doing spiritual good.
> (Because you believe, no fruit of the Spirit is given by those who have it not themselves;
> And, that those who have not faith are utterly blind, and therefore unable to guide other souls.)
> Whereas I believe,
> The way to attain it is, to wait for Christ and be still;
> In using all the means of grace.
> Therefore I believe it right, for him who knows he has not faith, (that is, that conquering faith,)
> To go to church;
> To fast;
> To use as much private prayer as he can, and
> To read the Scripture;
> (Because I believe, these are "means of grace;" that is, do ordinarily convey God's grace to unbelievers; and
> That it is possible for a man to use them, without trusting in them;)
> To do all the temporal good he can;
> And to endeavor after doing spiritual good.
> (Because I know, many fruits of the Spirit are given by those who have them not themselves;

> And that those who have not faith, or but in the lowest
> degree, may have more light from God, more wisdom
> for the guiding of other souls, than many that are strong
> in faith.)[1]

While the controversy centered on how one becomes a
Christian, the implications of it strongly affect the importance
of means of grace for the Christian life. The theological
preunderstandings which were brought to the conflict center
around four basic issues: (1) whether there are degrees of
faith, (2) the relation of immediate and mediated presence, (3)
the relation of Christ to means of grace, and (4) the role of
human activity in salvation.

(1) In a second lengthy passage just prior to that quoted
above, Wesley outlined the sharp disagreement over "degrees
of faith." According to Wesley, Molther asserts there is "no
justifying faith" prior to a new birth accompanied by a "full
assurance of faith." Those who testified to "the joy and love
attending" faith and yet lacked full assurance in actuality
lacked faith; their love and joy were "from animal spirits,
from nature or imagination," not from the Holy Spirit. For
Molther, then, faith is given fully and at once to those who
wait.

We have already seen how Wesley places the transformation of new birth within a more gradual process of change
beginning with prevenient grace and continuing as sanctification. He argues one "may have some degree" of faith without
full assurance, and that this is "a degree of justifying faith."
The source of the joy and love accompanying this is not
animal spirits, nature, or imagination, but God.[2] Faith may be
weak and yet be truly faith.[3] He had stressed faith as a gift of
God against Anglican formalism; now he stresses teleology
against his Moravian opponents.

The discussion of degrees of faith makes clear the sharp
distinction between nature and grace which underlies the
Moravian position. In a letter written to the Moravians in
Germany, Wesley accuses them of "mysticism" in that

you talk much, in a manner wholly unsupported by Scripture, against mixing nature with grace, against imagination, and concerning animal spirits, mimicking the power of the Holy Ghost. Hence your brethren zealously caution us against animal joy, against natural love of one another, and against selfish love of God; against which (or any of them) there is no one caution in all the bible.[4]

The effect of this nature/supernature discontinuity was to encourage doubt and despair among those who previously thought they had faith.[5] It was to shift the focus from the fruit of the Spirit as manifested in relation to God and neighbor to a passive waiting for a particular kind of experience. To Wesley, it meant that instead of persons growing in faith, they remained mired in doubt and prohibited from living a Christian life.

Wesley rejected this mutually exclusive understanding of nature and grace. While maintaining their distinctiveness, Wesley also maintained their interconnection. We have already seen this in the way prevenient grace is manifested as conscience and the "invisible world" encompasses the visible. It can also be seen in the way "heavenly" fruit of the Spirit takes on "earthly" ethical forms. The fruit of the Spirit are freely given by God through faith by way of our continual relationship with God, and their content or description is determined by the God who is their object (thus, love of God is quite different from love of mammon). Yet their very nature prohibits a withdrawal from the world; instead, they cannot but be manifested in our relationship both in the church and in the world itself.

(2) This distinct yet interconnected understanding of nature and grace is applied to the means of grace themselves. To return momentarily to Wesley's controversy with formalism, his Anglican opponents had taken exception to his claim of the "immediate inspiration" of the Holy Spirit. Not denying the charge, Wesley says he "cannot conceive how that

harmless word 'immediate' came to be such a bugbear in the world," and shows how he uses the word.

But all inspiration, though by means, is immediate. Suppose, for instance, you are employed in private prayer, and God pours his love into your heart. God then acts *immediately* on your soul; and the love of him which you then experience is as immediately breathed into you by the Holy Ghost as if you had lived seventeen hundred years ago. Change the term: say, God then *assists* you to love him? Well, and is not this immediate assistance? Say, His Spirit *concurs* with yours. You gain no ground. It is immediate concurrence, or none at all. God, a Spirit, acts upon your spirit.[6]

So to those who denied that God acted now as in the days of the Apostles, Wesley asserted the living presence and activity of God.

If those of a formalist tendency feared the word "immediate," the Moravians were unhappy with "mediation." Wesley's argument was the same to them as it was to the formalists: inspiration, though by means, is immediate; the means of grace are an occasion or locus for God's presence and invite interaction with God. Wesley's language of "seeing" and "feeling" God describes an experience which for him normally occurs by way of using the means of grace.

Wesley thus rejected certain commonplace associations of the words immediate and mediate. It was generally assumed that an immediate relationship was direct, and "inwardly" apprehended; the Moravians saw the directness as a check against self-deception, while the formalists saw the inwardness as an invitation to enthusiasm. Likewise, a mediated relationship was indirect and "outward," apprehended by senses and understood by reason, yet apart from the self. The formalists saw this as a check against enthusiasm, while the Moravians saw it as focusing on that which is not God, inviting formalism.

For Wesley, to be mediated through means of grace does not

mean that God is not immediately present. The means of grace directly relate us to God. The mistake is to separate the two terms, relating one to inward religion, the other to outward. The "outward" means of grace are means to "inward" religion, because they are the means whereby we receive and respond directly to God's grace; they are also the fruit of "inward" religion, manifested as both acts of piety and acts of mercy which relate us directly to God and our neighbor.

(3) The nature and grace issue also underlies the controversy over the relation of Christ to the means of grace. The Moravians insisted Christ is the only means of grace,[7] and the question was whether one trusted in Christ or in the means of grace. The Christian who has faith need not use them; the person without faith must not.[8] Some English Moravians advised persons that "you will never have faith till you leave running about to church and sacrament, and societies."[9] One woman told Wesley that, having "been hitherto taught of man," she was now "taught of God only," and "God told her not to partake of the Lord's Supper any more; since she fed upon Christ continually."[10]

To Wesley, the sharp distinction between Christ and the means of grace was "mere playing upon words," for Christ is a means of grace in a different way from prayer or the eucharist. The means of grace are channels "through which the grace of God is conveyed," while Christ is "the sole price and purchaser of it."[11] The power which works through the means of grace is the power of the Holy Spirit; the merit is that of the Son.[12]

Wesley agrees that it is a serious mistake to trust in the means of grace, but, against the Moravians, believes that one does not have to trust in them to use them. Rather, one may use them precisely because one's trust is in God. To use the means of grace in this manner is to look "for the blessing of God therein," to believe "that whatever God hath promised, he is faithful also to perform." Our trust is not in the means but in God's promise.[13] It is the category of promise which for Wesley dissolves the false dichotomy between Christ and the means of grace, while preserving divine sovereignty and initiative.

This desire to affirm Christ's presence without compromising divine freedom is characteristic of the Reformed sacramental theory of virtualism. By arguing that Christ is present in the Lord's Supper by virtue of the Holy Spirit, it "loosens" the automatic identity of the elements with Christ's presence while nonetheless insisting on Christ's efficacious presence in freedom. This perspective precludes confusing the elements with Christ, yet directs the participant to seek God's grace in the meal according to God's promise.

Virtualism corresponds to Wesley's description of grace as personal and relational: a personal God freely relates to humans, and enables their free response. Wesley extends this sacramental theory to all the means of grace, and deepens it through reconceiving the relationship between immediate and mediated presence.

(4) The Moravian understanding of nature and grace was also central to their distrust of human activity with regard to salvation. More specifically, they insisted the means of grace were works, and therefore inherently antithetical to faith.[14] Wesley was accused of "preaching up the works of the law" from which believers were not free.[15] We will examine the antinomian implications of this in the next chapter. Here we can note that Wesley saw Luther as the source of the Moravian error, "constantly coupling the Law with sin, death, hell, or the devil; and teaching, that Christ delivers us from them all alike." Wesley insists that Christ no more "delivers us from the Law of God, than . . . from holiness or from heaven."[16]

The concern to avoid works righteousness led the Moravians much further afield than Luther would have liked, for he would never have agreed to de-emphasize scripture or sacrament. Beyond this, Wesley charged the Moravians with undervaluing "good works . . . never publicly insisting on the necessity of them, nor declaring their weight and excellency." The Moravians only did good works if they were "moved" to do so.

> By this means you wholly avoid the taking up your cross,
> in order to do good; and also substitute an uncertain,
> precarious inward motion, in the place of the plain
> written word.[17]

Wesley argued that Christians are not free of the Law of
Christ, only the ordinances of Jewish law.[18] To use the means
of grace is not to expect salvation due to our own work, but
through the work of Christ who has promised to meet us in
the means of grace.

The Moravians apparently feared that to do anything other
than "be still" was to risk confusing our own nature with
grace, our own works with God's, to trust in ourselves instead
of Christ. If faith comes while we do nothing, then it must
have come from God.

To Wesley, this didn't remove nature from the picture, but
rather left one at the mercy of "precarious inward motion."
He refused to place "inward feeling" against scripture and
other means of grace. Wesley counseled activity, participation, interaction through the means of grace, to "neither
neglect nor rest in the means of grace";[19] indeed, one could
neither attain or remain perfected in love apart from using all
the means of grace.[20]

Here Wesley was re-affirming two traditions which he had
adopted as a participant in the Holy Club at Oxford. The
Anglican holy living tradition of Jeremy Taylor and William
Law had insisted the Christian life must be sought, that it was
a matter of the intention or will. The patristic ascetical
tradition saw the Christian life as involving spiritual discipline.
Wesley believed if one intended to live a Christian life, one
would freely undertake the discipline which nurtures that life.
For Methodists, that discipline involved participation in the
small groups, doing acts of mercy, and regularly using means
of grace in public worship and personal devotion.

In accepting Moravian arguments that faith was a gift of
God accompanied by an experience of assurance, Wesley did
not abandon these earlier beliefs. Rather, he saw that faith and

assurance could not be obtained as a result of dutifully living an outwardly Christian life, but were instead the foundation of the Christian life. Sanctification was not the means to justification, but a joyful response to the justification freely given by God. Furthermore, the intentional, disciplined life was also a normal precondition to experiencing forgiveness and new life, in that it placed persons with the faith of a servant into a continuing relationship with God.

Both the beginning and the continued growth of the Christian life depends on our reaction to divine activity. "The Spirit or breath of God" is received "into the new-born soul" and as

> it is continually received by faith, so it is continually rendered back by love, by prayer, and praise, and thanksgiving—love and praise and prayer being the breath of every soul which is truly born of God. And by this new kind of spiritual respiration, spiritual life is not only sustained but increased day by day. . . .[21]

In contrast to Moravian stillness, we may

> Infer the absolute necessity of this re-action of the soul . . . in order to the continuance of the divine life therein. For it plainly appears, God does not continue to act upon the soul unless the soul reacts upon God.[22]

Thus one should be "zealous of good works, of works of piety, as well as works of mercy,"[23] which are the means of grace.

Although it is clear Wesley did not understand means of grace as *opus operatum,* his frequent admonition to "use" them remains open to misunderstanding. For him, the means of grace were loci of divine activity and our reaction to that activity, of God's love and forgiveness and our love, praise, and gratitude. They are means of our worship even as they are means of God's grace. To fail to "use" the means of grace was to fail to maintain a continuing relationship with God, and thereby not progress in the Christian life.[24]

The Moravian position corresponds to the last two of the three varieties of enthusiasm described by Wesley in his sermon on that subject. The first variety, those who "imagine they have the grace which in truth they have not," Wesley applies to his formalist opponents[25]—the ones most likely to accuse Wesley of enthusiasm. The other two varieties, though descriptively distinct, are in practice closely related; Wesley encountered specific instances where they occurred together and reinforced one another.[26]

Wesley describes the second variety of enthusiasm as "those who imagine they have such gifts from God as they have not" or who "imagine themselves to be so influenced by the Spirit of God, as, in fact, they are not."[27] More particularly, these include all "who imagine that God dictates the very words they speak" so that "it is impossible they should speak anything amiss"; all "who imagine, they either do or shall receive 'particular directions' from God, not only in points of importance, but in things of no moment"; and all who expect "to be directed of God . . . in what is justly called an *extraordinary* manner," such as "by visions or dreams, by strong impressions or sudden impulses of the mind."[28]

His understanding of the freedom of the Holy Spirit leads Wesley to acknowledge that God may work in an extraordinary manner "in some very rare instances."[29] But he insists that a "sober Christian" inquires after the will of God by consulting scripture, which provides a general rule ("that we should be inwardly and outwardly holy") which reason and experience then applies to particular circumstances. It is through this process that we are assisted by the Spirit, though " 'tis not easy to say, in how many ways that assistance is conveyed."[30] But the Spirit does work through our use of scriptures, a means of grace.

Wesley further suggests that asking what is the will of God may be a misleading question; it would be better asked in each situation what will further one's own improvement or growth in grace, and what would make one most useful to God.[31]

Here Wesley moves from the potentially more abstract and arbitrary question of God's will to a more concrete and defined focus on our Christian character in our particular situation. The shift is away from seeking a particular direction from God and toward becoming the kind of persons who increasingly embody God's will; from transient feelings to "calm, standing tempers" which abide in the heart over time.[32]

The third variety of enthusiasm includes "those who think to attain the end without using the means, by the immediate power of God."[33] While a strong view of the freedom of the Spirit affirms that "God *can* give the end without any means at all," Wesley insists we "have no reason to think he *will*." Rather, we should "constantly and carefully use all these means which he has appointed to be the ordinary channels of his grace."[34]

If the religion of the heart is the antidote to formalism, then using the means of grace is the cure for enthusiasm. The failure of Methodists to use the means of grace was seen by Wesley as the cause of their enthusiastical tendencies. We "are not . . . more holy," he said, "because we are enthusiasts; looking for the end without using the means." Such means here included fixed times for private prayer and fasting;[35] elsewhere he notes the failure to search the scriptures (unnecessary, some thought, because they are now written on our hearts) or to attend preaching.[36]

In spite of Wesley's claim that God can act apart from any means, it is clear that he regarded the means of grace as not only normative but indispensable to the Christian life. But this does not exactly tell us why they are indispensable, and more specifically, why those particular activities, practices and disciplines singled out by Wesley as means of grace are indispensable.

Sometimes the means of grace sound arbitrary, as if their form or content contribute nothing to the work of the Holy Spirit. In opposing formalism Wesley will sharply distinguish between the form and the grace itself. "There is no *power* in this," he insists; in itself it is "a poor, dead, empty thing: separate from God, it is a dry leaf, a shadow."[37] But granted that bread and wine has no power apart from the Holy Spirit, that doesn't explain why the Holy Spirit chooses to work through bread and wine. Form without power is dead, but why does power work through certain forms and not others?

When we turn to Wesley's most positive statements concerning why we use the means of grace, we are disappointed. He characteristically gives two reasons for our using them. The first is Christ himself directs us to use these means of grace (here Wesley would include both the general and instituted means), and we must do so if we are to be obedient. The second (which would include the prudential means) is that we must use them if we are to receive their benefits.[38] Neither reason tells us what these means of grace themselves contribute to the Christian life.

We can, however, point to a partial answer implied in the discussion of enthusiasm. The problem at the heart of formalism was forgetting God, and the solution was the experience of God's love in an ongoing relationship. The parallel problem in enthusiasm is self-deception, an imagined experience or relationship which is not actually of or with God. The means of grace of the church—scripture, the Lord's supper, the prayer book—are the solution to this problem as they enable us to remember *who* God is and *what* God has promised. God's presence through them is "objective," in that it evokes affections and invites imagination while it resists the projections of our own imagination and desires on to it. Of course, the matter is more complex than this and the dangers more subtle, and this is the reason the means of grace form a mutually interacting pattern. The point here is that for Wesley, means of grace offer descriptive accounts of God's nature and work which counters enthusiasm, and at the same time invite a relationship with God which counters formalism. And, as formalism and enthusiasm can be seen to overlap, so

also are forgetting God and self-deception functions of one
another, and the activity of the Holy Spirit and the use of
means of grace mutually reinforcing.

To move beyond this to a more complete answer requires a
close examination of each means of grace and its role in the
Christian life, as well as the actual practices encouraged by
Wesley. That task is reserved for Chapters IV and V. But in
concluding this chapter, the direction such an answer will take
can already be seen.

When Wesley accused his Anglican opponents of enthusiasm while charging the Quakers with formalism, he was
attempting to break out of old dichotomies in order to present
the Christian life from a fresh perspective. Those who saw
religion as assent to certain doctrines, a minimal morality, or a
dutiful attendance of church and sacrament, had a Christianity
as imaginary as any enthusiast. Those who saw religion as
passive, as apart from all means of grace in order to be
"immediate," as purely inward feelings or impressions, had a
Christianity as dead and deceptive as any formalist.

Wesley saw in both of these misunderstandings a loss of the
living God, the God of scripture. Whether God is forgotten in
a dissipated life, supplanted by formalist activities, or confused with our own inward feelings or impulses, God becomes less distinctive and less real. The Christian life,
consisting as it does of affections which are related to their
objects, is not possible unless God is loved for who God
actually is. Thus the forgotten God must be remembered, the
living God distinguished from the imagined God, if there is to
be any true Christian life. The formalist whose life is
dissipated into the world and the enthusiast who confuses
God with themselves have no living relationship with God
because they no longer remember God.

The means of grace, if they contribute to the Christian life,
must therefore enable and encourage the presence and
growth of love through an ongoing relationship with God.
They will on one hand resist themselves becoming the object

of the relationship instead of God through them; on the other hand they will hinder the substitution of "precarious inward motion" for a true relationship with God. They will work against our forgetting God or confusing God with self; they will help us truly know who God is and, as a consequence, who we are before God and who God calls us to be.

Chapter III

The Ends of the Christian Life

1. THE HEART PERFECTED IN LOVE

When young George Whitefield entered Oxford in 1734, he was in search of a saving faith. As a result of his friendship there with John and Charles Wesley, Whitefield began preaching on the new birth, inaugurating the evangelical revival in London, Bristol, and elsewhere. When Whitefield went to serve as chaplain to the Georgia colony, his friends the Wesleys continued the revival.[1]

In America, Whitefield became accustomed to preaching in dissenting churches and in the open air. When he returned to England, he found Anglican pulpits increasingly closed to his message of new birth, and he initiated open air preaching in Bristol.[2]

However, Whitefield desired to return to America, and he urged John Wesley to lay aside his Anglican scruples against open air preaching and take charge of the revival in Bristol. United both by a common cause and a deep friendship, Whitefield and the two Wesleys deliberately muted the one point upon which they disagreed: the doctrine of predestination.[3]

After returning to America, Whitefield began to move away from that emphasis on sanctification which had been and would remain the central concern of the Wesleys. While himself warning against antinomian misunderstandings, he now stressed that Christ's own righteousness was imputed to believers.[4] This in itself was not strictly in disagreement with

John Wesley, but Whitefield's own struggle with indwelling sin had made him pessimistic about the holiness for which believers might hope. Thus he became increasingly uneasy with the reports he received of Wesley's preaching in England.[5] There, Wesley was integrating his strong concern for sanctification and Christian perfection as the goal of the Christian life with his newer understanding of justification by faith, assurance, and the new birth.

Such shifts in emphasis have major soteriological repercussions. By relying on the doctrines of predestination and perseverance for his assurance, Whitefield undercut the centrality of sanctification, for the hope of heaven now rested solely in *past* divine activity. An emphasis of the fruit of the Spirit as a result of one's election becomes essential if antinomianism is to be avoided; but it could also become a legalistic criterion of those anxious to determine if they are, in fact, among the elect.

For Wesley, Christian perfection was the holiness without which none shall see God. Thus, he tied sanctification as a *present* divine activity securely to the *future* hope for both heaven and eschaton. The past activity of God in Christ is seen as the necessary foundation and precondition for salvation in the present. Of course, there can be misunderstandings of this approach as well, but these will be the subject of the third section of this chapter.

Whitefield never did understand what Wesley meant by Christian perfection, because he never made the distinctions between human frailty, voluntary transgressions, and dispositions of the heart which characterized Wesley's theology. Thus, Whitefield accused Wesley of arguing for sinless perfection,[6] and suggested that his friend's own spiritual struggles were due to his failure to rest on God's predestinating love.[7]

Having dealt for fifteen months with the antinomian danger of the Moravian stillness doctrine, Wesley was now forced to confront those same implications in Calvinist orthodoxy, many of whose advocates were far more willing to allow for sin in believers than Whitefield.[8] With some reluctance, and not mentioning Whitefield by name, Wesley made the debate public by publishing "Free Grace: A Sermon Preached at Bristol" in 1739;[9] Whitefield published an open letter to Wesley in reply,[10] and a controversy with Calvinism began which would continue until Wesley's death.

While he and Whitefield remained cordial (Wesley preached at Whitefield's funeral), the predestinarian polemic against Wesley was malicious and bitter: not to preach predestination was to not preach the gospel at all, but a system of works righteousness. None seemed to grasp Wesley's concern for holiness and fear of antinomianism, nor his attempts to ground these concerns precisely on the grace which is available from Christ alone. This was due primarily to their very different understandings of divine grace.

We saw in the last chapter how Wesley rejected a sharp discontinuity of nature and grace, while at the same time opposing an identification of grace with nature. Here I will be examining much more centrally his understanding of how God is active in human lives in the present, and for what one may or may not hope in the present age.

The problem of God's gracious activity runs through the three interlocking issues which structure the first two sections of this chapter. The first concerns the meaning of the imputed righteousness of Christ. This doctrine was promoted, though for different reasons, by the Moravians, the Calvinists, and some within Wesley's own movement; it was pushed to antinomian extremes through asserting that believers should have no righteousness of their own. This will be the subject of section 1.

The second was the doctrine of predestination which lay behind the Calvinist version of imputed righteousness. In conjunction with this were the differing descriptions of God held by Wesley and his Calvinist opponents.

A third issue has to do with eschatology. Here we shall see how Wesley's emphasis on both eschatological promise and its present reality in sanctification constitutes a fundamentally different theological approach than that which relies on eternal decrees. These last two issues will be discussed in section 2.

In all these issues, Wesley struggled against static concepts of God in favor of more dynamic and interrelational descriptions of God's activity. While himself assuming much of the classical theistic picture of God, Wesley nonetheless challenged any claim concerning God which undercut the scriptural assertion that God is love, for it is only as a response to God's love that the Christian life is a present possibility.

These descriptions of God's character and activity enabled Wesley to offer a more optimistic view of the Christian life than did his opponents. The danger of antinomianism was that it led to despair and complacency: despair that one could actually grow in the Christian life, and therefore a complacent acceptance of the life of sin as normative for the Christian. Against this danger Wesley counseled hope in God's promise of new life, even unto perfection in love.

The doctrinal roads to antinomianism were many, but they had in common the pushing of doctrinal positions to their logical extreme. Perhaps the most unusual and ironic instance were those perfectionists in Wesley's own movement who advocated a static state of perfection as an instantaneous gift of God to those who would "only believe."[11]

As we have seen, the Moravians exaggerated Luther's antimony of law and gospel, often to the point of passivity and moral quietism; their voiding of the law with grace also voided ethical concern. Wesley, accused of preaching law instead of gospel, was alarmed by their refusal to help persons in need unless "moved" to do so by God, by their suspicion of using the means of grace, and by their insistence that the "old creature" remains in those born anew until death.[12]

The Calvinists opened the door to antinomianism through their doctrine of eternal decrees: God had done all, so we can do nothing. The corresponding Christology is remarkably like that of the Moravians: we are saved through Christ's righteousness, not our own, through faith and not works, and corruption remains in the heart until death. The emphasis is on that which has been done in the past, and not that which God is accomplishing now or which might be expected in the future. While the Calvinist insistence on the third use of the law restrained the antinomian tendencies of this position, many of the less careful Calvinists became "properly Antinomians; absolute, avowed enemies to the law of God"; they preached Christ "without one word of either holiness or good works."[13]

Such complacency about sin was, of course, Wesley's great concern:

> . . . what we are afraid of is this: lest any should use the phrase, 'The righteousness of Christ', or the righteousness of Christ is 'imputed to me', as a cover for his unrighteousness. We have known this done a thousand times. . . . And thus though a man be as far from the practice as from the tempers of a Christian, though he neither has the mind which was in Christ, nor in any respect walks as he walked, yet he has the armour of proof against all conviction, in what he calls 'the righteousness of Christ'.
>
> It is the seeing so many deplorable instances of this kind which makes us sparing in the use of these expressions.[14]

In spite of Wesley's repeated explanation of his "sparing" use of these expressions,[15] his opponents continued to see in this a capitulation to works righteousness. At times, Wesley would insist that he and they were arguing for the same thing but merely using different words, and would offer to set the controversy aside if the Calvinists would warn their followers against antinomian misunderstandings of imputed righteousness.[16] Yet the continued vehemence of the Calvinist polemic pushed Wesley to see what his opponents had sensed all along: at stake was not the use of favorite expressions but a basic understanding of God's relation to humanity.

Wesley's opponents had a Christology which was static,

fixed, rooted in the past; the salvific effects of the atonement were accomplished in their entirety on the cross. To speak of Christ taking away our sins was for them to speak of a past transaction which makes present human activity irrelevant for salvation, an occasion for misunderstanding this gracious gift, and therefore perhaps even detrimental to faith. True faith links the believer to the atonement such that Christ's own active obedience is imputed to the believer as if it were the believer's own obedience.

The present and future orientation of Wesley's thought is indicated in his rejection of this position, which he called an "absurdity." Christ "will not put an end" to original sin "before the end of the world." As for actual sin, "if I now feel anger at you in my heart, and it breaks out in reproachful words" it is ridiculous "to say Christ put an end to this sin before it began. . . ."[17] Did Christ "heal the wound before it was made, and put an end to our sins before they had a beginning"?[18] Thus Wesley would refuse to interpret Rev. 13:8 and I Pet. 1:20 as speaking of Christ's sacrifice before the foundation of the world, for this would conform the atonement to predestinarian assumptions.[19]

The more careful of Wesley's opponents sought to avoid antinomianism by acknowledging the necessity of the fruit of the Spirit as a manifestation not of the believer's inward affections but of the holiness of Christ. To Wesley it was a contradiction to deny that there are any holy affections in the believer while the believer nonetheless bears, "both inwardly and outwardly, the fruits of holiness," and it was an error to deny that a believer may grow in this holiness.[20]

Wesley's position was that "God *implants* righteousness in every one to whom he has *imputed* it." Those "to whom the righteousness of Christ is imputed are made righteous by the Spirit of Christ, are renewed in the image of God. . . ." The "righteousness of Christ is the whole and sole *foundation* of all our hope," and it "is by faith that the Holy Ghost enables us to build upon this foundation."[21]

In their controversy Wesley and his opponents have tied

two different understandings of the divine/human relationship to two different understandings of sin. The Calvinists tended to see sin as so inextricably intertwined with one's fallen humanity that any divine action against sin necessarily meant a lessening of human activity and a supplanting of it by the divine. The Holy Spirit represses human nature and then acts through the human. The human self is thus superseded by Christ, and the fruit of the Spirit are Christ's holiness, not ours. We are holy only through imputation.

Theodore Runyon has clearly seen the import of the Calvinist position, and the Lutheran as well. For both, our *essential* humanity, in order to avoid works righteousness, is located with God or Christ, in a "transcendent realm," rather than in this world. Our good works become separated from our personhood, and are totally attributed to the Spirit or to Christ. "When action is no longer understood as the expression of the person who acts," Runyon notes, "it becomes difficult to show how the person is accountable for deeds that are extrinsic to him or her."[22]

While holding to the doctrine of original sin, Wesley believed prevenient grace had restored the possibility of moral intentions and actions. Thus sin was to an extent separable from humanity as such, and humans were to an extent changeable. In any event, it made no sense to Wesley to argue that God could not transform persons nor, given scriptural promises, that God would not. Through the Spirit, Christ does not suppress or supersede our humanity, but restores it and enables it to grow in love. The righteousness of Christ is implanted in us, increasing by grace and through faith until we have the mind of Christ.

Thus, as Clarence Bence has observed, for Wesley the finite is, to a significant degree, capable of the infinite,[23] and sanctification is therefore "the life of God in the soul."[24] It is "dwelling in God and God in thee," our being an "inhabitant of eternity."[25] The power and presence of God is actively introduced in human existence.[26] And, as Outler notes, we are not possessed by grace as if by an irresistible force, but are indwelt and led by the Holy Spirit.[27] Wesley observes that in the new birth Christ

> did not take away your understanding, but enlightened and strengthened it. He did not destroy any of your affections; rather they were more vigorous than before. Least of all did he take away your liberty, your power of choosing good and evil; he did not *force* you; but being *assisted* by his grace you, like Mary, *chose* the better part.[28]

We do not, therefore, rest in the finished obedience of Christ, but Christ through the Spirit enables us to increasingly appropriate the promised salvation in the present.

Wesley's position is reflected in his reluctance to give Christ's active obedience a role in our justification. John Deschner has shown that, while Wesley stresses the inseparability of active and passive obedience in his more careful and conciliatory writings, in others the emphasis falls almost totally on the passive obedience, and in his polemical writings he denies that active obedience has a role in justification.[29] Again, his concern was antinomian despair and complacency:

> For if the very personal obedience of Christ . . . be mine the moment I believe, can anything be added thereto? Does my obeying God add any value to the perfect obedience of Christ? On this scheme, then, are not the holy and unholy on the very same footing?[30]

The only specific positive role for the active obedience of Christ seems limited to a teaching ministry which reinforces the law's authority.[31]

Deschner sees this underdevelopment of Christ's active obedience as part of a general problem in Wesley's theology wherein the law is partially separated from Christ and God's justice separated from God's mercy.[32] Whatever the merits of this observation, it leads Deschner to misunderstand what Wesley was attempting, and consequently to miss certain strengths in Wesley's approach. By examining Deschner's argument, we can more clearly see the value of Wesley's position in contrast.

Deschner recognizes that for Wesley Christ is the "norm of sanctification"[33] and that "Wesley wants to learn the content of holiness from Jesus Christ."[34] But he argues that Wesley violates his own characteristic path from the cross to holiness by partially abstracting the "content of holiness" from "the person and revelation of Christ, even though its origin may ultimately be in Him, and His is the power which affects it." For Deschner, Wesley's use of "tempers" to describe Christian emotional and moral qualities implies "a more abstract, stylized kind of holiness."[35]

The solution proposed by Deschner is for Wesley to stress "a participation in the being of Christ's love" rather than human tempers apart from the person of Christ.[36] Then, each believer's "every particular act of obedience" would "be made contemporary with and conformed to Christ's own Good Friday and Easter."[37]

Antinomianism could be avoided through our communal participation, as the body of Christ, in Christ's ongoing intercessory ministry. Deschner believes this was the actual practice of Wesley's classes and bands, though not reflected in Wesley's theology. Thus the answer to "Christ has done all; we need do nothing" need not be "Christ has not done all."[38]

There is some merit in Deschner's suggestion, especially in light of Wesley's view of the Christian life as continual prayer (see Chapter IV). However, Deschner has missed certain essential emphases of Wesley, for his own perspective seems to share elements with those of Wesley's Calvinist opponents. We shall shortly examine Deschner's misunderstanding of Wesley's doctrine of God and his undervaluing of Wesley's eschatological approach; here we will examine the Christology.

Deschner's description of the problem is in the past tense: whether Christ has or has not done all. But Wesley sees Christianity not only as a participation in a past salvific event, but—as Wesley never tires of insisting—the experience of a present salvation. Christ is not only in the past, but the risen Christ is present through the Holy Spirit sanctifying human lives, moving them forward. Wesley quotes St. Augustine— "who is generally supposed to favour the contrary doctrine"— with approval: "he that made us without ourselves, will not save us without ourselves."[39]

Thus there is an appropriateness in saying "Christ has not done all," for Christ is now at work bringing to reality that which has been promised, and that work will only be completed in the eschaton. Even then, however, God will not cease to be active; there is a sense in which our dynamic, transforming relationship with God continues for all eternity. For Wesley, the Christian life is rooted in the atonement but does not rest there; instead it strives forward into the future.

Consistent with Wesley's orientation to the present and future, he could have tied Christ's active obedience more strongly to the ongoing work of Christ through the Holy Spirit. The stress would not be on our participation now in Christ's past active obedience, but Christ's past and present active obedience increasingly becoming manifested in our own lives through sanctification, through growing in the love of God and of our neighbor. Wesley insists the disciple shall indeed be as the Master, "free from all sinful tempers," and he refers concretely to the purity, lack of self-will, humility, lack of anger, patience, etc., which characterized the life of Christ as those which are the goal of the Christian life as well.[40]

Wesley does not, as Deschner fears, sever the connection between Christ and the present life of a Christian. It is not only that Christ affects holiness, but that the holiness takes the form of tempers or affections which are of necessity relational. They cannot be, as Deschner imagines, dispositions apart from Christ (or from God's love for us in Christ), for then they change. They are truly our affections, but are only Christian affections if they remain continually related to God as their object. The importance of this continual reliance upon Christ will be seen more fully in the third section.

This means, too, that we should not be misled by the word "law." Wesley does not mean legalism but the law written on the heart; to obey God's law is for him to have the love of God and one's neighbor as a governing affection.

The place of Christ's active obedience in Wesley's Christology is not as detrimental to his intention to make Christ the norm of sanctification as Deschner believes. It is not only the avoidance of antinomianism but the affirmation of the present activity of Christ in the Christian life which shapes Wesley's christological emphases.

Far more significant for the normativeness of Christ's life for the Christian life is the largely christological language he uses to describe it. Wesley's emphasis on the work of the Holy Spirit and his variety of synonyms for Christian perfection may cause us to miss this emphasis. For example, in some passages Wesley can tie the Son to the atonement and justification, and the Spirit to renewing persons in the image of God.[41] Only an awareness that for Wesley such renewal is the work of the "Spirit of Christ,"[42] and that the entire Trinity is at work in all aspects of redemption, will give us the christological and trinitarian context of the passage.

We might also think christological description is only one of many ways Wesley pictures Christian perfection.

> In one view, it is purity of intention, dedicating all the life to God. It is the giving God all our heart; it is one desire and design ruling all our tempers. . . . In another view, it is all the mind which was in Christ, enabling us to walk as Christ walked. . . . It is the renewal of the heart in the whole image of God, the full likeness of Him that created it. In yet another, it is the loving God with all our heart, and our neighbor as ourselves.[43]

One can take Christian perfection "in which of these views you please" for "there is no material difference" in any of them.[44] But this is the point: having the mind that was in Christ is identical to perfect love or pure intention, for these were and are descriptive of Jesus Christ. This is why our having the mind that was in Christ is one of Wesley's most characteristic descriptions of the Christian life.[45]

In a recent dissertation, J. Blake Neff has drawn attention to the christocentric language which dominates Wesley's descriptions of sanctification. By way of a metaphoric cluster analysis, Neff compares Wesley's language to that of his theological ally, John Fletcher. Neff concludes that while Fletcher abounds in pneumatological metaphors for the Christian life, Wesley's language is overwhelmingly christological.[46]

Since both Wesley and Fletcher were stressing the power and activity of the Holy Spirit, it is remarkable that Wesley did not follow Fletcher in shifting to Spirit language in describing the Christian life. Wesley is apparently intent upon firmly grounding the Christian life in the life and death of Jesus Christ. This avoids the temptation to enthusiasm of pneumatocentric language which speaks of empowerment but leaves descriptively open the content and goal of the Christian life.[47] Thus Wesley says,

> 'Let this mind be in you which was also in Christ Jesus.' For although this immediately and directly refers to the humility of our Lord, yet it may be taken in a far more extensive sense, so as to include the whole disposition of his mind, all his affections, all his tempers, both toward God and man.[48]

Deschner's criticism was a concern that Wesley was undermining his own intent to make Christ the norm of sanctification. In a more positive discussion, Deschner notes that "there may be an even more immediate correspondence between Christ's history and ours in Wesley's thinking" than a doctrinal connection between Christology and soteriology.

> Christ is born of God; we are made children of God by the Holy Spirit. Christ inherits as the Son; we also, in being born again, become joint heirs with Him. Christ suffers and is glorified; our sanctification is a path of

suffering and glory. . . . It is doubtful whether Wesley
anywhere develops this correspondence between
Christ's history and our order of salvation, as a whole,
but parallels of specific moments are not lacking.[49]

Indeed, descriptions of Christ's character and history deci-
sively inform the Christian life for which believers hope. But
Christ is more than a pattern for our lives. In opposition to
William Law, Wesley insisted that Christ is our example only
after we are justified and born anew; only after we have come
into a faith relationship with the living Christ does the
imitation of Christ become possible for us through the work
of his Spirit within us. Thus for Wesley, Christianity as a
system of doctrine first describes this Christian "character in
all its parts, and that in the most lively and affecting manner."
Then, it "promises this character shall be mine, if I will not
rest till I attain it." Thirdly, it tells me "how I may attain the
promise; namely by faith."[50]
    The biblical descriptions of Christ, and especially the
narratives of Christ's death and resurrection, are the means by
which Christian affections such as faith, hope and love are
evoked and deepened. It is in being affected and renewed by
Christ that we are enabled to become like Christ.
    There are some necessary distinctions which must be made
here between God in Christ as the object of our affections and
the imitation of Christ as depicted prior to the resurrection.
What Wesley makes clear is the latter rests on the former. We
shall consider this again in Chapter V, where I will show how
the means of grace provide the descriptions which enable this
distinctive experience of the crucified and risen Christ, as well
as normative descriptions of the Christian life itself.

2. AGAINST ANTINOMIANISM: THE PROMISE OF NEW CREATION

While Wesley might have sometimes been ambivalent
concerning the use of the term "imputed righteousness," he

was consistently clear in his rejection of predestination. He considered the doctrine a dangerous error, and while he could work with any predestinarian who stressed sanctification, he could never agree to it.[1]

The logical consequence of predestination was "it directly and naturally tends to hinder the inward work of God in every stage of it";[2] it has "a natural, genuine tendency . . . either to prevent or obstruct holiness." Wesley claimed that the effects of this tendency were observable in the vast majority of persons who adopted the Calvinist perspective.[3]

The detrimental consequences of predestination were due to misunderstandings of God's activity and character which were logically derived both from the doctrine itself and from its theological offspring, "irresistible grace and infallible perseverance."[4] As has been shown, Wesley objects to depicting God's activity or grace as irresistible, as this implies a corresponding passivity on our part as we experience God's grace. It undercuts the active interrelationship of God and humanity which Wesley's soteriology requires. Salvation is not the resolution of a conflict of divine and human wills in favor of the divine, it is the movement, enabled by the divine, to divine/human cooperation.

Predestination also rules out human moral responsibility, thereby opening the way to antinomianism. If there is no human free will (even as a gift of grace), and everything is indeed done for us by God in an eternal decree, then sanctification through an ongoing relationship with God is inessential to salvation. This calls into question God's justice:

> . . . God is a rewarder of them that diligently seek him. But he cannot reward the sun for shining, because the sun is not a free agent. Neither could he reward us, for letting our light shine before men, if we acted as necessarily as the sun.[5]

The doctrine of predestination also encouraged a misunderstanding of God's character. This was a fundamental concern for Wesley, for while there "may be a right opinion of God, without either love, or one right temper toward him," it is certain that "right tempers cannot subsist without right opinion."[6] We have seen in the last chapter how God as the object of our affections qualifies the very nature of those affections.

Moreover, our description of God influences our expectation of God and our relationship with God. An arbitrary God, or a God who has already predetermined all things, is more inaccessible to our prayers and desire for salvation than a loving God who may yet act on our behalf. The question of what we may expect from God is central in a soteriology which depends on human openness and response to grace.

Thus Wesley's uneasiness with predestination was in the implications of that doctrine for God's character. Insisting that "the holy God cannot be the author of sin,"[7] he resisted any description of God's sovereignty or omnipotence which seemed to have the contrary as its logical conclusion. While not intending to abandon classical theism, Wesley was here engaged in questioning certain assumptions concerning God's nature which have dominated western Christianity since Augustine.

As an alternative rendering of the tradition, Wesley argues God is revealed as both Creator and Governor; while these are not inconsistent with one another, they are totally different. God as Creator "has acted, in all things, according to his own sovereign will." Since justice cannot have any place here, "for nothing is due to what has no being," God may "in the most absolute sense, do what he will with his own."[8] Wesley allows a great deal to God's creative sovereignty, including the different strengths and weaknesses, both physical and intellectual, with which each person is born. However,

> . . . the difference cannot be so great, as to necessitate one to be good, or the other to be evil; to force one into everlasting glory, or the other into everlasting burnings. This cannot be, because it would suppose the character

> of God as Creator, to interfere with God as a Governor;
> wherein he does not, cannot possible act according to his
> own mere sovereign will; but, as he has expressly told us,
> according to the invariable rules both of justice and
> mercy.[9]

By keeping the ideas of God as sovereign Creator and just
Governor distinguished, "we give God the full glory of his
sovereign grace, without impeaching his inviolable justice."[10]

The predestinarian confuses the two, applying the concept
of absolute sovereignty to God as Governor. This leads to an
understanding of divine grace wherein if the human does
anything, then God did not do it all, and therefore God
cannot have all the glory. Against this "confused, unscriptural
notion" of God's glory, Wesley insists that the "glorious
attributes of God, more especially his justice, mercy, and
truth" are more manifest in empowering all to be saved if they
will, than in irresistibly saving some and condemning others.[11]
God does "not necessitate us to be happy,"[12] but influences
all, "without destroying the liberty of his rational creatures."[13]

Within the sphere of God's role as Governor, Wesley
insists that God's justice and mercy are inseparably joined and
apply equally to all.[14] But above all, and qualifying all else, is
love as God's supreme characteristic.

> God is often styled holy, righteous, wise; but not
> holiness, righteousness, or wisdom in the abstract as he
> is said to be love; intimating that this is . . . his reigning
> attribute, the attribute that sheds an amiable glory on all
> his other perfections.[15]

By "abstract" Wesley does not mean God's love has no
concrete scriptural description, but that it is "without
bounds," or "without any exception or limitation"; God's
"love extends even to those who neither love nor fear him."[16]

From this perspective Wesley challenges other predestinarian arguments. When they insist God is unchangeable, and
thus unchangeably "loves" some but "hates" others (based on

the story of Jacob and Esau), Wesley argues that God unchangeably loves holy tempers and hates sinful tempers, "his unchangeableness of affection properly and primarily regards tempers and not persons; and persons . . . only as those tempers are found in them."[17] God loves all persons and seeks to give them new life; those who are impenitent receive God's just wrath only because of their unholy tempers, and not because God chose to "hate" them as persons.

Because of this unchangeable love and justice, God makes a "proportionable change in all the divine dispensations" to each person in accordance with their response to God's grace.[18] Thus Wesley's synergism of grace did not make God changeable as the Calvinists supposed, but showed a God of unchangeable character to be actively and reactively involved in relationships with persons.

Wesley uses the same approach in his interpretation of God's faithfulness. God is not faithful to a select group of persons chosen before creation, but to God's promises to all persons. These promises are seen as conditional or covenantal: God's faithfulness extends to those who, empowered by God, fulfill the conditions of the promise.[19] Here again, the Calvinist emphasis on a past sovereign choice establishing a static relationship is replaced by seeing God as actively interrelating with persons in the present, in the context of a conditional promise.

What Wesley has done, in effect, is not to ignore God's sovereignty and freedom in redemption but to change the locus of that activity from eternal decrees to eschatological promise. God is sovereign in that God can and will do as promised, and God is free to interact with persons in freedom as they seek fulfillment of those promises in their lives.

In spite of Wesley's affirmation of much of classical theism, the difference between his picture of God and that of the Calvinists is striking. The love of God receives redemptive priority over the sovereignty of God, present salvation over past decision, actual transformation over eternal decrees, divine interaction over excessive dualism, and divine activity over static transcendence. When we recall that the precondition for holiness and happiness is the knowledge of God, and that our love for God and our neighbor is fundamentally a response to God's love, we can see how important our concept of God is for Wesley. The predestinarian God could neither be called upon in terms of conditional promise, nor experienced as the loving object of our affections. For Wesley, the promise of new life only made sense if it was given by the God who is love: the Christian, "remembering that God is love . . . is conformed to the same likeness."[20]

Wesley identifies the "fundamental principle" of the predestinarian as "God has from eternity ordained whatsoever should come to pass."[21] The consequence of this principle is not only to make God the author of sin and to rule out human moral responsibility, but to make the last judgement a mere formality.[22] In his own understanding of the final justification, Wesley insists both faith and, opportunity permitting, works as the fruit of faith are necessary. While the righteousness of Christ is necessary to *"entitle"* us to heaven and give us "a *claim* to glory," it is only personal holiness which can *"qualify"* us for heaven and gives us "a *fitness*" for glory.[23] As Clarence Bence has put it, Wesley sees the final justification as "a moment of destiny."[24] The future is very much open in Wesley's thinking.

Wesley accounts for predestinarian language in scripture by arguing that Paul is not "describing a chain of causes and effects" but "simply showing *the method in which God works— the order* in which the several branches of salvation constantly follow each other." This he believes will be clear to anyone who surveys the work of God "either from the beginning to the end, or from the end to the beginning";[25] but it appears most clearly when viewed "backward, from the end to the beginning."[26]

In an attempt to reconcile an open future with classical theism, Wesley uses the category of divine foreknowledge. Strictly speaking, God has "no foreknowledge, no after-knowledge" but "sees and knows . . . all that is, that was, and that is to come, through one eternal now." Thus to God, "nothing is either past or future, but all things equally present."[27] Time is "a fragment of eternity, broken off at both ends."[28] This enables Wesley to claim that persons are not believers because God knows them to be, but God knows them as believers because, from an eternal perspective, they are. Persons "are as free in believing or not believing as if he did not know it at all."[29]

While the future is open, God's promise has in the end provided consequences for human freedom. Holiness, or sanctification, makes us fit to be participants in glory, gives us the character of a citizen of the Kingdom of God. There is a teleological thrust to Wesley's soteriology, where salvation in the present is a preparation for the kingdom and, as we shall see, also a present realization of the life of the age to come.

Harald Lindstrom, in his classic study of Wesley's theology of sanctification, has argued that while Wesley's soteriology has an overall "teleological structure,"[30] at the same time "a causal view impinges on the teleological."[31] By teleological, Lindstrom is observing how each element is seen as a means to the end of Christian perfection and the eternal kingdom. The causal view refers to Wesley's incorporation of the instantaneous transforming experience of God's grace into this more gradual context. I have noted this feature of Wesley's thought, and some of the tensions inherent in it, in the previous chapter. But in view of Wesley's admonition against "a chain of causes and effects," care must be taken in describing the role of this "causal" element.

John Deschner is aware of the admonition, but nonetheless orients Wesley's theology toward the past. He emphasized the tension identified by Lindstrom, but resolves it in favor of the causal element. Arguing that Wesley's soteriology is grounded in the atonement, or the priestly work of Christ, Deschner hopes to avoid the implication that Christ is only the means toward some greater end by rooting salvation in the past, completed work of Christ.[32]

This is to put the question wrongly. The assumption is that

for Christ's atonement to be the foundation, all must be oriented toward Christ's past activity. However, if the crucified Christ is risen and presently active, and if that same Christ is coming again, then the atonement itself is oriented toward a future to which it points. This misunderstanding is evident in Deschner's use of Wesley's eternal decree language, where he held, in opposition to the Calvinists, that God has decreed all who believe shall be saved. Deschner sees in this a grounding of the atonement in an Arminian eternal decree.[33] But Wesley's polemical use of "eternal decree" should not be allowed to obscure that this is the language of promise, which offers a future to those who respond to God's grace in faith. What we have in Wesley is a soteriology oriented toward the future and emphasizing the present activity of Christ; the atonement serves as the foundation of the promise of perfect love for which the believer hopes.

In contrast to Deschner, Theodore Runyon and Clarence Bence see eschatological promise as the context of Wesley's soteriology. Their different reading of Wesley is not only due to a divergent interpretation of texts, but to basic decisions as to which texts are significant. Deschner deliberately focuses on the historic theological norms of Methodism: the Twenty-Five Articles of Religion, the 53 standard sermons and the *Notes on the New Testament*.[34] But Runyon and Bence have seen how Wesley's second series of sermons, published as a group when Wesley was 85 years old, provide a way to see conversion and sanctification "in their organic relation to creation and kingdom."[35] In particular, these sermons invite an eschatological reading of Wesley, the appropriateness of which is shown by its harmony with the major emphases of the earlier sermons.

Runyon expresses the significance of this eschatological perspective quite clearly:

> If we ask, in comparison with Luther and Calvin, what was determinative for Wesley's orientation, the uniqueness of his approach becomes more apparent. Whereas

for Calvin the eternal counsels of God provide from the
beginning the context within which our knowledge of
ourselves and our destiny unfolds, and whereas for
Luther the reconciliation of God and the sinner which
takes place at the midpoint of history in the cross and is
appropriated through justification by faith provides the
center from which any system must be constructed, for
Wesley it is renewal and re-creation in anticipation of,
and participation in, the future that is determinative.[36]

Thus, in contrast to most eighteenth century thinkers,
Wesley does not "view the kingdom of God as referring
exclusively to heaven or to life after death"; rather the "first
fruits of the Kingdom are available now."[37] As Wesley himself
says,

The kingdom of heaven and the kingdom of God, are
but two phrases for the same thing. They mean, not
barely a future happy state in heaven, but a state to be
enjoyed on earth; the proper disposition for the glory of
heaven, rather than the possession of it. . . .[38]

Here we see Wesley's characteristic use of the word "heaven"
to denote the age to come; the "seat of happy spirits" prior to
the coming of the kingdom is called "paradise."[39]

Wesley underscores this present participation in the future
age through his distinction between a pledge and an earnest.
While a "pledge is to be restored when the debt is paid," an
"earnest is not taken away, but completed." The Holy Spirit is
the earnest or "first fruits" of the future,[40] and our "love to
God" is "both the earnest and the beginning of heaven."[41]

The present participation in the kingdom begins with faith
as a new epistemological capacity. Wesley can define faith as
the "spiritual sight of God and the things of God," of "things
not seen; that is, of past, future, or spiritual things. . . ."[42] Faith
is the remedy for another form of dissipation, "this unspeak-
able folly, this unutterable madness, of preferring present
things to eternal," and for our "natural blindness to futurity."
We are "not at all affected" by the "beauties or terrors of

eternity" because "they are so distant from us" and thus "appear to us as nothing, as if they had no existence."[43] The believer, in contrast, "lives in eternity and walks in eternity."[44]

However, as I have indicated, more is involved than a new eschatological perception. The believer not only lives and walks in eternity, but begins to live the life of eternity, the life of love which characterizes the Kingdom of God. The connection with Wesley's description of sanctification is explicit in his picture of the age to come.

> Hence will arise an unmixed state of holiness and happiness far superior to that which Adam enjoyed in Paradise. . . . As there will be no more death, and no more pain or sickness . . . no more grieving for or parting with friends; so there will be no more sorrow or crying. Nay, but there will be a greater deliverance than all this; for there will be no more sin. And, to crown all, there will be a deep, an intimate, an uninterrupted union with God; a constant communion with the Father and his Son Jesus Christ, through the Spirit. . . .[45]

While recognizing the future end to death and suffering, Wesley considers even more important the elimination of sin and the loving communion with God. These are precisely the aspects of this coming kingdom which are realizable to a significant extent in the present.

The continuity with and distinction between the two ages is expressed by Wesley through the terms *kingdom of glory* and *kingdom of grace,* which are both part of the one Kingdom of God.[46] When we pray "Thy kingdom come," we pray that "the kingdom of Christ may come" to "a particular person," that "the Kingdom of God" will be "begun below, set up in the believer's heart. . . ." But we also pray "for the coming of his everlasting kingdom, the kingdom of glory in heaven, which is the continuation and perfection of the kingdom of grace on earth."[47]

Christian perfection is a point of culmination in the process

of sanctification. From the perspective of the coming kingdom, it is also a decisive point in the participation in the life of
the age to come. This is not to say no further growth is
possible, for Wesley emphatically sees Christian perfection as
yet a new beginning. But the presence of perfect love for God
and one's neighbor in the life of the believer, and the
consequent elimination of intentional sin, is the arrival of the
fullness of the life of the kingdom as the ruling disposition of
the heart.

I have described the Christian life in terms of affections
which are dispositional and relational. In this view, original sin
is seen as deprivation of a relationship with God as the object
of our affections, and the consequent absence of those holy
tempers which that relationship enables. As the previous
chapter has shown, this is the dominant language Wesley uses
to describe the Christian life. Christian perfection, then, is
love fully taking the place of or transforming those affections
previously centered on things rather than God, on this life as
if there were no eternity, for "as long as love takes up the
whole heart, what room is there for sin therein?"[48]

Yet in conjunction with the relational language Wesley
uses a substantial description of original sin. Here sin is seen
as "the evil root, the carnal mind" which can only be
destroyed by an instantaneous act of God.[49] Thus in Christian
perfection, original sin, or some significant aspect of original
sin, no longer exists. It should be noted, however, that in spite
of this substantial language, those who do not continue
responding to God's grace will regain the root of sin;[50]
teleology remains the context for this more "crisis" oriented
view.

My intent here is not to further the discussion of this
problematic terminology, but to note how it indicates
Wesley's commitment both to the depth of original sin and
the power of God's grace over sin. Christian perfection is a
dramatic instance of God's eschatological power in the
present age, a "little eschaton" (as Runyon has so aptly
phrased it) in the life of the believer.[51]

As important as Christian perfection is for Wesley's theology, personal salvation is not the only arena of eschatological activity. Runyon and Bence have shown how Wesley's individual soteriology must be understood within a broader eschatological context that includes both the church and the world.[52] While the Kingdom of God at times signified a future reality, it was also for Wesley "a society to be formed, which was to subsist first on earth, and afterwards with God in glory."[53] The Jerusalem church of Acts 2, in which all things were held in common, was seen by Wesley as an eschatological community.[54] But as humanity fell, so the church was corrupted, largely by wealth and success.[55] It is the recovery of this primitive community, as is the case in the recovery of the lost image of God, that is necessary if Christians are to begin again to move toward the eschatological goal. I will show how Wesley puts this intent into practice in Chapter IV, where I discuss the classes and bands.

Perhaps even more striking than Wesley's claims for Christian perfection and Christian fellowship as present experiences of the eschaton is his insistence that the life of the kingdom consists of a holiness and happiness beyond that of Adam before the Fall. Since for Wesley the new creation surpasses the original,[56] God's original intention in creation can only be understood from the perspective of the end, the coming kingdom. This is the reverse of the Calvinist approach, in which all is given at creation; in Wesley new possibilities are continually opened through the creative power of the Holy Spirit.[57]

The focus on new creation does not point to the destruction of the old, but to its deliverance and transformation; "annihilation is not deliverance."[58] The very matter of creation shall be changed but not destroyed.[59] Thus there is a continuity between this world and the world to come.[60]

What is true for creation in general is most especially true for humanity in particular. Here Wesley must speak of the recovery of the image of God,[61] but this recovery is not seen as simply a return to an Adamic state before the Fall. The restoration of the image of God is actually to "gain infinitely more than we have lost," to attain "higher degrees of holiness" than would have been possible had there been no Fall.[62] The orientation is not that of returning to the past but of moving forward, toward the eschatological goal.[63]

As Bence has noted, there is an ambiguity in the extent of this restoration, for "bodily weakness, sickness, and lack of intellectual understanding . . . still persist in even the holiest persons." As these are for Wesley results of the Fall, "Christian perfection is not Adamic perfection,"[64] and the eschatological promise that these human problems will be overcome is not realized in the present.

Yet for the central characteristics of the kingdom, holiness and happiness, Wesley can assert that in salvation we do exceed the character of Adam. Because this is "an infinitely greater happiness than" we "could possibly have attained if Adam had not fallen," God allowed the Fall.[65] Now, persons can be more holy and happy on earth and in heaven.[66]

Wesley argues that if Adam had not sinned, there would have been no necessity for the incarnation, and "no room for that amazing display of the Son of God's love" to humanity in the cross,[67] "which has, in all ages, excited the highest joy, and love, and gratitude from his children."[68] As a consequence, whatever faith and love we would have would be far less than faith and love as a response to God's love for us in Christ. Since we love God because God first loved us, our faith and love are greatest only in response to God's greatest act of love for us.[69] Additionally, since we love one another as Christ has loved us, "our benevolence to all" humanity increases "in the same proportion with our faith and love of God."[70] Thus there is now available a new level of human relationships than was possible in Eden.

Wesley even sees in the pain and suffering of fallen creation (caused he believes by human sin) the purpose of God in allowing a context within which the love that both endures all things and manifests itself in good works has an opportunity to flourish.[71] Thus out of the fallenness of creation itself God en-

ables an increase of holiness and happiness which corresponds
to the very life of God, revealed in the life and death of Christ.
Having examined the connection between the eschaton
and its present realization in history and in human lives, we
turn to the process by which we appropriate it in the Christian
life. The argument here will build on the discussion of
sanctification in Chapter II, viewing it now from an eschatological perspective.

Bence has convincingly proposed a teleological hermeneutic as a way of understanding Wesley's theology. He discards
Lindstrom's causal/teleological distinction for a more goal-
oriented approach, which contains

> a dialectical tension between present attainment and
> future expectation throughout the entire order of salva-
> tion. This tension creates a joyous assurance of divine
> accomplishment while at the same time urging the
> individual and society forward to the promise of a
> relative perfection in this world and complete perfection
> in the world to come.[72]

In this approach, each "attainment of a specific goal" is
counterbalanced with "an immediate expectation of a new
goal which transcends and at the same time extends that which
has already been realized."[73] In opposition to soteriology as a
"stop-frame sequence of ends," Bence sees each accomplish-
ment not as an end in itself, but as an invitation and incentive
to continued growth.[74] Thus Wesley advises Christian perfection be preached "scarce at all to those who are not pressing
forward," but to "those who are, always by way of promise;
always drawing, rather than driving."[75]

Having already described the element of present attainment in this process as continual growth toward "perfect" love
and beyond it remains only to note the importance of joyously
recognizing present attainment at any point along the way.
Satan, warns Wesley, attempts to dampen this joy by constantly holding before us what we have not attained. The goal,
instead of an invitation to growth, then becomes a sign of our

failure and an occasion for despair.[76] Thus our progress in the Christian life must be celebrated as a gift of God in its own right as well as a means to a greater end.

Attainment must be linked with expectation if the Christian life is to move forward. Wesley was aware the expectation of Christian perfection as an instantaneous act of God actually provided the incentive for active participation in the more gradual process of growth.

> They are "saved by hope," by this hope of a total change, with a gradually increasing salvation. Destroy this hope, and that salvation stands still, or, rather, decreases daily. Therefore whoever would advance the gradual change in believers should strongly insist on the instantaneous.[77]

Because, as Runyon notes, with Christian perfection "a fundamental hope is engendered that the future can surpass the present," a "holy dissatisfaction is aroused with regard to any present state of affairs," which thereby keeps the process moving.[78]

Thus the celebration of attainment and the dissatisfaction with the present exist side by side in Wesley's soteriology. Together they evoke a hope which preserves the Christian "from striking upon either of those fatal rocks, presumption or despair."[79]

Wesley therefore regards fallen creation as a means to growth in love beyond that possible in Eden, and believes the hope of Christian perfection provides a particular incentive to a more gradual increase in love. However, one should not conclude by this that his teleology ends with Christian perfection. Rather, a processive structure pervades Wesley's theology from beyond Christian perfection through all eternity. There is no perfection

> which does not admit of a continual increase. So that how much soever any man has attained, or in how high a degree soever he is perfect, he hath still need to 'grow in grace', and daily to advance in the knowledge and love of God his Saviour.[80]

Some reasons for this will be examined in the next section. It is important here to note that the teleological dynamic extends not only beyond Christian perfection, but beyond death to Paradise[81] and to the eternal kingdom itself.[82]

But one cannot fall from Paradise or the kingdom; one can fall from Christian perfection. Thus to those who have gone on to perfection Wesley gives this advice:

> Yea, and when ye have attained a measure of perfect love, when God has . . . enabled you to love him with all your heart and with all your soul, think not of resting there. That is impossible. You cannot stand still; you must either rise or fall. . . . Therefore the voice of God . . . to the children of God, is, 'Go forward!'[83]

These first two sections of this chapter have identified certain dangers to and necessities for the Christian life. Despair and complacency are dangers because they encourage the acceptance of sin as normative while decreasing any present expectation of God's presence or power. Necessary to the Christian life are a broad range of narrative and imagic descriptions of God's promise of new life as a present gift.

Chapters IV and V will show how the means of grace contribute to the Christian life through countering these dangers and providing what is necessary. Here, those discussions will be briefly anticipated.

The means of grace in the Methodist movement, which were used to avoid formalism, also assist in avoiding despair and complacency through undermining static, finished, or irresistible depictions of God's grace. In community with others, they enable persons to experience the reality of new birth and sanctification, both in their own lives and in the lives of others. At the same time they encourage an expectant hope in God's promise and a receptivity and responsiveness to God's present activity.

The means of grace of the church, which were seen as the antidote to enthusiasm, also assist in avoiding despair and complacency through providing descriptive access to God's character, activity, and promises. The remembrance of who God is and what God has promised evokes the hope which seeks to grow in the Christian life. Through narrative portrayals of the life and death of Christ, these means of grace offer concrete descriptions of the Christian life itself.

Optimistic claims for the Christian life—especially claims which use the language of perfection—run certain risks. The temptation is to claim too much, or to think one has fully attained without further expectation, or to think the "already" has exhausted the "not yet." By locating primary descriptions of God and the Christian life in the means of grace, Wesley works against presumptive claims: narratives, images, and metaphors resist and critique attempts to fully restate their content in propositional form. Because their meaning is inexhaustible, they cannot be replaced by rational doctrines or experiential testimonies.

Yet the danger of presumption persists, for the unsubstitutable nature of narratives and images may in practice be ignored, and the discontinuity between the present age and the coming kingdom may be denied. Does Wesley recognize this danger in his theology, and do the means of grace themselves offer a corrective? Section 3 will show how Wesley responded to presumptive claims for Christian perfection within his own movement.

3. AGAINST PERFECTIONISM: A CONTINUAL RELIANCE ON CHRIST

When we focus on Wesley's doctrinal and ecclesiastical innovations, it is easy to forget that he was a High Churchman, an Anglican traditionalist. Thus when young convert Thomas Maxfield began to shift from testifying to preaching, Wesley was immediately concerned: Maxfield was not ordained. Yet his preaching was effective, not only impressing Lady Huntingdon but (of much greater importance to Wesley) evoking responses from those in the humbler classes.

Wesley's mother urged him to think carefully before prohibit-
ing Maxfield from preaching, for "that young man is as surely
called of God to preach as you are." Upon hearing him for
himself, Wesley agreed, and Maxfield became one of the first
of a number of lay preachers used by Wesley, ministers of the
word but not of the sacraments.[1]

Wesley loved Maxfield, who became one of the leaders of
the movement. Wesley introduced Maxfield to the woman
who would be his wife, and managed to have a bishop ordain
Maxfield as priest.[2]

But in Maxfield, and his associate George Bell, the Anglican fears of lay preaching and Whitefield's warning against
teaching perfection came together. Maxfield began gathering
around him a group of "entirely sanctified" Methodists, who
used the evidence of dreams and visions to bolster their claim
to this special state. George Bell went even further, attempting to work miracles and eventually prophesying that the end
of the world would occur on February 28, 1763.[3]

In writing to Charles, John Wesley confided: "If Thomas
Maxfield continues as he is, it is impossible he should long
continue with us. But I live in hope of better things."[4] His
love for Maxfield restrained him; it was over a year later when
the final breach came.[5] Even Bell was held in affection. When
a woman asked Wesley why he could not discard a servant like
Bell who will not follow directions, he answered "It is right to
discard such a servant; but what would you do if he were your
son?"[6]

The Wesleys, through both meetings and correspondence,
tried to dissuade Maxfield and Bell from their enthusiastic
version of Christian perfection; they replied, however, that
until Wesley himself had such an experience of perfection, he
could not teach them.[7] At the same time, others of Wesley's
opponents were using the enthusiasm of Maxfield and Bell to
tarnish the whole movement.[8] Thus separation had to come,
for once again the very nature of the Christian life had
become an issue. In a letter to Maxfield, Wesley listed the
problems he saw with his and Bell's approach to Christian

perfection. As with the Moravians, we shall hazard a long quotation of selections from this letter to have the advantage of Wesley's clear statement of the issues.

> I like your doctrine of Perfection, or pure love; love excluding sin; your insisting that it is merely by faith; that consequently it is instantaneous (though preceded and followed by a gradual work,) and that it may be now, at this instant.
>
> But I dislike your supposing man may be as perfect as an angel; that he can be absolutely perfect; that he can be infallible, or above being tempted; or that the moment he is pure in heart, he cannot fall from it.
>
> . . .
>
> I dislike your directly or indirectly, depreciating justification; saying, a justified person is not in Christ, is not born of God, is not a new creature, has not a new heart, is not sanctified, not a temple of the Holy Ghost; or that he cannot please God, or cannot grow in grace.
>
> I dislike your saying that one saved from sin needs nothing more than looking to Jesus; needs not to hear or think of anything else; believe, believe, is enough; that he needs no self-examination, no times of private prayer; needs not mind little or outward things; and that he cannot be taught by any person who is not in the same state.
>
> . . .
>
> . . . I dislike something which has the appearance of pride, of overvaluing yourselves, and undervaluing others. . .
>
> I dislike something that has the appearance of enthusiasm, overvaluing feelings and inward impressions; mistaking the mere work of imagination for the voice of the Spirit; expecting the end without the means; and undervaluing reason, knowledge, and wisdom in general.
>
> . . .
>
> But what I most of all dislike is, your littleness of love to your brethren . . . your want of union of heart with them, . . . your impatience of contradiction; your counting every man your enemy that reproves or admonishes you in love, . . . your censoriousness, . . . in one word, your divisive spirit.[9]

These points can be summarized as follows: First, they denied the teleological context within which Wesley had placed the instantaneous. Thus they demeaned that which preceded Christian perfection as less than Christian, and thought further growth unnecessary.[10] Secondly, as growth in grace was denied, so too were self-examination and the means of grace which aided in that growth.[11] In their place was put a version of the "only believe" doctrine discussed in section 1, here applied not to new birth but to Christian perfection. Third, they had a static, finished view of perfection which claimed a far greater escape from human finitude than Wesley would allow, a perfection "as an angel." Finally, the evidence for this perfection was feelings of joy[12] and extraordinary spiritual experiences rather than "humble love," a grain of which is "better than all these gifts put together."[13] It is their lack of love which Wesley dislikes more than all else, for in that they have missed the content and goal of the Christian life.

The examination of these issues shall begin by once again placing Christian perfection in its eschatological context. There it will be shown how the theme of discontinuity between the kingdom and the present age is as essential to Wesley's thought as the continuity discussed in section 2.

This will be followed by a more specific examination of what Wesley says perfection is not. The implications of Wesley's distinctions are perhaps further reaching than he was aware.

This will show why for Wesley there is never any point of growth of maturity in the Christian life which can stand apart from a continual reliance on the grace of Christ. Thus he insists on the need for continued repentance on the part of believers, even those whose hearts are perfected in love.

In both his vision of the coming kingdom and his denial that we recover all that Adam lost in the Fall, Wesley insists certain aspects of our eschatological hope are not realizable in the present. What we cannot escape is our finitude, manifestations of which include ignorance, sorrow, and death.

Bence is aware of these discontinuous elements in Wesley's thought, and nicely summarizes several of Wesley's sermons on the subject. The themes of continuity and discontinuity are both present, but not in the same degree in each sermon. Thus "The General Spread of the Gospel" is a highly optimistic portrayal of God's increasing triumph in history, as the world becomes progressively more holy and happy. In contrast, "The End of Christ's Coming" which precedes it focuses on personal salvation as the locus of God's triumph over sin, while noting the victory over ignorance, infirmities and death awaits the general resurrection. And, in "The New Creation" which follows "The General Spread of the Gospel" Wesley rules out any evolutionary transition to the kingdom; rather there is an apocalyptic break between the two ages, and an inbreaking of God from without to establish the kingdom.[14]

Wesley's pervasive optimism of grace leads Bence to stress the continuities in Wesley between present and future salvation. He rightly insists that Wesley is no apocalyptic doom-sayer, and thus concludes that Wesley de-emphasizes "the apocalyptic elements of eschatology in favor of a hope for universal salvation in this age. . . ."[15]

But in making this claim, Bence undervalues the importance of the tension between continuity and discontinuity in Wesley's thought. The question is not whether Wesley was a present optimist or a doom-sayer, but the content of our hope: For what may we hope, and for what may we not hope? What has God promised to us in this age, and what in the age to come? Or, to be more exact, which aspects of the coming kingdom are presently attainable, and which are not?

Now there is no question Wesley was highly interested in that which could be attained through grace in the present. But the danger of presumptuous misunderstandings of Christian perfection necessitated the placing of a corrective tension between the "already" and the "not yet" alongside the teleology of attainment and expectation. This apocalyptic element was not only designed to check the excesses of a Bell or Maxfield, but more importantly to aid growth in the Christian life itself through evoking humility or repentance.

> But it may be observed that the Son of God does not destroy the whole work of the devil in man, as long as he remains in this life. He does not yet destroy bodily weakness, sickness, pain, and a thousand infirmities incident to flesh and blood. . . . both ignorance and error belong to humanity. He entrusts us with only an exceedingly small share of knowledge in our present state, lest our knowledge should interfere with our humility, and we should again affect to be as gods.[16]

Wesley's identification of those aspects of the kingdom which are wholly future corresponds to his important discussion on what perfection is not:

> We willingly allow, and continually declare, there is no such perfection in this life, as implies either a dispensation from doing good, and attending all the ordinances of God, or a freedom from ignorance, mistake, temptation, and a thousand infirmities necessarily connected with flesh and blood.[17]

Although in 1741 Wesley made a number of excessive claims for Christian perfection which he soon retracted, including a freedom from temptation,[18] the above quote seems on the whole to represent Wesley's views throughout his ministry. Because of their importance for an understanding of the means of grace, we shall examine some of these qualifications of Christian perfection.

First, Christians "are not perfect in knowledge" so "as to be free from ignorance."[19] Neither the holy angels nor Adam prior to the Fall were perfect in knowledge; in this Christians should not hope to exceed them.[20] Moreover, because Christians are limited by a corruptible body, "they must at times think, speak, or act wrong; not indeed through a defect of love, but through a defect of knowledge."[21] These mistakes have moral consequences, frequently occasioning "something wrong, both in our temper, and words, and actions." Thus we may "love a person less than he really deserves" through "mistaking his character;" and we then "are unavoidably led to speak or act, with regard to that person" in a manner contrary to the perfect law of God.[22]

This observation brings us to one of the most important and problematic aspects of Wesley's theology. For while each "mistake is a transgression of the perfect law" and would, except for the atonement, "expose to eternal damnation," these mistakes are "not sin, if love is the sole principle of action."[23] Put differently, they are not "sin, properly so called," a "voluntary transgression of a known law" in thought, word, or deed; but "sin, improperly so called," an "involuntary transgression of a divine law, known or unknown."[24]

Wesley is aware of at least some of the dangers in making this distinction: in not calling these involuntary transgressions sins, persons may think they "are in such a state as that can stand before infinite justice without a Mediator." Yet if Wesley joins Luther and Calvin in confounding "these defects with sins, properly so called," then the hope for Christian perfection in this life becomes difficult to sustain.[25]

This shows more clearly why Wesley insisted Christian perfection was not a resting state but a new beginning within a continuing process of growth. As Bence has noted, Christian perfection provides "an integrative center to the personality" which extends "into all areas of one's life":

> those aspects of one's life that are perfected (intention, motive, love) will necessarily cause an on-going improvement of imperfect dimensions of life (actions, understanding, interpersonal relations).[26]

But it also shows why the apocalyptic tension between the "already" and the "not yet" is equally essential to Wesley's theology, for it is here that presumptive misunderstandings of perfection are corrected.

Indeed, today it is not the necessity of this tension which we might question, but whether it is sufficient as a corrective. For in our century, taught as it is by Freud and Marx, "involuntary transgressions" have taken on a power and a moral significance in human life much greater than that assumed in the eighteenth century. We may well question whether these are not, in fact, the dominant and most pervasive ethical influences in our life, even should we be perfected in love.

In a perceptive article on systemic evil and holiness, Albert L. Truesdale has seen the importance of the eschatological "not yet" in Wesley's theology. While admitting Wesley's own view of involuntary transgressions was too "passive," his distinction nonetheless provides contemporary theologians with a Wesleyan framework within which they can deal responsibly and credibly with the problem of systemic evil.[27]

However, in a reply to Truesdale, William Hasker concludes that "the reality of systemic evil makes any thought of individual spiritual perfection extremely problematic." This is because our problem is not simple ignorance but "a deeply motivated failure to recognize evils whose recognition would cost us something." Though there may be a solution through "consciousness-raising," it must certainly be a purely gradual process which would rule out a "crisis experience of sanctification."[28]

But the problem is actually deeper than this, for even if Christian perfection is acknowledged as a real possibility in this life, whether through a crisis experience or not, the question of its moral significance remains. Only if there is a critical principle at work in the life of the Christian which enables a continuing awareness and growing freedom from these deep and deceptive "involuntary" motivations and prejudices is the Christian life as Wesley envisioned it a possibility. And, if love is to truly characterize the Christian life, it must have a way to overcome, heal, or direct these more hidden aspects of who we are.

Chapters IV and V will argue that the means of grace provide such a critical principle, both in the life of the

Christian and in the Christian's relationship with society. It is our neglect of the full range of these means of grace, or of their interrelationship, which accounts for superficial or partial realizations of the Christian life in this age. In this section I will set the stage for that later argument by discussing the continuing need for Christ and the repentance of believers.

Prior to this, another important way in which Christians are not perfect, that of not being free from temptation, will be examined. Wesley acknowledges that those newly reborn may for a time not experience temptation; this may account for his earlier, over-optimistic claims for Christian perfection in this area. "But this state will not last always," Wesley warns, for "the Son of God himself, in the days of his flesh, was tempted even to the end of his life. Therefore so let his servant expect to be. . . ."[29]

While Wesley does not offer a systematic account of temptation in the Christian life, he is aware that, besides the ongoing temptation connected with living in the world (dissipation), there are those temptations peculiar to the Christian life, such as spiritual pride. "Watch and pray continually against pride," Wesley warned, "It is full as dangerous as desire."[30] Pride is the parent of enthusiasm and enthusiasm is the parent of antinomianism.[31] Therefore, we must be "open and frank," and "always ready to own any fault"; by this we do "not hinder, but adorn, the gospel."[32]

Pride is a temptation because it is self-deceptive. One may ascribe all we have to God, yet engage in pride through thinking "we have what we really have not." You might, for example, "humbly" ascribe all your knowledge to God, and yet think you have more knowledge than others; or that as you are taught of God, you no longer can be taught by others who have less knowledge.[33] Thus progress in the Christian life, rather than lessening temptation, gives rise to new forms of temptation.

Both the subtleties of temptation and the hidden potency of involuntary transgressions require, even for those perfected in love, a continual reliance on Christ. Certainly this is in part due to the nature of grace: "it is a free gift" from Christ, received "as his purchase, merely in consideration of the price he paid."[34] Grace rooted in the atonement remains the foundation of the Christian life. But there are several additional reasons for the continuing need for grace, all related to the "not yet" of salvation.

"We have this grace," Wesley notes, "not only from Christ, but in him"

> For our perfection is not like that of a tree, which flourishes by the sap derived from its own root, but . . . like that of a branch which, united to the vine, bears fruit; but, severed from it, is dried up and withered.[35]

Thus even those perfected in love "still need Christ as their King; for God does not give them a stock of holiness"; without Christ, "nothing but unholiness would remain."[36] Most fundamentally, sanctification is not substantial but relational, by faith. The Christian affections or holy tempers cannot exist apart from their relation to Christ which gives them their distinctive form or shape.

Additionally, even the "holiest of men still need Christ, as their Prophet," for Christ "does not give them light, but from moment to moment"; when Christ withdraws, "all is darkness."[37] Given our discussion of temptation and involuntary transgression, there is an obvious need for a continuing, prophetic, critical work of Christ in the life of the believer.

The priestly work of Christ remains significant in two ways. First, all our temporal, spiritual, or eternal blessings "depend on his intercession for us, which is one branch of his priestly office"; for this "we always have equal need." Secondly, even the most holy "still need Christ . . . to atone for their omissions, their shortcomings, . . . their mistakes in judgement and practice, and their defects of various kinds."[38] They do not, to be sure, need Christ "to restore the favour of God, but to continue it."[39] But it follows that even these must pray for themselves as well as others "Forgive us our trespasses."[40] Thus none "feel their need of Christ" like those perfected in love, "none so entirely depend upon him. For Christ does not give life to the soul separate from, but in and with, himself."[41]

Our continual need for Christ is due to our unending potential for growth and our limitations as fallen human beings in this age, as well as to the relational character of those affections which constitute the Christian life. Complementary to this emphasis is Wesley's insistence that there be continuing repentance in believers, both prior to and following Christian perfection. So far, I have in this chapter examined the implications of eschatological discontinuity for the Christian life, and how these are manifested in Wesley's understanding of perfection. In my discussion of repentance I shall broaden the scope of my inquiry to show the need of a critical principle with regard to that "inward sin" which is fully supplanted by love in Christian perfection. The focus, then, will be on the role of repentance in the process of sanctification.

As with the repentance prior to justification, this ongoing repentance is "one kind of self-knowledge—the knowing ourselves sinners, yea, guilty, helpless sinners, even though we know we are children of God"; it is essential for one's continuance and growth in grace.[42] There are several "branches" of repentance.

One is the conviction of guiltiness, the sense that one deserves punishment. But in the believer, this conviction does not lead to fear of punishment, for there is no condemnation for those who are in Christ.[43] It "implies no guilt, no sense of condemnation, no consciousness of the wrath of God,"[44] that is, no feeling of guilt before God's judgement due to the forgiveness and reconciliation experienced in justification.

Another "branch" of repentance is a conviction of our utter helplessness. This is a double helplessness: first, an inability on one's own to do good or resist evil (that is, to resist outward sin), except by the grace of God given moment to moment;

and second, an inability to overcome inward sin which remains in one's heart and thus be delivered from guiltiness without the grace of God.[45] Thus the sense of helplessness directly reinforces our need to continually rely upon Christ.

A third "branch" is a conviction that sin remains in the heart of the believer, although it does not reign.[46] The focus here is on inward sin, our intentions and dispositions rather than our actions. Repentance is "a conviction of our proneness to evil," of "the tendency of our heart to self-will, to atheism, or idolatry; and above all to unbelief, whereby in a thousand ways, and under a thousand pretences, we are ever 'departing' more or less, 'from the living God'."[47]

Inward sins are one form of voluntary transgression. At times Wesley identifies other types of voluntary transgressions for which believers need repentance: outward sins,[48] sins of omission,[49] and spiritual sloth. The latter is a "want of striving" which "keeps your soul in darkness," an unconcern for sin and neglect of repentance.[50]

A final "branch" of repentance is the conviction that, "as sin remains in our hearts, so it *cleaves* to all our words and actions"; they are "mixed with sin" if not "sinful altogether." The "very *intention*" underlying the speech of believers is not free from "unholy mixtures," whereby they speak both to please God and "partly to please themselves," to do the will of God and "their own will also." And "their good actions, so called, are far from being strictly such; being polluted with . . . a mixture of evil. . . ." Actions of mercy and piety both suffer from mixed motives, unholy tempers, and wandering thoughts.[51]

This description of repentance in believers has largely focused on the Christian life prior to Christian perfection. It has shown that repentance has a different focus for Wesley at different points in the process. Prior to justification and new birth, the focus is on outward sins; afterward it is on inward sins. Christian perfection, provided one remains in it, is the end of inward sin, and so the focus shifts to involuntary transgressions. But throughout this process, involuntary transgressions also cleave to our words and actions, in the way Wesley has described for inward sin above.

Thus all along the way, the Christian life requires self-knowledge, and therefore submission to a critical principle wherein hidden deceptions, mixed motives, and societal conditioning can be exposed. It is no wonder that Wesley reacted so strongly against Bell's insistence the perfect Christian no longer needed self-examination.

The means of grace provide practices which facilitate critical self-awareness. What follows will anticipate the more complete discussion in Chapters IV and V.

The means of grace in the Methodist movement counter presumptive claims through encouraging accountable discipleship, self-examination, and repentance within a community of forgiveness and love. The discipline and practices of the community presuppose the complex and deceptive nature of sin, and necessary relation of humility to love.

The means of grace of the church assist in avoiding presumption through a continuing presentation of the atoning and mediational work of Christ and the "not yet" nature of the coming kingdom. These evoke repentance, which is both shaped and expressed through prayers and hymns of confession.

As was true of formalism and enthusiasm, the opposing misunderstandings of antinomianism and perfectionism often share common assumptions. Both have static conceptions of grace, as past event and irresistible will (antinomianism) or as an instantaneous act of grace apart from and outside a process of growth (perfectionism); for both the cry was "only believe." Their understanding of sin does not allow a distinction between intentional and involuntary transgressions; thus their idea of perfection is of an absolute sinlessness and a finished state. This leads the antinomians to claim too little for the Christian life and the perfectionists to claim too much.

As he did with formalism and enthusiasm, Wesley sensed and rejected the common underlying assumptions of these two misunderstandings. He pictured grace as a dynamic,

ongoing process of divine/human interaction and cooperation. He rejected any description of perfection as either
absolute or finished, and chose instead to focus on the reign of
love in the heart, which even as perfect love can infinitely
increase and deepen. This is only possible through living one's
life in the midst of God's gracious activity. It is the means of
grace which provide such a context for the Christian life.

Chapter IV

The Means to the Presence of God

1. REMAINING IN THE CHURCH: *ECCLESIOLA IN ECCLESIA*

According to Wesley, God raised up the Methodist movement "Not to form any new sect; but to reform the nation, particularly the church; and to spread scriptural holiness over the land."[1] His beginning with a disclaimer acknowledges the sectarian risk which accompanied his movement. It was a risk he took unhesitatingly in the face of Anglican accusations that he was splitting the church, while at the same time he forcefully opposed those within the movement who sought to form a new Dissenting church. It was "the peculiar glory of the people called Methodists," that in "spite of all manner of temptations, they will not separate from the Church."[2]

Wesley's commitment to a distinctive movement and his reluctance to leave the church should not be understood as contradictory tendencies but as united in his passion for the Christian life. This chapter is concerned with the means of grace associated with the renewal movement; that is, with those practices which countered the formalism of the Anglican church by encouraging a living faith which sensed the presence of God, and an expectant hope in God's promise of sanctification. But these means of grace, and the faith and hope they encourage, are dependent on those other means of grace which tell the story of the activity and promises of God, and thus give faith and hope their content. Because of this dependence, I begin by examining more particularly Wesley's own reasons against separation from the Church of England, and how the Methodist movement was intrinsically related to the means of grace of the larger church.

Wesley gives two main reasons against separation. The first concerns the end or goal of the Christian life, and applies to "schism" in general. Schism, says Wesley, "is both evil in itself, and productive of evil consequences." To separate from "a body of living Christians" is "a grievous breach of the law of love";[3] such separation, whether from a religious society or the Church of England, is only permissible when continuing therein would lead to "breaking a commandment of God."[4]

But this permissible cause of separation is for Wesley such an unlikely occurrence he can insist that, while the "pretenses for separation may be innumerable," the "want of love is always the real cause."[5] Thus "to feel, and much more to express, either contempt or bitterness" towards the clergy of the Church of England "betrays an utter ignorance of ourselves and of the spirit which we especially should be of."[6]

> We are not Seceders, nor do we bear any resemblance to them. We set out upon quite opposite principles. The Seceders laid the very foundation of their work in judging and condemning others: We laid the foundation of our work in judging and condemning ourselves.[7]

Schism is a denial of the life of love which Methodists profess to be seeking, and toward which the means of grace point. Thus while the fellowship of the Methodists is exclusive in terms of discipline, it must remain inclusive in terms of love or it will contradict its purpose as a means of grace.

The second reason against separation concerns the means to the Christian life. Wesley thought it especially beneficial that God had given the Methodists both those "spiritual helps" which "are peculiar to their own society" and "those which are enjoyed in common by other members of the Church of England."[8] Thus while Methodists "call sinners to repentance in all places of God's dominion; and . . . frequently use extemporary prayer, and unite together in a religious

society" they are not Dissenters, for they do not "renounce
the service of the Church," Methodist worship does not
supersede "the Church service; it presupposes public prayer.
. . . " As a church service Methodist worship "would be
essentially defective," lacking the "four grand parts of public
prayer, deprecation, petition, intercession, and thanksgiving."[9]

> If it be said, 'But at the Church we are fed with chaff,
> whereas at the meeting we have wholesome food', we
> answer: (1) The prayers of the Church are not chaff—
> they are substantial food for any who are alive to God.
> (2) The Lord's Supper is not chaff, but pure and
> wholesome for all who receive it with upright hearts.
> Yea, (3) In almost all the sermons we hear there, we hear
> many great and important truths.[10]

Thus Wesley saw the means of grace associated with the
church as complementary to those of the societies, and as
themselves necessary to the Christian life.

Aware of the sectarian tendencies within an organized
renewal movement, Wesley was "greatly afraid" of "a narrowness of spirit," that "miserable bigotry which makes many so
unready to believe that there is any work of God but among
themselves." Resolved "to use every possible method of
preventing" this, Wesley allotted one evening a month to read
to the societies "the accounts I received from time to time of
the work which God is carrying on in the earth," including
that among those of "various opinions and denominations."[11]

The concern to avoid narrowness and the affirmation of the
value of the means of grace of the church find their unity in
Wesley's presupposing the church as the context for his
societies. As David Lowes Watson has perceptively observed,
the affirmation of the doctrine and ordinances of the larger
church as "inherently valid and necessary" enabled those in
the societies to respond with integrity "to the inner prompt-
ings of the Spirit."[12] Conversely, to reject the structure of the
larger church would require the movement to "provide its

own, thereby losing the freedom of its spontaneity" and the advantages of a discipline grounded in tradition which could avoid the excesses of enthusiasm.[13]

The point is not that by presupposing the Church of England, Wesley was free to devote his energies to more pressing concerns. Rather it is that the means of grace of the church provide a context within which the societies can avoid sectarianism, and the religious affections can have as their object the distinctive God of scripture, eucharist, and tradition.

To separate from the church was to either become a new church, thus losing the disciplined fellowship of a voluntary society, or to invite sectarian narrowness and experiential enthusiasm. To remain in the church was to retain the discipline and community necessary for faith in a present God without losing that which provides narrative and descriptive identity of the God who is present. The experience of God's identity forms and shapes the conversation in the class meeting, the language of extemporaneous prayer, and the practice of general means of grace. The practices of the societies not only presuppose those of the church, they are pervaded by those of the church.

2. DISCIPLINE IN COMMUNITY: CLASSES AND BANDS

The voluntary communities of Methodism were concerned with the maintenance and advancement of the Christian life. While they embodied "Christian conference," an instituted means of grace, Wesley continually called them prudential: their particular organization was not a model for the centuries but a pattern of fellowship and discipleship related to their historical and cultural context. Yet while their exact structure is contextual, they are necessary for the Christian life in all times and places.

The concern for the Christian life evident in these communities was more particularly a concern for those affections which characterize that life: a living faith, an expectant hope, a humble love for God and one's neighbor. There were checks against both presumptive claims for the Christian life and despair or complacency in pursuing that life. Above all, members were made continually aware that they lived their lives in the presence of God, and at the same time in the midst of a world in which God had been forgotten. This latter element is the unique feature of Wesley's voluntary communities. Monastics and Moravians formed voluntary communities as places of residence and occupation for their members. By withdrawing from the world with its temptation to dissipation, they hoped to then give undistracted attention to those sinful desires within their hearts. It would be unfair to accuse monasticism of being unconcerned about the world; rather their withdrawal was often a means of becoming increasingly clear as to the needs of the world before God.

Wesley rejected the idea that growth in the Christian life was limited to monastics and others who could escape the vicissitudes of .everyday life. Christian perfection was a reasonable hope for any Christian and leaving one's home or occupation was not its precondition. Nor was growth in the Christian life the prerogative of persons of leisure or of the upper classes, as held by many Anglicans and Dissenters. The problem was not lack of time or resources, but lack of attention to God; the lower classes were if anything less tempted to forget God in their need than the wealthy in their abundance. The task of Wesley's voluntary communities was to nurture faith and counteract dissipation among persons who continued to live and work in the world at large.

This can be seen in Wesley's account of the origin of the Methodist societies. Those who responded to his open air preaching soon found themselves "surrounded with difficulties" for "all the world rose up against them," warning against becoming overly righteous or enthusiastic. Living daily in a context in which "every one strove to weaken, and none to strengthen," a number of Methodists sought Wesley's advice. He suggested they strengthen one another through mutual conversation and prayer;[1] that is, gather together from time to time as a distinctive Christian community. However, as they also desired Wesley himself to talk and pray with them, he eventually began weekly meetings on Thursday evening, and termed the group a *society.* Those in the society united

> in order to pray together, to receive the word of exhortation, and to watch over one another in love that they might help each other to work out their salvation.[2]

The advantages of the society became clear to Wesley when he observed that, after a few months, those who had not united "fell back," while those who had united continued forward.[3] Upon reflection, Wesley noted that the society had functioned similarly to the catechumenate of the ancient church.[4]

Here, at the beginning, are a number of features which will characterize the smaller classes and bands as well. This first is the society as a temporary yet essential haven from a hostile world. It was not a place of permanent escape, but a means by which Christians could strengthen one another's faith and obtain renewed clarity as to the content of faithful discipleship in the world.

Second, they watched over one another in love; that is, they were accountable to one another concerning their discipleship. Here we find anticipated that mutual accountability which David Lowes Watson has identified as the most central feature of the early class meetings.[5]

Third, and related to the second, they were mutually responsible for one another: they helped each other work out their salvation. This is for Wesley an essential characteristic of true Christian fellowship.

Finally, they accepted Wesley as a spiritual director. As the movement grew in size, the role of spiritual director was increasingly shared, but it remained a constant feature of Wesley's communities.

It was the phenomenal growth of Methodism which made the *class meeting* necessary. The several societies were too large, and their membership too geographically extended, for Wesley to be in regular contact with each member. Several Methodists "grew cold, and gave way to the sins which had long easily beset them," becoming simultaneously a temptation to Wesley's followers, an obstacle to Wesley's hearers, and an inspiration to Wesley's critics. The detection of these "disorderly walkers" became an increasingly serious concern.[6]

The solution came inadvertently, by way of a plan by the society in Bristol to pay off the preaching-house debt. The proposal was to divide the society of over 1000 members into classes of 12, each with a leader. Every week the leader would visit the class members to collect a penny from each, and would pay on behalf of any who were too poor to pay anything. In the process of these visits, the leaders discovered some members who did not live according to the Methodist discipline. Wesley shifted the primary purpose of the classes from the collection of money to the detection of "disorderly walkers," hoping to turn them "from the evil of their ways" but determined to "put away from us" those who persisted. Classes were soon organized in the society in London and elsewhere.[7]

For a number of reasons, visitation of class members was sometimes difficult or impossible. It was therefore decided that each class should meet together weekly rather than be visited individually by the leader. This class meeting became the point of entry into the Methodist society:

> Nothing can be more simple, nothing more rational, than the Methodist discipline. . . . Any person determined to save his soul may be united . . . with them [the Methodists]. But this desire must be evidenced by three marks: avoiding all known sin, doing good after his power, and attending all the ordinances of God. He is then placed in such a class as is convenient for him, where he spends about an hour in a week. And the next quarter, if nothing is objected to him, he is admitted into

the Society. And therein he may continue as long as he
continues to meet his brethren and walks according to
his profession.[8]

The class meeting was now—in a more intentional way—
fulfilling the original role of the society and exhibiting the
four features noted above. Those who responded to the
sermons, often with the faith of a servant, were placed in
classes. There were no doctrinal conditions, but each member
was expected to live according to the three-fold discipline of
the General Rules of the United Societies.[9] It was this
discipline that distinguished the Methodists from the world
and formed them in a way of life. The great majority of
experiences of new birth occurred in the class meetings.[10]

Because they met together in groups of 10 to 12, the sense
of accountability to one another was even stronger than in the
first societies. However, the mutual accountability was sec-
ondary to their accountability to the leader.

The experience of fellowship or mutual responsibility was a
highly significant feature of the class meeting. One of the
original reasons for having the class meet was that one
member "affirmed what another denied" and "little misunderstandings and quarrels . . . frequently arose" which
necessitated face to face meetings. The result more than
corrected the cause: not only were quarrels and misunderstandings removed, but many "now happily experienced that
Christian fellowship of which they had not so much as an idea
before."[11]

> They began to 'bear one another's burdens', and 'natu-
> rally' to 'care for each other'. As they had daily a more
> intimate acquaintance with, so they had a more endeared
> affection for, each other. And 'speaking the truth in
> love, they grew up into Him in all things. . . . '[12]

Most important of all was the role of the class leader.
Originally the leader visited each person once a week

in order to inquire how their souls prosper; To advise, reprove, comfort, or exhort, as occasion may require. To receive what they are willing to give toward the relief of the poor.[13]

At the weekly meeting, the leader continued to exercise the responsibilities of pastor and spiritual director. The health of the class in large measure depended on the maturity and perceptiveness of the class leader.

The heart of the class meeting was what Watson calls a catechetical exchange between the leader and each member. The intent was not to "press for an intensive confessional," but to invite from each "a straightforward accounting of what had taken place during the preceding week."[14] Rather than an inward inquiry, the class member gave an account of his or her discipleship during the week in accordance with the three General Rules, with the leader then "articulating what was felt to be the point which would most profitably be shared by the other members."[15] A person could admit being beset by sin without specifying the exact nature of that sin.

Although the meeting focused on discipleship, each leader was encouraged not only to see "how each person observes the outward Rules," but also to "inquire how every soul in his class prospers," how each "grows in the knowledge and love of God."[16] The leaders were required to place beside the name of each member an appropriate notation as to their spiritual progress, whether one was awakened, doubtful, professed justification, or professed the perfect love of God.[17]

While the class meeting was ideal for the newly awakened Methodist who was seeking new birth, it had certain limitations for those in the process of sanctification. These "felt a more tender affection" for one another than before, and had "such a confidence in each other that they poured out their souls into each other's bosom." This they found to be a necessity, for "temptations were on every side," often "of such a kind" that could not easily be spoken of in a class of "young and old, men and women."[18]

These therefore wanted some means of closer union: they wanted to pour out their hearts without reserve, particularly with regard to the sin which did still 'easily beset' them, and the temptations which were most apt to prevail over them.[19]

To meet this need Wesley divided them into groups of six to eight called *bands,* "putting the married or single men, and married or single women together."[20] The bands originated with the Moravians, but were adopted by Wesley only with significant modifications. In particular Wesley disliked the rigid spiritual supervision of the band monitors, and instead stressed mutual accountability and the selection of the leader by the band.[21] The emphasis on mutuality is clear in Wesley's description of the bands as obeying the scriptural injunction to "Confess your faults one to another, and pray one for another, that ye may be healed."[22]

The band meeting was a more intimate and intensive experience than the class. The highly confessional character of the bands required an openness and vulnerability on the part of the members which was only possible in a context of mutual forgiveness and love. Each member was both the recipient of the advice and prayers of the others and a spiritual director for the others. The fellowship in the bands was thus much closer than in the classes.

At the same time, appropriately for those moving on to perfection, the three General Rules involve a more demanding discipline in the "Directions Given to the Band-Societies." Members are to "carefully" avoid evil, "zealously" do good works, and "constantly" observe the ordinances of God.[23]

In spite of the advantages of this "closer union" for the many who "were strengthened in love,"[24] some "fell from the faith," either immediately through "known, wilful sin, or gradually, almost insensibly, by giving way in what they call little things," such as sins of omission or sins of the heart. These *penitents* Wesley placed in separate meetings in which the "hymns, exhortations, and prayers are adapted to their circumstances,"[25] that is, adapted to those who once had faith as a spiritual sense but now had fallen back to a more dissipated way of life. This experience of backsliding had a salutary effect on many, who not only "recovered the ground they had lost" but also "rose higher than before." They were "more watchful than ever," now being "stronger in the faith that worketh by love."[26]

The "small number" of persons who progressed in the Christian life beyond the average band members were gathered by Wesley into a *select society*. His design was "not only to direct them how to *press after perfection*" and "to incite them to love one another more, and to watch more carefully over each other," but also to have a group in which he "might unbosom myself on all occasions, without reserve."[27] Because they had "the best rule of all in their hearts," Wesley only provided them with three directions:

> First, let nothing spoken in this society be spoken again. (Hereby we had the more full confidence in each other.) Secondly, every member agrees to submit to his Minister in all indifferent things. Thirdly, every member will bring once a week all he can spare toward a common stock.[28]

Unlike the classes and bands, the meetings of the select society were unstructured, having no required or recommended questions to be asked. Everyone had "an equal liberty of speaking, there being none greater or less than another." The advantage of this "free conversation" was that each learned from the others, and "in the multitude of counsellors there is safety."[29]

The select society was the culmination of trends which began with the classes and extended through the bands. The discipline begun in the classes and intensified in the bands was now a way of life; correspondingly, in this progression of small communities there is increasingly less structure and more mutuality in spiritual direction. As the capacity for repentance grows, it becomes more spontaneous in its exercise. Likewise, an increased sensitivity to the presence of God seems related to a growing disposition and ability to love one another and those in the world at large.

The select society was also the fullest social realization of the Christian life, toward which the class and band communities pointed. The desire to establish a "common stock" is both a recovery of the primitive Christian community of Acts 2 and an anticipation of the Kingdom of God itself. Despite the absence of an outward command, the early Christians had all things in common. The reason, says Wesley, was

> the command was written on their hearts. It naturally and necessarily resulted from the degree of love which they enjoyed. . . . And wheresoever the same course shall prevail the same effect will naturally follow.[30]

Although even here the Methodists remained actively in the world, the unity in love found in the select society nonetheless promoted distinctive social and economic relationships at variance with the larger social order. Growth in love and a corresponding deepening of Christian fellowship thus had for Wesley implications that extended beyond the specifically religious to all areas of human life.

In the Methodist communities, disciplined living was the fruit of desire for salvation,[31] and desire was the fruit of faith. It was faith—usually the faith of a servant—which brought persons into the class meeting. With this faith was a desire for salvation, that is, a desire for the assurance of forgiveness and to grow in the love of God and neighbor. The rules of discipline were means of grace through which God continually enabled and invited a mutual divine/human relationship of love.

The communities thus presupposed the faithful intention of their members, at least "a desire to flee the wrath to come, to be saved from their sins."[32] Their life was characterized by a disciplined faith, a striving to enter the "narrow gate" through the use of the means of grace.[33]

This life of discipline was both a response to grace received and an expression of desire for grace promised. It was a response to God in the relationship initiated by God, and a precondition for the continuation of and growth in that relationship. As such, it reflected both the necessity of divine initiative and the necessity of divine/human reciprocity for there to be an ongoing relationship with God.

The danger to this relationship was dissipation, the life of divided and thereby conflicting loyalties. Through dissipation one could lose faith, for dissipation distracts and clouds the vision of faith. To lose the sense of God's presence made possible by faith would be to replace the religion of the heart with formalism.

For faith to be maintained and increased, it must be disciplined. In the context of the mutual accountability and fellowship of the Methodist communities, the rules of discipline focused one's attention on God, and this served as means of participation in the relationship. Through their common struggle to live a disciplined life, the members of the class or band helped each other to keep a "single eye" on God in the midst of a world full of distraction.

It is no wonder failure to attend class or band meetings and failure to live according to the discipline were treated as serious matters. "With regard to any such person," Wesley said, "we will admonish him the error of his ways; we will bear with him for a season."[34] But persistent failure to keep the discipline brought expulsion from the society, facilitated by the practice of issuing membership tickets each quarter. The tickets, which Wesley associated with the letters of commendation mentioned in the New Testament, distinguished members from nonmembers and provided "a quiet and inoffensive way of removing any disorderly member."[35]

To not live according to the discipline was to invite dissipation, to allow other desires to compete with the desire for God, to risk a loss of faith. While Wesley did not presume to directly judge the hearts of others, he assumed that faith provided the motive for discipline, and discipline provided the means to maintain and deepen faith. Thus he did not claim for himself, as some opponents charged, the gift of the miraculous judgement of spirits. He wanted his class leaders to inquire as to the spiritual progress of their members, but not as a matter of discipline. The question of discipline "is not concerning the heart, but the life." The "general tenor of this," said Wesley, "cannot be hid without a miracle."[36]

While the Methodist communities presupposed faith on the part of those joining, they were designed, through mutual accountability to discipline and responsibility for one another, to both protect and increase that faith. This discipline was threefold: avoid all known sin, do all the good one can, and attend the ordinances of God. The instituted ordinances of God will be discussed in later sections in this and the following chapter. The first two rules will structure the remainder of this section: confession and the avoidance of sin, doing good within the fellowship, and doing good within the world.

To adopt the Methodist discipline was to turn from one way of life to a new way of life. The admonition to do no harm and avoid evil "in every kind"[37] concerns the first part: the turning away. It is the practice of rejecting all that dissipates one's life and distracts one's attention from God. Faith—even the faith of a servant—is a sensing of God's reality and presence; the practiced turning from sin avoids that which can cloud the vision of faith.

Wesley specifically lists those evils which are "most gener-ally practised" as a guide to what he means by doing no harm. He includes practices which directly turn our attention from the reality of God's presence: "taking the name of the Lord in vain; the profaning of the day of the Lord. . . . " But he also includes those which either harm or place us in enmity with our neighbor:

> Drunkenness, *buying or selling spirituous liquors; or drinking them* (unless in case of extreme necessity). *Fighting,* quarreling . . .; brother, 'going to the law' with

brother; returning evil for evil, or railing for railing; . . .
uncharitable or unprofitable conversation. . .; Doing to
others as we would not they should do unto us. . . .[38]

These practices are prohibited because they directly contradict the life of love for God and neighbor, and thus draw one
away from seeing ourselves and our neighbor in the light of
God's presence.

A related concern was the problem of moral honesty.
Wesley warned against "the 'using many words' in buying or
selling; The *buying or selling uncustomed goods;* The *giving or
taking things on . . . usury,*" and either "Borrowing . . . or
taking up goods without a probability of paying for them."[39]
He had no sympathy for the profit motive and the shrewd
business practices admired by many, both then and now.

But beyond this, Wesley insisted that Methodists turn away
from a way of life which invited dissipation: from the wearing
of gold or costly apparel, "The *taking of such diversions* as
cannot be used in the name of the Lord Jesus; Softness and
needless self-indulgence; Laying up treasures upon earth.
. . . "[40] This is a direct challenge to a life of acquisition and
consumption, corresponding to his well-known opposition to
what Outler calls "surplus accumulation,"[41] the coveting or
possessing wealth beyond the reasonable needs of self and
family. Wesley warns Christians to

> seek not to *increase in goods.* 'Lay not up for thyself
> treasures upon earth.' This is a flat, positive command,
> full as clear as 'Thou shalt not commit adultery'.[42]

The danger of surplus accumulation is twofold. First, one
tends to trust in riches rather than God; second, one tends to
seek happiness in them rather than God.[43] They easily replace
God as the object of one's faith and love, and in addition
prevent that generosity to the poor which characterizes the
Christian life.[44]

The failure to live by this discipline was seen by Wesley as

the reason personal religion was "amazingly superficial"
among Methodists:

> How little faith is there among us! How little commu-
> nion with God! How little living in heaven, walking in
> eternity. . . . How much love of the world; desire of
> pleasure, of ease, of getting money! How little brotherly
> love! What continual judging one another! What gossip-
> ing, evil-speaking, tale-bearing! What want of moral
> honesty! . . . who does as he would be done by, in buying
> and selling, particularly in selling horses![45]

The decrease in faith, communion with God, and love of
neighbor is directly related to the continued practice of
speaking ill of one another, moral dishonesty, and surplus
accumulation.

Wesley was concerned with more than refraining from a list
of sins. He sought the abandonment of an entire way of life
rooted in the values of society but subversive of faith. The
Methodists were accountable to a countercultural discipline,
but as persons who nonetheless actively lived in that culture.
The culmination of this countercultural tendency is seen in
the select society, with its goal of pooling personal economic
resources into a common stock.

The dissipated life of acquisition, consumption, and competition pervaded not only society but the habits, perceptions,
and desires of individuals. This inner reflection of the cultural
norms could not simply be overcome by a response to field
preaching, or even by new birth; it required a struggle within
the heart, and the Methodist communities were where that
struggle was engaged.

The disguised persistence of dissipation was most straightforwardly recognized in the bands. At each meeting every
member was asked "What temptations have you met with?"
and "What have you thought, said, or done, of which you
doubt whether it be sin or not?"[46] The members of the band
endeavored together to discern the ways in which dissipation
still had a hold on their affections and actions. They were

encouraged to critically examine one another and themselves in order to increase awareness of those practices and desires which continued to cloud the vision of faith and divide the heart.

The class meeting was more concerned with those practices against which Wesley warned. Yet even here, in the process of questions and answers, the discerning class leader or member could begin to deal with the more hidden aspects of the dissipated life.

This necessary struggle against the persistence of cultural values and perceptions in the heart is in contrast to understandings of the Christian life which posit a point of arrival or completion. Because perfectionists assume that temptation and actions contrary to the will of God are no longer a problem, they become open to those very influences they presume to have overcome. Integral to the life of the communities was the critical examination of any presumptive claim for the Christian life.

Correspondingly, the practice of confession in community was a central feature of Methodist discipline. In the classes, confession occurred in a general, nonspecific form; in the bands and select society there was a more intimate probing of the depths of sin. As the danger of presumptive claims increases after the new birth, the confessional practices likewise intensify.

The practice of mutual confession was not simply a seeking of hidden attitudes and values. It was most centrally a mutual experience of forgiveness, a freeing from guilt in order to grow in love. The members of a class or band stood together before God as both sinners and as those promised new life. Each Christian life was not the solitary project of the individual, but the common responsibility of the fellowship. It was the communal context of grace and forgiveness which enabled persons to increasingly open their lives to others, and become increasingly honest with themselves.

Although fellowship might seem to be the governing characteristic of Methodist communities, Watson has persuasively argued that the purpose of the class meetings was accountability. It was only as this accountability was practiced that persons "began to realize they were indeed on a common journey," and fellowship was engendered.[47] This seems to be the case, both historically and logically. But while fellowship may depend on the prior purpose of accountability or (in the bands) confession, its emergence was a central reason Methodist communities were means of grace, and in turn permitted accountability and confession to become increasingly effective.

The classes, bands, and select society were, to use Howard Snyder's phrase, "eschatological communities"[48] insofar as they embodied in themselves and in the world the social relationships of the age to come. While persons came to the classes and bands concerned with their own salvation, through meeting together they recognized their need for fellowship and responsibility for one another. Salvation must occur in community if it was to occur at all.

These communities of love stood over against life in the larger society. Although the classes and bands were by no means perfect embodiments of the kingdom, their members experienced a mutual caring which contrasted significantly with the competitiveness, acquisitiveness, and social dividedness of everyday life.

The tension between the Methodist communities and the larger culture encouraged members to be mutually supportive. Wesley was not optimistic about the world's response to the religion of heart, expecting such Christians would suffer loss of friends, business, and employment.[49] Even when they were employed or trusted, it was not out of love but a desire for profit. Thus, "setting aside what exceptions may be made by the preventing grace or the peculiar providence of God," the world hates Christians "as cordially and sincerely as ever it did their Master."[50] This tension sheds light on Wesley's General Rule that Methodists do good "especially to them that are of the household of faith, or groaning so to be," through employing and doing business with one another, for "the world will love its own, and them only. . . . "[51]

In addition to giving mutual support, Methodists were to avoid those practices which undermined fellowship. We have already seen Wesley's rule against uncharitable and unprofitable conversation.[52] He defines uncharitable conversation as "repeating the faults of absent persons"; unprofitable conversation is that which does not edify or minister grace to hearers.[53]

As Outler notes, persons with pietist leanings are tempted to a "high-minded censoriousness" which would threaten "the closeknit fellowship of the Methodist class meetings. . . ."[54] Realizing this, Wesley warned that uncharitable conversation, or evil-speaking, "attacks us in disguise," for we see ourselves speaking out of an indignation against sin; "We commit sin from the mere hatred of sin!"[55] This endangers not only the fellowship but the Christian life, for there "is scarce any wrong temper . . . which may not be occasionally gratified by it, and consequently incline us to it."[56]

Wesley advises Methodists to confront directly anyone seen to be at fault, speaking straightforwardly, but always in the spirit and manner of love. Correspondingly, they should in the process avoid even the appearance of pride, arrogance, disdain, contempt, anger, and hatred.[57]

Mutual responsibility and charitable conversation were practices through which Christians learned how to love one another. As the recipients of such love, they also learned how to gladly receive the love of others. Thus Christian affections associated with love of neighbor were both expressed in concrete acts of love, and evoked and deepened through the experience of being loved.

Insofar as love was experienced in the Methodist communities, their members had a foretaste of the Kingdom of God. The life of the community countered complacency or despair through being an experienced anticipation of that which is promised for all, and nourished faith through providing in the midst of the world a vision of eternity.

Christianity for Wesley is a way of being in the world which is rooted not in the world but in the Kingdom of God. Thus the Methodist communities endeavored to become free of those cultural values, desires, and assumptions which remained in their lives, while at the same time seeking to reflect in their fellowship the life of the coming kingdom. Methodists were not only to live the Christian life in the meetings, but also to live daily in a world whose values and practices conflicted with Christianity.

It was necessary for Christians to willingly face the conflict in order to actively love their neighbor and to themselves grow in love. The one who loves as God loves

> cannot confine the expressions of it to his own family, or friends, or acquaintance, or party; or to those of his own opinions; no, nor to those who are partakers of like precious faith; but steps over all these narrow bounds that he may do good to every man; that he may . . . manifest his love to neighbors and strangers, friends and enemies.[58]

Love which is not exercised to all is less than the love which God calls us to have and promises to give; to not love all persons is to not live the Christian life. Christianity, says Wesley, "is essentially a social religion, and to turn it into a solitary one is to destroy it. . . ."[59]

Methodists were expected to do good at every opportunity and in every circumstance by

> everything which we give, or speak, or do, . . . whereby another man may receive any advantage, either in his body or soul. The feeding the hungry, the clothing the naked, the entertaining or assisting the stranger, the visiting those that are sick or in prison, the comforting the afflicted, the instructing the ignorant, the reproving the wicked, the exhorting and encouraging the well-doer; and if there be any other work of mercy, it is equally included in this direction.[60]

As in the fellowship, but now within a much wider context, the Christian learns through practicing love what it means to love one's neighbor. Works of mercy are means of grace through which the active expression of love in the world both increases sensitivity to human need and deepens the capacity to love.

Increased sensitivity to human need corresponds to an increased clarity in seeing the world and a diminishing of dissipation. Wesley argued that involvement with the poor was a precondition for a real love for the poor, as it broke down false assumptions about the reality and seriousness of poverty.

> One great reason why the rich in general have so little sympathy for the poor is because they so seldom visit them. Hence it is that . . . one part of the world does not know what the other suffers. Many of them do not know, because they do not care to know: they keep out of the way of knowing it—and then plead their voluntary ignorance as an excuse for their hardness of heart.[61]

Far from equating involvement in the world with dissipation, Wesley saw the active practice of love as a means of growing in faith and love.

As we have seen, involvement in the world by way of increasing riches was another matter. Wesley wanted the Methodists to be "patterns of *diligence* and *frugality*," both for their own sake and so that they would not discredit the gospel.[62] But with industry and frugality comes riches, and riches in turn leads to "pride, anger, and love of the world in all its branches."[63] Wesley's famous solution to the problem of surplus accumulation and its accompanying threat of dissipation was for those who "gain all they can" and "save all they can" to likewise "give all they can,"[64] that is, "*give alms* of such things as you possess, and that to the uttermost of your power."[65] Christianity, both for the sake of the poor and the Christian life, required a radical, voluntary redistribution of wealth, through which love is expressed and dissipation avoided.

While the need to practice love concretely in the world is

similar to that in the fellowship, the experience of love is vastly different. In the fellowship love is both given and received; in the world it is given to the neighbor but often not given back in return. Love in the fellowship mirrors the mutuality of the divine/human relationship of love; love in the world more often mirrors the cross. The experience of the love of God and neighbor in the community is foundational to works of mercy in the world, and these require that foundation because they lack the experienced mutuality.

Yet even the hostility Christians face when they try to love as Christ loved is essential to the Christian life. Wesley argues that "some intercourse even with ungodly and unholy men is absolutely needful" for the development of such Christian tempers as poverty of spirit, meekness, and love of enemies.[66] The attempt to turn a disposition such as meekness "into a solitary virtue is to destroy it from the face of the earth."[67]

Works of mercy were means of grace through which love of neighbor was formed, deepened, and expressed. They were at the same time reminders of God's presence and involvement in the world. Christians undertook works of mercy as a response to God's love for them and in recognition of God's love for the world. Through their experience of practicing love, Christians deepened their knowledge of what God's love for a fallen creation entails. As they increasingly experienced the depths of God's love, the vision of their faith and the strength of their love grew as well.

To provide a list of rules inevitably invites legalism, in which the rules, instead of serving as means of grace, become ends in themselves. Wesley's own attitude toward these rules of discipline is revealed by his comments on a letter he received from Thomas Willis, who wrote to him concerning the Directions for the Band Societies. In publishing the letter, Wesley commends Willis' approach with these prefatory remarks: "See a pattern of true Christian simplicity! His name is still precious to all who knew him. He was for many years an ornament of the Church of England and of the Society in Kingswood."[68]

Given this praise by Wesley, it is noteworthy that Willis opens his letter by saying if anyone should

> ask me if I did follow all the directions given to the Band Societies, I must answer, No. For I believe one general rule for all sorts of people, in all conditions of life, though all seeking salvation, cannot be performed without some exception. . . . [69]

The letter goes on to examine each rule, describing how Willis has or has not been able to follow the directions. For example, he obeys the rule "Neither to buy nor sell anything at all on the Lord's day" exactly, except for the selling of milk. Willis reasons that even on Sundays cows need milking, children need the milk, and the milk would spoil if left to Monday. Wesley then adds his own comment: "Quite right."

As for the direction "be at a word both in buying and in selling," Willis seeks always to speak the truth with his neighbor. He notes, however, that in country business, because prices continually fluctuate, "buying and selling cannot be at one word." Wesley comments, "All right."

Willis partially objects to the direction, "to pawn nothing; no, not to save life." While having kept this rule "to perfection" because he hates extortion, he does "believe it is better to save life than to destroy." Wesley answers, "You need not take the phrase literally."

Beyond this, Willis confesses that he does at times "mention the fault" of someone "behind their back," but only for edification, so "that others may take warning, and be more careful for the future." He also is not at the Lord's table every week, but goes once a month in his parish church, "which is as often as it is administered there."[70]

While avoiding legalism concerning the directions, Willis nonetheless took the rules seriously. This, I believe, is why Wesley approves of his approach. Willis sought to apply the rules to his own circumstances, and in the process made appropriate or necessary exceptions concerning milk, country markets, and the Lord's Supper. More importantly, his application of the directions was governed by the rule of love "which our Saviour gave in his Sermon on the Mount" which "can be performed by all people, in whatsoever condition of life, if they have faith."[71] To do unto others as you would have them do unto you meant for Willis that children needed milk on Sunday, saving lives always took priority, and persons needed warning about the dangers to the Christian life which others had faced. To deny this approach to the rules of discipline would give them authority over that to which they are a means, which is the life of love. Such formalism Wesley was determined to avoid.

The discipline of the Methodist communities included accountability, confession, fellowship, and works of mercy; each was essential to the others. Accountability was foundational, for through it persons were encouraged to maintain the discipline. Accountability and confession aimed toward increased honesty and knowledge of the self, particularly avoiding naive or presumptive claims about one's own Christian life. The fellowship in turn made confession possible, strengthened the members for service in the world, and provided a present experience of love that would counteract temptations to despair. Works of mercy brought one in contact with the life of the world and its needs, working against willful ignorance and complacency and strengthening the need for confession, forgiveness, and supportive fellowship.

The communities were also necessary to maintain and increase faith. In various ways the disciplined life sought to avoid dissipation and to uncover the disguised ways in which it influences lives. At the same time, attention was focused on the presence of God in the world and in the community: confession was before God, fellowship was with God, works of mercy were in the service of God. The presence of God was experienced in and through the community, and from there in the world at large.

The classes, bands, and their accompanying discipline were prudential means of grace, and highly attentive to the needs of the Christian life in Wesley's own time and place. Christians in other contexts may justly question the applicability of Wesley's discipline to their own situation. But whatever form the danger of dissipation and the practice of love may take, the necessity to avoid the former and do the latter remains. Growth in the Christian life requires a disciplined context, in which the promise of the gospel and the actual practice of Christianity mutually inform one another and critically deepen our understanding of both. And in all times and places, the Methodist communities are a reminder that the Christian life is not a solitary project; the Christian life is nurtured in a community of mutual accountability and responsibility, and in service to a world in need of love.

3. PRAYER AND FASTING

Prayer, said Wesley, is "the grand means of drawing near to God"; all other means are helpful "as they are mixed with or prepare us for this."[1] Prayer thus pervades the other means of grace, as both preparation and content. But prayer also pervades the Christian life itself.

For Wesley prayer is a way of life. The Christian prays without ceasing, in that the "heart is ever lifted up to God, at all times and in all places. . . . "[2] It is connected with the practice of the presence of God, for so "much as we really enjoy the presence of God, so much prayer and praise do we offer up *without* ceasing;" prayer is "the breath of our spiritual life."[3]

On one hand, faith is a prerequisite to prayer, as it is a prerequisite to our enjoying the presence of God. Prayer without faith is dead and formal; prayer in faith is communion with God. While faith as a spiritual sense is necessary for prayer without ceasing, it is a "blasphemous absurdity" to assume faith "in the full Christian meaning" is necessary for prayer. The only faith absolutely necessary for one who prays is "not doubting God heareth his prayer, and will fulfil the desire of his heart,"[4] even if "through fear and shame he scarce knows what to say."[5] Thus those with the faith of a servant should pray for the assurance of forgiveness and new birth,[6] those with the faith of a child should pray for sanctification. Only whenever one prays, "see that it be thy one design to commune with God, to lift up thy heart to him, to pour out thy soul before him. . . ."[7]

On the other hand, prayer is a prerequisite for increasing the faith and love one has, and is therefore a means through which God enables and invites a deeper communion and growth in the Christian life. Wesley thought it "wisdom to force ourselves to prayer; to pray whether we can or not,"[8] seeing prayer as an efficacious means of grace apart from one's feelings at the moment. There are three reasons prayer increases faith and love:

First, because prayer is communion with God, it invites a conscious, intentional relationship with God. As has already been noted, such a relationship is necessary for the Christian life to grow in love, and is at the same time the expression of that love.

Second, prayer is absolutely necessary if we would receive any gift from God,"[9] and this most especially includes the soteriological gifts of new birth and Christian perfection, as well as the more gradual growth in the affections. Here prayer presupposes scripture, for the content of prayer is informed by the remembered promises of God.

Third, the act of praying itself gives shape to the relationship and the Christian life: God is the one who gives in love, we are the ones who are open to receive God's gifts and respond in love. The end of our praying

> is not to inform God, as though he knew not your wants already; but rather to inform yourselves, to fix the sense

of those wants more deeply in your hearts, and the sense
of your continual dependence on him who only is able to
supply all your wants. It is not so much to move
God—who is always more ready to give than you to
ask—as to move yourselves, that you may be willing and
ready to receive the good things he has prepared for
you.[10]

The "one great office of prayer" is to produce "a fit disposition on our part to receive his grace and blessing" and "to
increase our desire of the things we ask for. . . . "[11]

In contrast to the Moravians, Wesley saw prayer as the
integration of activity and receptiveness. Because we seek
God and ask for promised gifts of grace, we become increasingly aware of God's presence and open to God's transformation of our lives. And as we respond in love, our relationship
with God grows.

It is no surprise that Wesley found the neglect of prayer to
be a central hindrance to the Christian life. The failure to ask
for increased holiness in prayer is one reason persons fail to
grow in the Christian life;[12] the "neglect of private prayer" is
the most frequent cause of Christians losing their faith.
"Nothing can be more plain," he argues, "than that the life of
God in the soul does not continue, much less increase, unless
we use all opportunities of communing with God. . . . "[13]

Wesley identifies four elements of prayer: supplication
(petition, discussed above), deprecation (confession), intercession, and thanksgiving (equated with praise). Like supplication, each of the other three involves a particular form of
interaction with God.

Deprecation and intercession correspond to the practices in
the classes and bands. As one is accountable to and makes
confession in the community, so one is directly accountable to
God and makes confession to God in prayer. The practices in
community assist the prayer of confession through enabling a
deeper awareness of sin and an increased clarity of vision;
accountability before God in prayer assists communal prac-

tices by raising new doubts, concerns, and perspectives on the meaning of love of God and neighbor. Through confession the Christian life takes shape before God: the one who prays is a sinner in need of forgiveness; God is the one who judges and yet forgives in love.

As one does acts of mercy in the community and in the world, so one intercedes for the needs of the community and world to God in prayer. The practices in community assist the prayer of intercession through enabling an increased sensitivity to human need and a broader vision of a changed world; the prayer of intercession assists communal practices by placing the needs of the community and world before the God who is love and then bringing the practice of love into closer accord with God's own loving will. Through intercession the Christian life takes shape before God: God loves the world; the one who prays actively loves that which God loves.

Thanksgiving is the fruit of rejoicing in prayer for the love of God in Christ.

> Thanksgiving is inseparable from true prayer; it is almost essentially connected with it. He that always prays is ever giving praise, whether in ease or pain, both for prosperity and for the greatest adversity.[14]

While one might take exception to Wesley's giving praise *for* all circumstances, it is consistent with his view of prayer that Christians give thanks *in* all circumstances. Through thanksgiving the Christian life also takes shape before God: the one who prays is the joyful recipient of a gift; God is the one who has given freely in love.

Thus Christian prayer necessarily includes this full range of elements because the relationship with God is itself multidimensional.[15] All focus the attention of the one who prays upon God, but in ways that nurture different affections: hope, humility, love of neighbor, and gratitude, but in all cases love for the God who promises, forgives, serves, and blesses. In the full range of prayer, presumption is countered with honest confession, complacency with active love, and despair with expectant hope.

Wesley urged the Methodists to use both written and extemporary prayer. We can use Wesley's description of praying without ceasing, quoted at the beginning of this section, as a means to understand his insistence. If prayer is the lifting of one's heart to God, the written prayers provide descriptive access to the God to whom one prays. If prayer is to be made at all times and in all places, extemporary prayer discerns the presence of God in particular contexts and brings the needs of each situation before God.

The importance of written prayers will be discussed more fully in Chapter V. Here I simply note that Wesley used both and urged others to do the same, and in his own private devotions he characteristically made written prayers the context within which he prayed extemporaneously.[16] This no doubt aided the discipline of prayer at those times he did not "feel" like praying. But it is also a paradigm of the major thesis of this dissertation: prayer as descriptive identity and prayer focused on God's presence in concrete circumstances are mutually dependent and essential to an ongoing relationship with God; together they are one prayer to the one distinctive God who is present.

For Wesley, fasting and prayer are closely connected. Confronted by its continual neglect among Methodists, Wesley again and again insisted on its necessity,[17] and set an example by himself fasting regularly. Wesley did not urge an extreme fast and recognized "several degrees of fasting which cannot hurt your health."[18] One could fast for a number of days, a single day, or a half-day; one could abstain from all food, some food, or from pleasant foods.[19] The degree of fasting depended on circumstance and was prudential, but fasting itself was an instituted means of grace for all times and circumstances.

Wesley identifies five grounds or reasons for fasting: sorrow for sin, bodily health, avoidance of excessive consumption, self-punishment (of which scripture and tradition witness, but Wesley is reluctant to stress), and as an aid to prayer.[20] The union of fasting to prayer was especially important for Wesley, who saw it as a means

> of confirming and increasing, not only virtue, not chastity only (as some have idly imagined without any ground either from Scripture, reason, or experience), but also seriousness of spirit, earnestness, sensibility and tenderness of conscience; deadness to the world, and consequently the love of God and every holy and heavenly affection.[21]

While Wesley does not say why fasting is such an important aid to prayer, two of his reasons for fasting suggest an answer. First, he argues that "sorrow for sin, and a strong apprehension of the wrath of God" are the natural grounds of fasting. Preoccupied with this eternally significant concern, one forgets to eat, abstaining "not only from pleasant, but even needful food."[22] Here fasting is a recognition of oneself as a sinner before God and an expression of the resulting penitential and non-presumptive relationship.

Second, fasting is the avoidance of excessive consumption of food, along with a "carelessness and levity of spirit" and an increase in "foolish and unholy desires, yea, unclean and vile affections" which accompany such consumption.[23] This observation is in accord with the insights of patristic asceticism concerning the connection of eating with a more general rise in sensuality. The danger which fasting helps avoid is a dissipation of desire, and a corresponding turning away from God.

Both sorrow for sin and the avoidance of competing desires enable persons to focus their attention on God and clarify their true needs as they offer their prayers to God. A growing freedom from transient desires allows an increased passion for the eternal values of the kingdom; a diminished attention to one's own desires allows an increased attention to the needs of others.

Although fasting could be a source of self-righteousness, when rightly used it is a means of avoiding both presumptive claims for the Christian life and the dissipation which leads to formalism. When used with prayer in a context of mutual accountability and support, it enables Christians to attend to the presence of God, and to the needs of the world that God loves.

4. THE GENERAL MEANS OF GRACE

The general means of grace are closely related to the Methodist discipline. "Watching" and the "exercise of the presence of God" are connected to doing no harm and avoiding evil; "denying ourselves" and "taking up our cross" are specifically mentioned by Wesley as aspects of doing all the good one can.[1] They are distinguished from all other means of grace in that, while the others "may be used without fruit,"[2] one can never "use these means but a blessing will ensue." The "more you use them, the more will you grow in grace."[3] All other means of grace—including those such as class meetings and extemporary prayer—are subject to formalist abuse. I shall attempt to explain why the general means of grace are especially resistant to formalism through a discussion of their interrelationship with one another and with other means of grace.

Watching, says Wesley, is an "earnest, constant, persevering exercise;" it implies "steadfast faith, patient hope, labouring love, unceasing prayer," and "the mighty exertion of all the affections of the soul. . . ."[4] By this Wesley is not presupposing a certain degree of Christian maturity as a precondition to watching, but is insisting that at any point in the Christian life watching requires wholehearted effort.

Watching can be defined both negatively and positively. On one hand it is to "watch against the world, the devil, yourselves, your besetting sin."[5] It is a conscious, intended alertness to the deceptiveness of sin, an attentiveness to continued temptation and one's weakness in the face of it. As such, watching is an essential attitude underlying the disciplined accountability and confessional practices of the classes and bands, as well as prayers of confession. It counters presumptive claims for the Christian life and encourages a sense of continued dependence on grace.

On the other hand watching is inwardly attending to God in order to know God's will, "gain power to do it," and thereby grow in grace.[6] This shows its close relationship to the exercise of the presence of God, which is endeavoring "to set God always before you" and "to see his eye continually fixed upon you."[7] Here again is a constant, intended attentiveness, this time to the presence of God. Through this, faith is strengthened and formalism is avoided.

Watching and the exercise of the presence of God are thus mutually reinforcing. Watching helps faith continue and grow through avoiding that which blocks or distorts the vision of faith; exercising the presence of God informs faith of those remaining sins and temptations which need to be removed.

As watching is related to exercising the presence of God, so self-denial is related to taking up one's cross. Wesley makes this connection explicit:

> If we do not continually 'deny ourselves', we do not learn of him, but of other masters. If we do not 'take up our cross daily', we do not 'come after him', but after the world. . . . If we are not walking in the way of the cross, we are not following him. . . . [8]

While watching and the exercise of the presence of God opened one to God's presence, self-denial and taking up one's cross enables one to imitate Christ. This is why they are part of the discipline of doing good: to follow Christ is to love as Christ loved.

Self-denial, says Wesley, is

> to deny our own will where it does not fall in with the will of God, and that however pleasing it may be. It is to

deny ourselves any pleasure which does not spring from,
and lead to God. . . .[9]

Self-denial is a deliberate turning from a way of life contrary
to God or which leads away from God. It is an abstinence
from those practices or possessions which the world calls
pleasing but which do not constitute true happiness. Self-
denial thus avoids the sources of dissipation which lead to
formal religion.

The practice of self-denial is vital in the face of increasing
riches. Without self-denial, Wesley observes, persons generally decrease in grace in the same proportion as they increase
in wealth.[10] Such persons, due to their increasing love of
pleasure, are correspondingly unable to take up their cross
and endure hardship on behalf of others.[11]

Self-denial is the precondition for taking up one's cross. A
cross, says Wesley,

> is anything contrary to our will, anything displeasing to
> our nature. So that taking up our cross goes a little
> farther than denying ourselves; it rises a little higher,
> and is a more difficult task . . . it being more easy to
> forego pleasure than to endure pain.[12]

Wesley further distinguishes between bearing a cross, in
which "we endure what is laid upon us without our choice,
with meekness and resignation," and taking up a cross, in
which "we voluntarily suffer what is in our power to avoid"
through embracing the will of God.[13] Taking up one's cross is
turning toward and accepting the way of love in the world no
matter what the cost. It avoids complacency in the Christian
life, challenging the minimal morality of formalism with the
radical claims of the gospel.

Self-denial and taking up one's cross are mutually reinforcing. Self-denial prepares the way for taking up one's cross
through renouncing all that tempts one to avoid love through
pleasure; taking up one's cross in the world enables one to

become increasingly aware of those undenied temptations and practices which still remain as obstacles to a life of love.

Given Wesley's call to wholehearted intention in using the general means of grace, it might seem that fundamentally an act of will is more important to the Christian life than the gift of faith. But this would remove the general means of grace from the context of the Christian life as understood by Wesley.

These practices are not basically acts of will but graced responses to grace received. At a minimum, persons using the general means of grace are already within a relationship with God through prevenient grace; nearly if not all have at least responded to the gospel with the faith of a servant. Consequently the general means of grace do not precede faith but presuppose it and strengthen it.

Faith, Wesley insists, is made perfect by works; "otherwise it will insensibly die away."[14] Those with the faith of a servant quickly relapse into a "fatal insensibility" through a lack of self-denial; in the same way those with the faith of a child can "make a shipwreck" of their faith.[15] Without the general means of grace, there is increasing dissipation, and faith is supplanted by formal religion.

To respond to grace through using the general means is to avoid dissipation and keep one's faith focused on God; it is to turn from competing objects of love to an increasing love for God and one's neighbor. The process is cyclical: watching and self-denial are critical practices which counteract dissipation; exercise of the presence of God and taking up one's cross are expressions of faith, hope and love. These latter practices in turn invite increased watching and self-denial in light of the actual experience of living a Christian life in the world.

Watching and self-denial are never abandoned, nor is there any point in which loving God or one's neighbor cannot deepen or grow. Thus the Christian is not self-sufficient in these practices but increasingly dependent on grace. The Christian life is marked by an active receptivity to God in which the general means of grace are practiced with all the devotion one has, but with the desire for an ability to practice them more faithfully. The Christian is increasingly aware of a continued need for God, and seeks to further the relationship with God.

The reason these means of grace are always efficacious is that they are themselves responses to grace and expressions of faith and love. If they are practiced wholeheartedly, they cannot but further the relationship with God which constitutes salvation. Together they are attitudes which underlie all the means of grace in this chapter, and the faith they strengthen is necessary to the means of grace in the following chapter.

They do not, however, stand alone. The general means of grace presuppose a Christian community in which individual practices can be critically evaluated and mutually reinforced. They also presuppose other means of grace which provide descriptive content to the character of the God whose presence is sensed by faith, and narrative portrayals of the love which is expressed through the taking up of a cross. It is to these means of grace I now turn.

Chapter V

The Means to the Identity of God

1. RENEWING THE CHURCH: EXPERIENCED IDENTITY

Wesley consistently refused to separate the experience of faith from the ordinances of God in the church. While he acknowledged that formalism abused the ordinances through mistaking the means for the end, he insisted with equal force that to seek the end without the means led to enthusiasm. Instead, he urged that

> the abuse be taken away and the use remain. Now use all outward things; but use them with a constant eye to the renewal of your soul in righteousness and true holiness.[1]

That is, use them with that faith which is both a response to God and a desire for God and the life God gives. Wesley sought not alternatives to the church but the renewal of the church.

This chapter is concerned with the means of grace associated with church and tradition; that is, with those practices which countered the tendency toward enthusiasm in the renewal movement through presenting those descriptions, actions, and promises which identify God and characterize the Christian life. But these means of grace, and the remembrance and promise they convey, are dependent on those means of grace discussed in the previous chapter. Because of this dependence, I begin by examining more particularly how those means of grace which maintain and strengthen faith and provide occasions for the practice of love serve as means to the renewal of the church.

The Christian life is not predicated on knowing that there is a God, but on knowing God. God is known for Wesley only in the union of the knowledge of God's identity or character with the experienced present reality of God. To have "experiences" which one attributes to either a generalized or partially described "God" is to court enthusiasm; to have information about God without experiencing the presence of God is to invite formalism.

Faith is the antidote to formalism because it seeks to avoid dissipation through focusing on God. There are degrees of faith, and even the sort of faith which responds to prevenient grace will experience scripture, eucharist, and public prayer as loci for encountering the living God. But normally, this "prevenient" faith is brought to hear the preaching of the gospel; from there it is either the faith of a servant or of a child which experiences God in scripture, eucharist, and prayer.

Whatever the degree, faith focuses attention on God. Christian experience was not an "inward" search for God, but the effect of an "outward" relationship with God. "You look inward too much, and upward too little,"[2] Wesley advises one class leader; faith directs attention toward God and away from preoccupation with one's feelings. Faith encourages persons to seek God in the means of grace, not personal experiences.

Yet, because faith is a spiritual sense, the God who is sought is experienced in the means of grace. The perceptiveness of faith varies with the degree of faith, and is always subject to increase. What Wesley says of the "pure in heart" can thus be applied in appropriate measure to all who have faith in God:

> But in a more especial manner they see God in his ordinances. Whether they appear in the great congregation to " . . . worship him in the beauty of holiness", . . .

> whether they search the oracles of God, or hear the
> ambassadors of Christ proclaiming glad tidings of salva-
> tion; or by eating of that bread and drinking of that cup
> . . . they find such a near approach as cannot be
> expressed. They see him, as it were, face to face, and
> "talk with him as a man talking with his friends". . . .[3]

Through faith, the identity and presence of God become one
in the experience of the person, even as they are in God. This
is why Wesley resisted the common identification of mediation with indirect experience; to experience God through
these means of grace is to experience directly (though not
exhaustively) the presence and identity of God.

The experience is transformative because it is an experience of the identity of God. As God is remembered and as the
promises of God are renewed, the Christian affections are
formed and shaped. Affections such as love and hope not only
increase in strength, but grow qualitatively richer as well.

Faith is a gift of God, but it is given by God in degrees.
Whether the faith is that of a servant or that of a child, it is
maintained and nurtured in disciplined communities. It is
used, however, as the means to experience God as mediated
through scripture, eucharist, and public prayer. Because faith
enables a relationship with God through these means of grace,
it enables the Christian affections to be formed and shaped by
the identity of God.

The God who is the object of the affections is most fully
described by the life and death of Jesus Christ. The Christian
"sees the light of the glorious love of God, in the face of Jesus
Christ,"[4] and the affections are formed and shaped in response.

But Christ is not only the one to whom we respond
affectively; Christ is also the one we follow or imitate. The life
and death of Jesus narratively portrays that love which we are
to have for others in the world.

The true test of our understanding of the meaning of
Christianity is not our ability to explain its doctrines but our

ability to practice its life. The disciplined communities contribute to the understanding of scripture, eucharist, and prayer by mutually encouraging and critically evaluating the actual practice of the Christian life.

The relationship between the two sets of means of grace is cyclical. The means of grace which convey identity both transform and provide narrative and descriptive accounts of the Christian life. The understanding of that life is demonstrated and deepened by its disciplined practice in the community and in the world. This deeper understanding is then brought back to the means of grace which identify God and the Christian life, leading to further affective transformation by and a richer appropriation of their narrative portrayal.

Both faith and Christian practice assist in avoiding formalism in using the means of grace in the church. They enable persons to experience the reality of God in the means of grace and the meaning of new life in the world. The church not only presupposes the faith and practices of the societies insofar as it resists formalism, but is continually pervaded by them in all of its life. It is this faith which enables the living experience of that reality which the church proclaims.

2. THE LORD'S SUPPER

Identity and presence are not two different qualities which must somehow be united, but aspects of the one God which must be discerned. Through faith, the two are experienced in their unity in the Lord's Supper.

While Wesley called prayer the grand means of drawing near to God, he could also term the Lord's Supper the "choicest instrument" of grace:

> But none, like this mysterious rite
>   Which dying mercy gave,
> Can draw forth all His promised might
>   And all His will to save.[1]

The Lord's Supper has this distinction because participation in it involves a union of natural and spiritual senses corresponding to an experienced union of the tangible elements and the spiritual presence of Christ.

The best available analysis of Wesley's understanding of the Lord's Supper is by Ole Borgen; along with the primary texts, it shall provide guidance in this section. My central task is to examine how the Lord's Supper contributes to the Christian life through conveying the identity of Christ in remembrance and promise. But prior to this, I must first examine a problem in Borgen's own argument which calls into question a central thesis of this dissertation.

Borgen emphasizes that, for Wesley, the Lord's Supper is dependent for its efficacy on the agency of the Holy Spirit, over against Lutheran or Anglo-Catholic interpretations which see a union of Christ and the elements. He begins by showing how Wesley assumes the Augustinian distinction between the outward sign (*signum*) of the sacrament and inward grace, or the thing signified (*res*);[2] by grace Wesley means Jesus Christ and all his benefits.[3] Sign and grace are not the same, but neither are they separable; grace gives life to the sign, while the sign points to Christ as the source of grace.[4]

Although Wesley's position on the sacraments is in some ways unique, on a more general level it is a variation of the Reformed doctrine of virtualism, mediated through Anglicanism. Virtualism holds that the elements remain unchanged but Christ is nonetheless present through the Holy Spirit, using the elements as means of grace:

> Feeble elements bestow
>   A power not theirs to give
> Who explains the wondrous way,
>   How through these the virtue came?
> These the virtue did convey,
>   Yet still remain the same.[5]

Borgen argues that Wesley avoids a "static" relationship between the sign and the grace through seeing grace not as automatically present (and thus at human disposal) but as given by a living, acting God working through the means of grace. More than a Reformed doctrine of real presence, Wesley posits a dynamic or living presence; for Wesley, says Borgen, "where God acts, there he is."[6]

Borgen supports his reading of Wesley by an analysis of the Wesleyan eucharistic hymns. There he finds three types of invocation: that the elements be made a real and effective sign, that the sign become a means of grace, and that those who partake of this means of grace be sanctified.[7] Borgen is impressed by those hymns which long for the sacred sign to become a means of grace as well:

> How long, Thou faithful God, shall I
> Here in Thy ways forgotten lie?
> When shall the means of healing be
> The channels of Thy grace to me?
> In vain I take the broken bread,
> I cannot on Thy mercy feed;
> In vain I drink the hallow'd wine,
> I cannot taste the love Divine.[8]

Here the distinction between the sign and the grace in the sacrament seems to become a distinction in the experience of those faithfully seeking grace in the sacrament. Borgen contends that while it is a sacred sign for all who partake in faith, it may or may not be a means of grace, for that depends on the sovereign action of the Holy Spirit.[9] While the believer is dependent on spiritual union with God through the Lord's Supper, this

> by no means implies that the true worshipper receives this "food" at all times or, as it were, automatically. God dispenses his grace and uses his means as he will, and in his own time.[10]

Borgen's interpretation challenges my own at this point. I have argued that, for Wesley, grace enables and invites an ongoing relationship with God; Borgen, in order to emphasize the freedom of God over the sign, describes grace as more occasional. The issue is not whether the Holy Spirit is free apart from the sign, but the meaning of God's promise to use the Lord's Supper as a means of grace. In order to sustain my own argument I shall have to account for Borgen's observations without drawing his conclusions.

I begin by asking if the reason the Lord's Supper does not always seem to be a means of grace is that God is sometimes present and sometimes absent. A few of the hymns cited by Borgen seem to imply this, but such a supposition runs counter to much that Wesley says elsewhere. First, as Borgen rightly insists, Wesley consistently rejects any interpretation of the Lord's Supper as merely symbolic or as "real absence." Second, this presence or absence of grace seems not to vary from service to service, but from participant to participant in each eucharistic celebration. Third, Wesley agrees with Daniel Brevint that at "the holy Table the people meet to worship God, and God is present to meet and bless His people."[11] Thus the language of those hymns which suggest absence is most appropriately understood as an expression of human experience rather than reflections on divine decision.

But if God is present, and the partaker of the holy meal has a degree of faith, then there will be a unity of presence and identity in the eucharist, for the elements become revelatory of who it is that is present. The experience of this presence is both gracious and transformative, for it enables an ongoing relationship with God. The precondition is not God's decision to be present but the human use of the gift of faith:

> Lift your eyes of faith, and look
> On the signs He did ordain![12]

Borgen would agree that faith perceives the elements as a sacred sign, but would argue this is not necessarily gracious. He sees in Wesley a distinction between the sacred sign and God's making the sign a means of grace. The distinction is certainly there, but the inference that the Lord's Supper is sometimes not a means of grace for a person who has faith is incorrect.

To understand these hymns we must recall Wesley's distinction between the gradual work of God in the Christian life and the instantaneous work. Wesley considered gradual growth dependent upon a yearning for the instantaneous: those with the faith of a servant sought justification and new birth; those with the faith of a child sought Christian perfection. The longing for grace expressed in the hymns is a longing for the instantaneous work, not a denial of the eucharist as an ongoing means of grace. Many hymns explicitly call on God for the "double grace" or the "double life":

> Proceeds from Thee the double grace;
>   Two effluxes, with life Divine
> To quicken all the faithful race,
>   In one eternal current join.[13]

> Long we for Thy love have waited,
>   Begging sat by the wayside;
> Still we are not new-created,
>   Are not wholly sanctified.[14]

The instantaneous work is a direct act of God, sought in faith but occurring according to God's own timing.

The gradual work, however, occurs through a continual process of grace and response. One does not sometimes receive grace, but is rather placed in a context of grace through a continuing relationship with God. In another series of hymns Wesley refers to God's "constant" or "continuing" grace:

> All my hopes on Thee depend,
> Love me, save me to the end,
> Give me the continuing grace,
> Take the everlasting praise.[15]

> Our needy souls sustain
>   With fresh supplies of love,

> Till all Thy life we gain,
>   And all Thy fullness prove,
> And, strengthen'd by Thy perfect grace,
> Behold without a veil Thy face. [16]

The instantaneous work occurs within the context of the gradual, as is implied by the fact that hymns longing for the "double grace" are addressed to God with whom the singer is already in relation.

Borgen is aware that the Lord's Supper provides "a continual supply" of grace, giving one "strength to remain in God's love and endure to the end";[17] that is, its function is not limited to the instantaneous "double grace." My contention, however, is that it is *always* a source of transforming grace for one who participates with a degree of faith.

This does not compromise the freedom of the Holy Spirit, and can be seen as analogous to Wesley's understanding of prevenient grace. Persons may be theoretically described in a "natural state" as totally bound by original sin, but in fact none are without prevenient grace; so the eucharistic elements may be theoretically described as devoid of grace, but in fact are always means of grace. Yet within this context of grace God acts freely, giving the "double grace" and otherwise relating to and transforming persons' lives according to the degree of faith and the mystery of divine decision:

> The gospel ordinances here
> As stars in Jesus' church appear;
> His power they more or less declare,
> But all his heavenly impress bear. [18]

God's power may "more or less" manifest itself in each eucharist celebration, but God is always present, and the Lord's Supper is always a means of grace. The degree of efficacy depends on God, but the lack of efficacy is not due to the absence of God but to the absence of faith. It is the "*manner* of using them, whereon indeed it wholly depends whether they should convey any grace at all to the user. . . ."[19]

The distinction between the sign and the grace itself was used by Wesley to avoid formalist misunderstandings. But it is as much a mistake to claim elements can be sacred signs without being means of grace as it is to claim grace is given through the means but not received by the faithful. The three-fold invocation noted by Borgen distinguishes between three moments in a single event: the elements becoming sacred signs, the partaking of the elements as receiving grace, and the beneficial effects of the grace received. These distinctions were meant to avoid confusing the sign with the grace or the means with the end, not as an indication that one of these movements can occur in the Lord's Supper without another.

The distinction between sign and grace, or sacrament as sacred sign and as means of grace, can be misleading if it implies two separate though parallel acts of the Spirit; rather the grace is conveyed by means of the sign. This unity of sign and means is evident in Wesley's definition of means of grace as

> Outward signs, words, or actions ordained of God, and appointed for this end—to be the *ordinary* channels whereby he might convey to men preventing, justifying, or sanctifying grace.[20]

In the Lord's Supper, the elements as signs, along with the accompanying words and acts, are used by the Holy Spirit as means of grace.

This unity of sign and grace in the work of the Spirit enables a corresponding unity of sign and grace in the experience of the participant. The grace is received in the encounter with God at the table; the sign enables the identity of the God encountered to be experienced as remembrance and promise. The sign reveals now the character and activity of God which will be directly perceivable when God is seen face to face in the age to come.

To pursue further the contribution of the sign to the grace I will especially examine the *Hymns on the Lord's Supper* with its accompanying extract from Daniel Brevint's *The Christian Sacrament and Sacrifice.* The extract can be taken as an expression of Wesley's own view, as he uses it both to introduce and to organize the hymns, and because his editorial practice was always to remove objectionable material as well as to abbreviate and clarify.

Brevint begins, as the title implies, by distinguishing between the Lord's Supper as a sacrament and as a sacrifice. As a sacrament it is used by God to offer "us the Body and Blood of His Son, and all the other blessings which we need to *receive*"; as a sacrifice it invites us to "offer up to God our souls, our bodies, and whatever we can *give.* . . ."[21] That is, the Lord's Supper enables through grace a grateful response to God. I shall first focus on the eucharist as a sacrament, reserving its sacrificial nature for discussion later in this section.

The extract continues with a further distinction: as a sacrament, the Lord's Supper was ordained

> 1. To *represent* the sufferings of Christ which are *past,* whereof it is a *memorial.* 2. To *convey* the first fruits of these sufferings, in *present graces,* whereof it is a means; and 3. To *assure* us of *glory to come,* whereof it is an infallible *pledge.*[22]

Faith perceives that which is not seen, whether of the past, present, or future;[23] the Lord's Supper as a sign presents to faith the objective reality of God's actions in the past, present, and future. In experiencing the sign, the participant encounters the presence of God and receives grace thereby.

> O what a soul-transporting feast
> Doth this communion yield!
> Remembering here Thy passion past,
> We with Thy love are fill'd.[24]

> And can we call to mind
> The Lamb for sinners slain,
> And not expect to find
> What he for us did gain,

What God to us in Him hath given,
Pardon and holiness and heaven?[25]

Pardon, holiness, and heaven are the benefits of Christ's
atonement. More particularly, these benefits cover the entire
Christian life, including grief for one's sins, justification
(forgiveness), sanctification (including new birth and Christian perfection), and everlasting life.

But the benefits are received because the participant in the
Lord's Supper partakes of Christ, who is "a true and real
Presence" in the sacrament.[26] The death of Christ is commu-
nicated to the participant as both an offering to God and an
offering to humanity. As an offering to God, the partaker of
Christ is made one with Christ's sufferings, which in turn
"leads to a communion in all His graces and glories."[27] The
participant is thus united in the present with both the past and
future of Jesus Christ. As an offering to humanity, the
partaker of Christ receives "those mercies which are sent
down from His Altar,"[28] that is, "the graces that spring
continuously both from His everlasting Sacrifice and from the
continual intercession that attends it."[29] Here the participant
receives the aforementioned benefits, and with them the life
of God itself, as revealed in Jesus Christ.

Now, Lord, on us Thy flesh bestow,
And let us drink Thy blood,
Till all our souls are fill'd below
With all the life of God.[30]

Wesley, as an heir of the debate over transubstantiation,
uses the Reformed language of spiritual eating. Today one
might say that in the giving of bread and wine God gives
God's own self to the recipient; it is the present reception of
that self-giving love of God which was made manifest in the
cross of Jesus Christ. To partake of the Lord's Supper is to
gratefully receive God's love in Christ as given by way of the
elements.

Wesley recognized the consuming of the bread and wine

took place within a larger context of words, actions, and signs; it is this larger context which gives meaning to the reception of the elements. It is through partaking the elements within this context that the identity of the God who gives in love is experienced in remembrance and promise.

Remembrance and promise do not simply provide additional information about the God who is present in the Lord's Supper; rather they are present experiences of past and future actions of God which reveal the character of God. Borgen rightly describes remembrance for Wesley as "a dynamic drama of worship in which both the believer and the Holy Spirit are actively involved."[31] One does not observe at a distance but participates in that which is remembered and promised, and experiences God thereby.

In remembrance the participant experiences by means of the sacrament the death of Christ on the cross. The process begins with the words, actions, and signs which analogically represent the atonement. The combination of "the great and dreadful passages" of scripture and the visible elements invites the worshipper to "observe on this Altar" something "very like the Sacrifice of my Savior." The breaking of the bread and the pouring of the wine point to the broken body and shed blood of Christ; the offering of the elements by the minister invites one to conceive "that this God himself hath both given His Son to die, and gives us still the virtue of his death."[32]

Far more than a mere calling to mind, the "express design" of the sacrament is to "expose to all our senses, His sufferings, as if they were present *now*."[33]

> Christ revives His suffering here,
>   Still exposes them to view;
> See the Crucified appear,
>   Now believe He died for you.[34]

The participant, through the power of the Holy Spirit (the "Remembrancer Divine"[35]), experiences anew the one histori-

cal death of Christ. Through this present experience of the
past event, Christ intends

> to invite us to His sacrifice, not as done and gone many
> years since, but as to grace and mercy, still lasting, still
> *new,* still the same as when it was first offered for us.[36]

As Borgen perceptively notes, through faith "the worshipper transcends both time and space, and finds himself, as it
were, at the foot of the cross" where "the horror and tragedy,
as well as the immensity of Christ's great sacrifice, is brought
personally and existentially home. . . ."[37]

> Crucified before our eyes
>   Faith discerns the dying God,
> Dying that our souls might live,
>   Gasping at His death, Forgive![38]

And, at the same time, the past event of the cross is
experienced as efficacious in the present.

This experienced remembrance of Christ forms and shapes
and deepens two sets of Christian affections. The first set
includes the humility, repentance, and remorse which is
intrinsic to the Christian life. In the Lord's Supper the
worshipper perceives it was his or her own sins "which were
the nails and spears that pierced" the Savior:

> Yes, our sins have done the deed,
>   Drove the nails that fix Him here,
> Crown'd with thorns His sacred head,
>   Pierced Him with a soldier's spear,
> Made His soul a sacrifice;
>   For a sinful world he dies.[39]

As the reality of human sin and its terrible consequences for
God are experienced, grief and repentance are evoked. It
serves as a continuing invitation to evaluate critically one's
own life to discover any remaining sin before God.

The second set of affections includes love for God and love

for one's neighbor. The central affection is our love for God, which is in response to God's love for us in Christ, and which takes the form of gratitude.

> How deep and holy is this Mystery: What thanks should we pay for those inconceivable mercies of God the Father, who so gave up His only Son! and for the mercies of God the Son, who thus gave Himself up for us![40]

Wesley marvels at the love expressed in the death of God for sinful humanity:

> Tremendous love to lost mankind!
> Could none but Christ the ransom find?
>   Could none but Christ the pardon buy?
> How great the sin of Adam's race!
> How greater still the Saviour's grace,
>   When God doth for His creature die![41]

The sacrament is thus appropriately eucharistic, because gratitude is the most basic response to this infinite, sacrificial love. That the loving response is active and also directed to one's neighbor will be clear in the discussion of sacrifice below.

When participants receive the bread and wine, they receive them as concrete expressions of the love experienced in remembrance. In partaking of the Lord's Supper they meet again and again the God who, out of love, died that they might live.

Today, some would broaden the scope of remembrance to include the life of Jesus which led to the cross and especially the resurrection of Jesus from the dead; and with the early church see the eucharist most centrally as a meal with the risen Christ. This would not be foreign to Wesley, who in many ways recovered the *joyful* celebration of the eucharist, but it would nonetheless be a shift from the dominance of crucifixion imagery typical of the eighteenth century.

However much this remembrance might be broadened, it is

doubtful it could be experienced more deeply. For Wesley, the Lord's Supper invites an experience of faith which powerfully forms and shapes the affections, and a relationship with a God who freely gives God's own self out of love for sinners.

Wesley, with Brevint, recognized three uses of the Lord's Supper:

> The first is, to set out as new and fresh the holy sufferings which purchased our title to eternal happiness; the second is, both to represent and convey to our souls all necessary graces to qualify us for it; and to assure us that when we are qualified for it, God will faithfully render to us the purchase.[42]

Here the three uses are seen from the standpoint of the third, which is "the crown of the other two,"[43] and that toward which they aim. For all who faithfully partake of the life offered in the Lord's Supper, the sacrament is an assurance or pledge of future glory.

Wesley notes an important distinction between a pledge and an earnest: "an *earnest* may be allowed upon *account* for part of that payment which is promised, whereas *pledges* are taken back." Zeal, love and degrees of holiness are therefore earnests, for they will continue in heaven, but sacraments are pledges which shall be unnecessary when God is seen face to face.[44]

Both pledge and earnest are aspects of promise. The earnest is that part of the life of the kingdom which is promised now; the pledge is an assurance that those who have received the earnest will receive the kingdom in its fullness, including life everlasting.

As with the past in remembrance, the participant in the Lord's Supper experientially transcends time and space with regard to the future:[45]

> By faith and hope already there,
> Even now the marriage-feast we share. . .[46]

> How glorious is the life above,
>   Which is this ordinance we *taste;*
> That fullness of celestial love,
>   That joy which shall for ever last![47]

It is thus not only a pledge that whoever rightly partakes of
the Lord's Supper will likewise partake of the marriage feast,
but in partaking the worshipper experiences in the present
the reality of that promised future.

At the same time, as a means of grace, the Lord's Supper
conveys to the recipient the life of heaven, as an earnest of the
life to come:

> Happy the souls to Jesus join'd
>   And saved by grace alone;
> Walking in all Thy ways we find
>   Our heaven on earth begun.
>
> Thee in Thy glorious realm they praise,
>   And bow before Thy throne;
> We in the kingdom of Thy grace,
>   The kingdoms are but one.[48]

This earnest of the life to come is not only a present
realization of the promised future but a training and qualifica-
tion for that future. Only those who stand with Christ now will
stand with Christ then:

> Preserve the life Thyself hast given,
> And feed and train us up for heaven.[49]
>
> These are they that bore the cross,
>   Nobly for their Master stood,
> Sufferers in His righteous cause,
>   Followers of the dying God.[50]

There is an interplay of the necessity of suffering love and the
joy of salvation running through this collection of hymns.
This reflects Wesley's insistence that true happiness now and

in the future is inextricably tied to having and living that love which takes up the cross.

The earnest, then, is the gift of a life lived now in continuity with the age to come. The Lord's Supper as a pledge recognizes that the kingdom is promised, but has not yet come. The earnest as promise and reality counters antinomian resignation; the pledge as promise and recognition of the "not yet" counters perfectionist optimism.

In the Lord's Supper God is experienced as the one who promises in faithfulness. A response of loving gratitude is evoked for this promise of new life; a response of joyful hope is evoked for both the expectation of present transformation and the assurance of feasting with God in the future kingdom. The life shaped by gratitude recognizes salvation as a gift which it is open to receive, while the life shaped by hope looks joyfully and expectantly to the future, actively participating in the means of grace.

Thus, through both remembrance and promise, the participant in the Lord's Supper experiences the identity of the God who is present. The character and activity of the trinitarian God is revealed through an affective encounter with the story of Jesus in both its past and future dimensions. To partake of the bread and wine is to be united with that story and to experience anew the love of God in Christ.

Earlier in this section I noted that for Wesley the Lord's Supper is both a sacrament in which blessings are received from God, and a sacrifice in which our souls and bodies are offered to God.[51] These two aspects are united in the ongoing relationship with God which constitutes the Christian life: through the sacrament God acts to enable and invite a response; through sacrifice a response is made which continues the relationship.

The response is dependent on God's prior act of grace in Christ. Wesley and Brevint make this clear by beginning their discussion not with our sacrifice but with the Lord's Supper as a commemorative sacrifice. Commemoration is closely associated with remembrance, but while in sacramental remembrance the reality of the atonement is experienced and God's love is graciously received by faith, in commemorative sacrifice the worshippers now set forth the atonement of Christ "before the eyes of God His Father" as the ground of their own acceptability.[52]

> Father, see the victim slain,
>   Jesus Christ, the just, the good,
> Offer'd up for guilty man,
>   Pouring out His precious blood;
> Him, and then the sinner see,
> Look through Jesus' wounds on me.[53]

In singing the hymns the worshippers pray to God the Father to see them not according to their own righteousness but according to the righteousness of Christ. United with their pleas are the prayers of Christ, interceding before the Father for the faithful:

> For us He ever intercedes,
> His heaven-deserving passion pleads,
>   Presenting us before the throne, . . .[54]

Just as the participants in the Lord's Supper present the sacrifice of Christ before God the Father, so Christ presents them and their sacrifices before God.

It is the sacrifice of Christ which alone redeems humanity. But too many "who are called Christians live as if under the Gospel there were no sacrifice but that of Christ on the Cross." The effect of Christ's atonement was not to make our own sacrifice unnecessary but to make it acceptable to God; "though the sacrifice of ourselves cannot *produce* salvation, yet it is altogether needful to our *receiving* it."[55] Faithful participants in the Lord's Supper are thus at one and the same time "faithful disciples," of Christ their Master, "true members" of Christ their Head, and "penitent sinners" saved by Christ alone.[56] The necessity of a response counters antinomian complacency; the insistence that participants remain penitent sinners counters the illusions of perfectionism.

To offer ourselves in response to and in union with Christ's offering is to conform our lives to Christ's, "to follow Him as much as in us lies, through all the parts of His life, and every function of His office."[57]

> Jesus, we follow Thee,
> In all Thy footsteps tread
> And pant for full conformity
> To our exalted Head;
>
> We would, we would partake
> Thy every state below,
> And suffer all things for Thy sake,
> And to Thy glory do.[58]

While following Christ is living one's life in light of the entirety of Christ's story, it is most especially "the bearing of His cross"[59] and the sharing in Christ's sufferings:

> For without doubt we shall follow Him into heaven; if we will follow Him on earth; and shall have *communion* with Him in glory, if we have *conformity* with Him here in His *sufferings*.[60]

What Wesley means by bearing a cross and sharing in Christ's sufferings here is virtually identical to what he means by self-denial and taking up a cross as general means of grace.

The sacrifice of ourselves consists of three interconnected moments. First, there is grief in experiencing the death of Christ as caused by our sins:

> O what a killing thought is this,
> A sword to pierce the faithful heart!
> Our sins have slain the Prince of Peace;. . .[61]

Then, there is the response of self-denial, in which our sins which put Christ to death are themselves put to death:

> Our sins which caused His mortal smart
> With Him we vow to crucify;
> Our sins which murder'd God shall die![62]

Third, there is the offering of ourselves in service to God. Through these three moments of self-offering

> The saved and Saviour now agree,
> In closest fellowship combin'd
> We grieve, and die, and live with Thee,
> To Thy great Father's will resign'd;. . .[63]

Because this offering of ourselves is essential to our participation in the Lord's Supper, it is an ongoing feature of the Christian life. Every time the eucharist is celebrated, the participant dies to sin and rises to follow Christ in love. The intent is to live whole-heartedly for God, to offer all that we are and all that we have[64] to God:

> Take my soul and body's powers,
> Take my memory, mind, and will,
> All my goods, and all my hours,
> All I know, and all I feel,
> All I think, and speak, and do;
> Take my heart—but make it new.[65]

Just as he urged prayer without ceasing, Wesley insists on "constant" communion. This insistence is striking when seen in light of the eighteenth-century debate in England. Latitudinarians usually suggested the canonical minimum of communing three times a year; Puritans, who also communed infrequently, stressed preparation through earnest self-examination. The High-Church position, in contrast, insisted on "frequent" communion.[66] Wesley argued for

> 'constantly' receiving. For as to the phrase of 'frequent communion', it is absurd to the last degree. . . . For if we are not obliged to communicate 'constantly', by what argument can it be proved that we are obliged to communicate 'frequently'?. . . Every argument brought for this either proves that we ought to do it *constantly*, or proves nothing at all.[67]

As with prayer, the Lord's Supper was so essential to the Christian life that anything less than constant participation was inappropriate.

Participation in the Lord's Supper is an expression of the heart of the Christian life itself. The identity and presence of God is experienced through remembrance and promise; the response to the experience of God's self-giving love is to give ourselves in love to God and our neighbor. Its presentation of who God is helps avoid the imaginary projection of enthusiasm. But its containing within itself the experience of God's loving and transforming presence which enables and invites our loving response makes the Lord's Supper, when received in faith, an alternative to formalism as well.

3. SEARCHING THE SCRIPTURES

The purpose of scripture for Wesley is stated in the preface to his sermons:

> I want to know one thing, the way to heaven—how to land safe on that happy shore. God himself has condescended to teach the way: for this very end he came from heaven. He hath written it down in a book. O give me that book! At any price give me the Book of God! I have it. Here is knowledge enough for me. Let me be *homo unius libri*.[1]

Of course he did not mean by being a "man of one book" that he read only the Bible; he frequently alludes to classical and contemporary works of literature and theology in his sermons, and even in this preface. But he was insisting on the uniqueness and primacy of scripture for himself and, hopefully, for his readers as well.

And this meant, as Outler notes, that "Scripture would be his court of first and last resort in faith and morals."[2] While scripture was "interfaced with tradition, reason and Christian experience as dynamic and interactive aids in the interpretation of the Word of God in Scripture" in Wesley's theological method, scripture remained the "pre-eminent norm."[3]

But scripture had primacy not only as an authority for theological reflection, but as a context which formed and shaped the Christian life. Wesley's own life models this use of scripture. Wesley was immersed in the scriptures; as Gerald Cragg notes, "Scriptural language shaped his style; scriptural content governed his thought."[4] This is manifested in "his lifelong habit of interweaving scripture with his own speech in a graceful texture,"[5] a fact which has been especially challenging to those editing the new critical edition of Wesley's *Works*. But even more than style and the content of thought and speech, Wesley wanted the "word of Christ" to "dwell richly" in the Christian life: not to "make a short stay, or an occasional visit, but to take up its stated residence," and that in "the largest measure, and with the greatest efficacy; so as to fill and govern the whole soul."[6]

If prayer is the "breath" of the Christian life, a continuing relationship with the life-giving Spirit, then scripture is the heart of the Christian life, giving it a form and shape based on and in response to the character of God. The two are complementary, and their relationship is paradigmatic for that of the two sets of means of grace as a whole. Prayer opens us to the presence of God, permeating all other means of grace and providing the context within which scripture is read. Scripture portrays the identity of God and likewise permeates all other means of grace. It "in-forms" our prayers through showing us to whom we pray, and for what we should offer our thanksgivings, confessions, intercessions, and petitions.

Our interest is in scripture as a means of grace, which not only shows the way to heaven but is a way God uses to enable and invite persons to make the journey. Happily, we can thereby avoid the contemporary discussion of Wesley's understanding of the inspiration of scripture, in which (like Luther) he both affirms in general the lack of error in scripture due to the fact that the words are God's, and yet in particular instances can point to errors made by the writers or weigh the merits of certain passages against the whole. For our purposes, we simply note with Outler that scripture for

Wesley was not merely objective revelation but a "speaking book."[7] And, as Donald Dayton observes, the emphasis falls not on the "once-for-all givenness and absoluteness" of scripture but the "ongoing process of inspiration in the church and the present work of the Holy Spirit in making the Scriptures alive and vital today."[8] Wesley

> saw the Bible as a medium of a new source of life and power which changed persons and the world so that the application of the spirit of the Scripture could not be achieved by a mechanical application of the letter of the Scripture.[9]

Scripture is a means of grace for persons with any degree of faith, including "unbelievers" who are responding to prevenient grace.[10] Moreover, it is able to meet the varying and particular needs of those who read it. Wesley, quoting 2 Tim. 3:16–17, says that scripture

> 'is profitable for doctrine, for reproof, for correction, for instruction in righteousness'; to the end 'that the man of God may be perfect, thoroughly furnished unto all good works.'[11]

Thus far, we have seen that scripture is for Wesley a central means of grace. By "searching the scriptures," however, Wesley actually means more than the Bible itself. It includes "hearing, reading, and meditating,"[12] in which hearing refers to hearing the preached word.[13] Preaching will be discussed later in this section, while now I continue the discussion of scripture.

A clue to understanding how scripture functions as a means of grace is found in Wesley's advice as to the manner of searching the scriptures. Does one, he asks, search the scriptures by

> (i) Reading: Constantly, some part of every day; regularly, all the Bible in order; carefully, with the Notes;

seriously, with prayer before and after; fruitfully, immediately practising what you learn there?
(ii) Meditating: At set times? by any rule?[14]

This way of searching the scriptures must be examined in
more detail.

By "constantly," Wesley means to daily "set apart a little
time, if you can, every morning and evening for that purpose."[15] As with "praying without ceasing" and "constant
communion," scripture is an ongoing context within which
the Christian life is lived, an environment which nourishes
and sustains that life.

Reading "regularly" and "carefully" is connected to the
theme of identity. To read scripture regularly is to read it in its
entirety, preferably reading a chapter out of each testament
daily, or at least one chapter a day.[16] The reader is thus
encouraged to encounter the complete story and the full
range of images of God in scripture. A careful reading, using
Wesley's *Notes on the New Testament* and *Notes on the Old
Testament,* would make the reader aware how each passage
reflects the wholeness and unity of scripture:

> Have a constant eye to the analogy of faith, the connex-
> ion and harmony there is between those grand, funda-
> mental doctrines, original sin, justification by faith, the
> new birth, inward and outward holiness.[17]

As I shall show below, the "analogy of faith" refers to the
general sense of scripture as a whole. Scripture tells one story
of God and of salvation, and thus reveals the character of God
and the nature of God's promises.

If through a regular and careful reading scripture is a means
to identity, a serious and fruitful reading implies an openness
to God's presence. Scripture is read in the presence of God,[18]
therefore

> Serious and earnest prayer should be constantly used
> before we consult the oracles of God, seeing "Scripture

can only be understood through the same Spirit whereby it was given." Our reading should likewise be closed with prayer, that what we read may be written on our hearts.[19]

The prayer that God will write the scriptures on our hearts is in reciprocal relation to our intention to faithfully practice what is learned. The affections evoked by the scriptures enable practice; the practice deepens the affections and opens us further to scripture. Here again is the relationship of reciprocity, enabled and invited by grace, which characterizes the Christian life. It parallels the relationship already shown in the Lord's Supper between our experience of Christ's offering and our offering ourselves.

As with the Lord's Supper, meditation plays a key role in the process. To meditate on scripture "with all the attention and earnestness of which" the "mind is capable"[20] enables one to know God. To know of God is to experience God's love, and that leads to a "joyful experience of all the holy tempers described in this book," along with a corresponding outward holiness.[21]

Through meditation on scripture affections are evoked and strengthened. But meditation is also an occasion to resolve to practice what scripture teaches, and to obtain clarity as to how we might go about it. Is it not advisable, asks Wesley, to read scripture "with a single eye, to know the will of God, and a fixed resolution to do it?" And, he adds, it might also be useful to frequently pause and "examine ourselves by what we read, both with regard to our hearts and lives."[22] This self-examination not only gives clarity to Christian practice, but itself evokes affections in the presence of God, for it

would furnish us with matter of praise, where we found God had enabled us to conform to his blessed will; and matter of humiliation and prayer, where we were conscious of having fallen short. And whatever light you then receive should be used to the uttermost, and that immediately.[23]

The unity and reciprocity of affections and actions is shown in this passage; God's grace and our intentions are joined in the process of salvation.

Scripture portrays the identity of God and a corresponding picture of the Christian life. Wesley does not use terms such as story or narrative, but he expresses the single intention of scripture in such phrases as the "analogy of faith" or the "general" or "whole tenor" of scripture.[24] Likewise, Wesley does not discuss imagery and metaphor as means of rendering God, but together with his brother uses a full and rich range of biblical imagery in the hymns; the interconnection and mutual interplay of this imagery reflect Wesley's sensitivity to the whole tenor of scripture.

The general sense of scripture is, for Wesley, reflected in Christianity "as a scheme or system of doctrine." Christian doctrine "describes the character" of a Christian, "promises" that "it shall be mine, (provided I will not rest till I attain,)" and "tells me how I may attain it."[25] Scripture, and the doctrine derived from it, thus presents one life, one promise, and one means to that promised life.

The one character which scripture portrays is life centered in love. The religion of love

> is the *religion of the Bible,* as no one can deny who reads it with any attention. It is the religion which is continually indicated therein, which runs through both the Old and New Testament. Moses and the Prophets, our blessed Lord and his Apostles, proclaim with one voice, 'Thou shalt love the Lord thy God with all thy soul, and thy neighbor as thyself.'[26]

Christian doctrine "describes this character in all its parts, and that in the most lively and affecting manner." The "main lines of this picture," says Wesley, "are beautifully drawn in many passages of the Old Testament." In the New, these passages are "retouched and finished with all the art of God."[27]

Scripture is likewise united in the promise that all who seek that character shall attain it. "This is promised both in the Old

Testament and the New"; the New Testament is, "in effect,
all a promise."[28] Wesley sensed this overarching promise
most especially after his Aldersgate experience:

> All these days I scarce remember to have opened the
> Testament, but upon some great and precious promise.
> And I saw more than ever, that the Gospel is in truth but
> one great promise, from the beginning of it to the end.[29]

The promise of salvation is an expression of the one,
interconnected story which, in a general way, unites scripture.
Wesley quotes an unknown source with approval that "Scripture is *the history of God*."[30] The order of salvation of the
individual is seen within a larger context, running from
creation to eschaton. While Wesley readily affirms the salvation of the entire creation, he emphasizes human salvation as
the central theme of scripture:

> It runs through the Bible from beginning to the end, in
> one connected chain. And the agreement of every part
> of it with every other is properly the *analogy of faith*.[31]

The one story of God's saving intention and activity reveals
the character of God as love and faithfulness. And this in turn
is reflected in the Christian life, as both a recovery and a
deepening of the image of God.

In light of the one story, Wesley believes every command
of God "has the force of a promise"; the directive to live
according to the character of a Christian is at the same time a
promise by God to give one that character.[32] The law is not
the antithesis of faith but is established by faith. There is thus
no dichotomy for Wesley between the Old and New Testaments, or between Jesus' teachings and the grace of the
atonement; they are united in the intention of God to save
persons from sin and move them toward the life of perfect
love.

Scripture and Christian doctrine also affirm only one way to "attain the promise; namely, by faith."[33] We have described in earlier chapters Wesley's understanding of faith as a spiritual sense and a sure trust in God. But here again, he recognizes no faith/law dichotomy between the Old and New Testaments; those in the Old Testament at least had the faith of a servant, which is, as we have seen, saving faith.

Together, the character, promise, and faith described in scripture form the "analogy of faith" which for Wesley is the heart of the Bible, governing all else. The order of salvation is a personalized summary of this larger story of God's character and activity.

Outler has noted the "score or more brief summations" of the order of salvation which Wesley spreads throughout his writings. They were "never twice in the same form of words," and thus could not easily become doctrinal formulas abstracted from and used in place of the scriptures. But by pointing to the "soteriological core" of scripture, these summaries served to refocus the discussions in which they were placed on the central content of scripture, "which is to say, salvation."[34] Similarly, Timothy Smith has argued that the Wesleys saw love or holiness as an expression of "the wholeness of the central core of biblical teachings," a "way of thinking they believed they had not carried to Scripture but drawn from it. . . ."[35]

Wesley's understanding and use of scripture contributes to the Christian life in a number of important ways. Through meditation and personal application, scripture acts critically, countering presumptive claims for one's holiness or relationship with God. By taking the commands of God seriously, Wesley avoids complacency; by seeing them as promises, he avoids despair. His placing the use of scripture in the context of prayer encourages a sensitivity to God's presence, as an alternative to a more objective, uninvolved reading. And his constant reminder that scripture tells one story, shows us one Christian character, and portrays the one God who is love, together with his insistence that scripture be read fully and

with an eye to the analogy of faith, enables persons to know
who God is and who they are meant to be, and thus to avoid
enthusiastic projections of God and preoccupations with
passing feelings.

Wesley's advice concerning preaching closely follows that for
reading scripture. Does one search the scriptures, he asks, by

> (iii) Hearing: Every morning? carefully; with prayer
> before, at, after; immediately putting in practice: Have
> you a New Testament always about you?[36]

Preaching should thus be heard in the same way as scripture
is read, constantly and regularly, including attending the
services of morning prayer. It should be heard carefully,
comparing what is preached with the scriptures themselves.
Prayer and practice should provide the context of and
response to each sermon.

The advice to have a New Testament handy does, however,
point to the central difference between reading scripture and
hearing preaching. Scripture can be inadequately read, but in
itself scripture is always adequate as a means of grace.
Sermons, on the other hand, vary in adequacy; many, as we
shall see, are much narrower than the analogy of faith which is
at the heart of scripture. Wesley's insistence that the whole of
scripture be read with a sensitivity to its unity has its parallel
not in his advice to hearers but in his directions to preachers.

> The "best general method of preaching," he said, was (1)
> To invite. (2) To convince. (3) To offer Christ. (4) To
> build up; and to do this in some measure in every
> sermon.[37]

This in itself is almost a summary of the analogy of faith.
Sermons which were to be means of grace were expected,
whatever their focus, to in some measure tell the whole story
of salvation. This was necessary for three interrelated reasons.

First, it takes account of the varying degrees of faith among the hearers. Wesley is aware that because Methodists often preached in the open to unbelievers, many hearers first encountered the message of forgiveness in the sermons. From there, they were then pointed to other means of grace, such as scripture, prayer, eucharist, and class meeting. But it would be a mistake to restrict sermons to this alone, and as the movement grew, the need to preach holiness became more apparent.[38]

Second, and related to this, the whole story of salvation involves God's commands as well as God's forgiveness. As we saw above, Wesley believed God promises all that God commands, and thus sees the law in light of grace. He had no tolerance for sermons which offered forgiveness without the promise of sanctification as well:

> . . . I find more profit in sermons on either good tempers, or good works, than in what are vulgarly called Gospel sermons. That term has now become a mere cant word. . . . It has no determinate meaning. Let but a pert, self-sufficient animal, that has neither sense or grace, bawl out something about Christ, or his blood, or justification by faith, and his hearers cry out, "What a fine Gospel sermon!" Surely the Methodists have not so learned Christ! We know no Gospel without salvation from sin.[39]

This preaching, he wrote his brother, "naturally tends to drive holiness out of the world."[40] In opposition to this so-called "preaching Christ" Wesley advocated "practical preaching" which focused concretely on moral issues, values, and practices of daily living in light of the commands and promises of God.[41] He was determined to avoid antinomian and formalist complacency as well as enthusiastic escapism from the temptations and responsibilities of living as Christians in the world.

This means, third, that sermons truly preach Christ when they present the full identity of Christ as prophet and king as well as priest:

The most effectual way of preaching Christ, is to preach
him in all his offices, and to declare his law as well as his
gospel, both to believers and unbelievers. Let us
strongly and clearly insist upon inward and outward
holiness, in all its branches.[42]

Sermons can therefore tear down as well as build up the
Christian life. The so-called gospel preachers fed their hearers
"with sweetmeats, till the genuine wine of the kingdom seems
quite insipid to them." They "spread death, not life"; their
hearers seek "cordial upon cordial" while remaining "without
life, without power, without any strength or vigour of soul."[43]
By offering continued consolations, the gospel preachers
encouraged a passive complacency which hindered an ongoing, maturing relationship with God and a corresponding
growth in love. Instead, Wesley urges Methodists to love the
strictest preaching best; that which most searches the heart,
and shows you wherein you are unlike Christ; and that which
presses you most to love him with all your heart, and serve
him with all your strength.[44]

At the same time, sermons can harm the Christian life
through preaching the law divorced from promise, inviting
either a shallow presumption or a hopeless despair. Warning
that perfection can be preached too "harshly," Wesley urged
that it be placed "in the most amiable light," so that it may
excite only hope, joy, and desire."[45] The law is "not only a
command, but a privilege also, as a branch of the glorious
liberty" of the children of God. All "obedience springs from
love" to God, "grounded on his first loving us"; as such,
obedience "is not the cause, but the fruit" of our "acceptance
with God." Therefore, in preaching the law, the love of God
in Christ must be kept continually before the hearers.[46]

Like scripture, sermons which are means of grace present
the complete intention and promise of the loving God. A
diminished portrayal of God as the object of the affections
diminishes the affections themselves. Only sermons which
reflect the scriptural identity of God in its fullness are

adequate means to the Christian life lived in response to the God who loves in Christ.

4. TRADITION, PRAYERS, AND HYMNS

Both the Lord's Supper and searching the scriptures contribute to the Christian life through rendering the identity of God. By way of participation in narrative and imagery, the character and activity of the God who is present is experientially remembered, and this remembrance evokes and shapes the Christian affections. In the same manner God's eschatological promise is experienced, both as promise of the coming kingdom and of its present realization in the gift of new life. The story of God's love in Christ is at the same time the heart of the identity of God and descriptive of the Christian life of love.

In addition to the Lord's Supper and searching the scriptures, other means of grace functioned to portray the identity of God and the resulting identity of a Christian. Some belonged to the tradition of the church; others, composed by Wesley, were expressive of scripture and tradition. Not all were listed by Wesley as means of grace, but all clearly functioned as such in the lives of Christians. Thus both scripture and the Lord's Supper were surrounded by a larger ethos, rich in narrative and imagery. My discussion of these means of grace will be necessarily brief, but it will indicate how the concern to avoid enthusiasm through attention to identity was a dominant feature of both public worship and personal devotion.

As is well known, Wesley considered tradition, along with reason and experience, as theological authorities subordinate only to scripture. He did not, however, value all parts of the tradition equally. Of greatest significance were the writings of the ante-Nicene as well as certain post-Nicene church fathers. Also of great importance was Wesley's own Anglican tradition as expressed in the Book of Common Prayer, the Articles of Religion, and the Homilies. Finally, as shown by his *Christian*

Library, Wesley could range over the whole of the tradition for those writings which assisted persons in Christian growth.

The *Christian Library* contained abridgements, extracts, and translations of a wide range of devotional works, some describing various spiritual exercises and others portraying the lives of exemplary Christians. Wesley sought to avoid unintelligible, obscure, or controversial writings,[1] and felt himself "at full liberty" to omit or add "what was needful, either to clear their sense, or to correct their mistakes."[2] By this means he "endeavored to preserve a consistency throughout," that all might "conspire together" to advance the Christian life.[3] Here Wesley attempts to shape the tradition according to that same analogy of faith which governs scripture. Wesley thus considered the *Christian Library* "such a collection of English divinity, as (I believe) is all true, all agreeable to the oracles of God. . . ."[4]

In point of fact, the *Christian Library* contained a number of patristic and continental writings. And, although the great number were English, about half of these were Puritans.[5] Here again we find Wesley's concern to avoid narrowness by including writings of those not loyal to the central Church of England tradition.

The *Christian Library* was a resource for the devotional lives of Christians; Wesley urged his preachers to read it "in order with much prayer" from six to twelve in the morning.[6] Yet its use was not limited to this, for Wesley also wanted the preachers to "frequently read in public, and enforce select portions" of it.[7]

These devotional writings served to encourage persons to persevere in the Christian life, thus countering despair. At the same time, they helped avoid complacency and expose presumptive claims through concrete portrayals of the Christian life. And, through describing the character of a Christian, they undercut an enthusiastic focus on passing feelings and otherworldly consolations.

Although Wesley considered the "Prayers of the Church" to be "substantial food for any who are alive to God,"[8] he was not uncritical in his admiration for the Book of Common Prayer. In preparing the *Sunday Service* for the Methodists in America, he showed a sensitivity to patristic sources and an attentiveness to Puritan critique.[9] Yet it was on the whole a conservative revision, in the spirit of Wesley's statement in the preface:

> I believe there is no Liturgy in the world, either in ancient or modern language, which breathes more of a solid, scriptural, rational piety, than the Common Prayer of the Church of England: And though the main of it was compiled considerably more than two hundred years ago, yet is the language of it not only pure, but strong and elegant in the highest degree.[10]

One of Wesley's most radical revisions was the Psalter. In the preface he stated that there were "many Psalms left out, and many parts of the others, as being highly improper for the mouths of a Christian congregation."[11] According to James F. White, Wesley eliminates 34 of the 150 psalms in the Book of Common Prayer, and abridges 58 more.[12] In his dissertation, William N. Wade recognizes five categories of deletions:

> curses, wrath, killing, and war; descriptions of the wicked, lack of faith, or special personal circumstances; at odds with salvation by faith; concerns exclusively historical or geographical. . .; and references to the use of instruments or dance in worship.[13]

White notes that these revisions do not constitute a de-emphasis of the Psalter; it remains the "largest single item in the *Sunday Service*," and reflects Wesley's own daily recital of the psalms.[14]

Once again, Wesley's appreciation for the whole tenor of scripture has led him to abridge an original writing, this time a portion of scripture itself. Wesley is not concerned to remove psalms from the Bible, where they are a part of the larger whole. But at least the first three of Wade's categories invite misunderstanding if they are recited or prayed apart from their scriptural context. Thus Wesley thought them unsuitable as responses to God's love and as formative influences on the Christian life.

Wesley was most conservative in his retention of the Cranmerian collects and lections.[15] Because collects contain both scriptural descriptions of God and petitions warranted by those descriptions, they are especially suited to convey the identity of God and of the Christian life. To pray the collects over time is to become increasingly acquainted with who God is, and who God intends for us to be. The prayers of the church avoid enthusiasm through offering concrete scriptural descriptions of God, and thus evoke and shape affections, inform Christian practice, and provide language and direction for extemporaneous prayer.

Wesley's sense of the importance of written prayer carried over from public worship to personal and family devotions. Drawing upon existing prayers as well as writing his own, Wesley published four collections of prayers in his lifetime. The first, A Collection of Forms of Prayer, was first published in 1733, five years prior to Aldersgate; it went through nine editions and was placed by Wesley in his collected works in 1772. Consisting of his own compositions as well as selections from others, its continued usefulness was due to its bringing to expression in prayer the general means of grace, such as self-denial, and its recognition that holiness is the goal of the Christian life.[16]

In the middle of his life Wesley published A Collection of Prayers for Families and Prayers for Children.[17] With the growth of the Methodist movement, there was a need for family-oriented devotions as well as personal devotions. These two collections, together with the first, provided a comprehensive framework of written prayer within which extemporaneous prayer could be offered and the scriptures read.

The fourth collection, an abridgement and revision of a popular book of devotion by John Austin for the Christian Library, was intended for personal devotional use. Wesley considered Austin to have provided a complete system of Christian doctrine in devotional form.[18]

All the prayers were doctrinal in the sense that they provided descriptive accounts of the character and promises of God and the nature of the Christian life. They were not only prayers to God, but means through which the Christian life was formed and shaped. As such, they were devotional expressions of the analogy of faith which informed both the reading of scripture and the content of extemporaneous prayer.

I cannot here do justice to the Wesleyan hymns. Yet they must be considered, however briefly, for they were highly significant to the Methodist movement. The singing of hymns pervaded the worship and small group meetings, providing both a means of participation in all relationship with God and a form of instruction accessible to all.

Most of the hymns were written by Charles Wesley and then edited and published by John. Although a number of hymnals were prepared by the Wesleys, clearly the most important, both in their minds and in the opinion of Wesley scholars, is A Collection of Hymns for the Use of the People Called Methodists, published in 1780. It is a comprehensive hymnal, both as a summation of doctrine and as a means of grace.

In terms of doctrine,

> It is large enough to contain all the important truths of our most holy religion, whether speculative or practical; yea, to illustrate them all, and to prove them both by Scripture and reason.[19]

> In what other publication of the kind have you so distinct and full an account of scriptural Christianity?[20]

The doctrine contained in the hymns was not in the form of theological propositions but poetic description, an invitation to participate in and experience the reality which doctrine expresses. In the hymns, doctrine touches the heart.[21]

As means of grace, the hymns portrayed God and the Christian life in order to evoke affections and enable a relationship with God to continue over time. Wesley recommends the hymnal to the "pious reader"

as a means of raising or quickening the spirit of devotion, of confirming his faith, of enlivening his hope, and
of kindling or increasing his love to God and man.[22]

They were arranged according to the order of salvation (and
the analogy of faith), beginning with hymns which called on
sinners to return to God, then describing true religion, then
for those under conviction or backslidden, then for believers
struggling to live the Christian life and seeking perfection,
and finally for the society meeting as a whole.[23] Within these
larger groupings were smaller, more specific subcategories.
The hymns were designed, as means of grace, to deal with the
full range of the Christian life, from prevenient grace to
Christian perfection, whatever the need or degree of faith:

> The hymns are not carelessly jumbled together, but
> carefully ranged under proper heads, according to the
> experience of real Christians. So that this book is in effect
> a little body of experimental and practical divinity.[24]

The singing of the hymns enabled participation in a
relationship with God. Craig Gallaway has drawn attention to
the fact that most of the hymns take the form of a dialogue
with God, either as address to God or as God's address to
us.[25] In this the hymns parallel the general relationship of
prayer to searching the scriptures: prayer is our address to
God; through scripture and preaching God speaks to us.

As prayers addressed to God, the hymns include the full
range of thanksgiving, confession, petition, and intercession.
Each hymn describes God's character, activity, or promise
which evokes an appropriate response, while at the same time
giving concrete expression to that response.

Consider this hymn of thanksgiving:

> Thee, O my God and King,
> My Father, thee I sing!
> Here, well-pleased, the joyous sound,
> Praise from earth and heaven receive;
> Lost, I now in Christ am found,
> Dead, by faith in Christ I live.[26]

God is the agent of salvation, and this is the reason for praise. The experience of salvation evokes gratitude toward God, and the hymn then also serves as a means to express that gratitude.

The same pattern can be seen in another hymn, this time a petition for entire sanctification:

> Love divine, all loves excelling,
>   Joy of heaven, to earth come down,
> Fix in us thy humble dwelling
>   All thy faithful mercies crown!
> Jesus, thou art all compassion,
>   Pure, unbounded love thou art;
> Visit us with thy salvation!
>   Enter every trembling heart.[27]

God is described as compassionate, unbounded love, and as faithful to the promise that this love can dwell in human hearts. The response is a plea for God to transform the heart, nurturing a receptive and expectant hope.

The hymns through which God speaks to us are different only in that the hymn is not a means of our response. It is nonetheless clear that a response is sought, and many of these hymns are explicitly invitational:

> Sinners, turn, why will you die?
> God, your Maker, asks you why.
> God, who did your being give,
> Made you with himself to live;
> He the fatal cause demands,
> Asks the work of his own hands,
> Why, ye thankless creatures, why
> Will you cross his love, and die?[28]

God speaks here, as in the case of preaching and most of scripture, indirectly. The hymn evokes a recognition of our ingratitude toward a most gracious, just and loving God. The imagery of the cross signifies our rejection of God's love, which can only result in death. To turn to God is to receive life. Thus while not itself an expression of our response, the hymn evokes those affections that constitute our response.

The cross can also be used to show the depths of God's love:

> O Love divine! What has thou done!
> Th' immortal God hath died for me!
> The Father's co-eternal Son
>   Bore all my sins upon the tree:
> Th' immortal God for me hath died,
> My Lord, My love is crucified.[29]

This hymn invites persons to "Behold him, all ye that pass by,"[30] to see in the death of Jesus the love and consequent death of God for us. The range of affections to be evoked are unspecified, but most certainly could include love, gratitude, guilt, humility, faith and hope. Indeed, the hymn is appropriate at any point in the Christian life, and may evoke different affections at different times.

This pattern of response to descriptive renderings of God is certainly not unique to Wesleyan hymns. Its significance is in the central importance of hymnody to the Methodist movement. The singing of hymns was perhaps the most notable characteristic of Methodist gatherings.

Because of their pervasiveness and use of evocative imagery, some critics feared the Wesleyan hymns would invite enthusiasm. But this was to overlook the intrinsically relational nature of the affections evoked. The emotions were not due to introspective experiences or flights of imagination, but were in response to and connected with narrative and imagery in the hymns which provided descriptive access to the character and activity of God. And, because Methodists sang a great variety of hymns, they experienced God through a wide range of imagery.

The hymns, then, contain as a body the larger pattern of means of grace. They enable and invite participation in a relationship with God for persons at all points along the way of salvation. They are sung in the presence of God who is addressed and who addresses us, and they descriptively render through narrative and imagery the identity of the God who is present. Some invite self-examination and repentance before God; others invite commitment to serve God. The character and activity of God is experientially remembered, and the promises of God evoke expectant hope. It is in this context that persons experience God's love, and in response themselves grow in the love of God and their neighbor.

The singing of hymns, searching the scriptures, participation in the eucharist, and praying the prayers of the church all demonstrate the fundamental relatedness which is at the heart of Wesley's understanding of the experience of God. Enthusiasm results not from emotions in themselves, but from either a focus on having certain feelings or a narrow or superficial picture of God. Wesley uses means of grace to shift the attention to a God who is other than us, and who possesses an identity distinct from our own. Christian affections are either in relation to this God, or they are not Christian at all.

The depiction of God through narrative and imagery provides depth to this relationship. Because narrative and imagery are determinate (i.e., connected to a certain range of affections), they guard against enthusiastic renderings of God; because their meaning is inexhaustible, they continually challenge propositional statements about God. God is neither the projection of our subjective experience nor the possession of our reasoned doctrines. Rather, narrative and imagery invite us into an ever richer experience of God's character and activity, a continual deepening of our relationship with God, and a constant growth in those affections which constitute the Christian life.

Chapter VI

The Means of Grace and the Christian Life

1. PATTERNS OF INTERACTION IN THE MEANS OF GRACE

To say the Christian life depends upon the grace of God is not enough. Wesley insisted God's grace was normally mediated through means of grace, and to neglect any of the means of grace available was both disobedient (in the case of those means instituted by Christ) or unwise. The means of grace countered such dangers to the Christian life as formalism and enthusiasm, despair and presumption; they demonstrated their importance through enabling Christians to grow in love and the other affections. Wesley provided a full range of means of grace for the Methodists, and urged their continual participation in all the means.

I have explored the reasons why it was so important for Wesley to insist on this full range of means of grace. While Wesley was a careful observer of the effects of using or ignoring various means of grace, he did not offer an explanation as to why they were essential to the Christian life. It was enough that God has promised to use the instituted means, and was now clearly using both instituted and prudential means to further growth in the Christian life and to form Christian community.

It is necessary in our day to explore more deeply the value of these means of grace, for while much has changed, the dangers to the Christian life identified by Wesley remain. A contemporary concern for the Christian life requires not a

strict adherence to Wesley's own viewpoint, but an understanding of how the means of grace functioned in the lives of
Christians. Some of the means of grace, and the concrete
forms of most means of grace, are, as Wesley recognized,
prudential; but the manner in which those means of grace
functioned is a necessary context for the Christian life in all
times and places.

I have argued that the means of grace are essential to the
Christian life because they give form to a distinctive, continuing relationship with God. Taken together, their pattern of
mutual interaction and interdependence constitute a context
within which the Christian life is formed and shaped. To
participate in the means of grace is to be increasingly open to
the presence and transforming power of God.

The role of the means of grace in the Christian life involves
two sets of patterns of interaction. The first set concerns the
relationship between Christians and God through the means
of grace. The second set includes the various ways the means
of grace are related and interactive, providing a dynamic ethos
within which growth in the Christian life is enabled and
invited, formed and shaped.

The relationship between the Christian and God may be
expressed by one general pattern, of which there are many
variations. At its heart, it consists of God's gracious initiative
which enables and invites a human response. The response
involves both an openness to and desire for God, which
furthers the relationship.

Wesley's language describing grace is sometimes substantial but always relational. Thus, he can at times talk of grace as
a substance or quantity: to receive more grace one must use
the grace one has. But even here, the effect of the grace is
personal, and the admonition to use the grace one has is
directed to furthering the relationship with God. Grace is
never described as something which, having been already
received from God, one can now possess apart from God's
continuing love and sustaining power.

Prevenient grace is given on God's prior initiative to enable human response, which takes the form of obedience to conscience. Convincing, justifying, and sanctifying grace all share with prevenient grace the common pattern of God taking the initiative, and the human responding to that initiative. But in contrast to prevenient grace, God's presence and activity is then normally experienced through means of grace, in which God is known in terms of a distinctive identity. The response of faith is a response to this God, and is formed and shaped by God as the object of the affections.

Thus grace enables and invites a faithful response; faith in turn is open to God and desires a relationship with God. Since God normally meets persons in the means of grace, those who desire God in faith participate in the means of grace. A true desire for God is not a desire to "get" grace, as if God could be possessed; rather, it is a desire to know God and to live in response to God's love. It is a giving of ourselves to God, in response to God's self-giving love. The means of grace are means by which we express our love and gratitude to God, our love in service to our neighbor, our trust and hope in God's promises, and our repentance in light of God's purposes.

Faith, then, involves active receptivity and response; it seeks through the means of grace the God who has already sought us in love. This experience of God through means of grace continues to evoke, shape, and deepen the Christian affections, enabling us to grow in faith and love. Increased faith leads to increased openness and desire, which leads to a deeper participation in the means of grace, and this in turn leads to increased faith. Thus, the relationship with God not only continues, but increases in intimacy and love.

This general pattern is actually a complex of relational patterns, corresponding to the Christian life as a pattern of affections. Experiencing God's love increases our own love for God. Remembering what God has done for us increases our gratitude to God. Receiving anew God's promises increases our hope. Seeing ourselves honestly before God increases our humility and evokes repentance. Seeing others and the world before God increases our love for our neighbor and elicits works of mercy.

The interaction between the Christian and God through the means of grace is maintained through the patterns of interaction among the means of grace themselves. They do this in two ways. First, they help avoid misunderstandings of the Christian life which distort the relationship with God and thereby hinder growth. Second, they enable and invite a distinctive relationship with God, and provide a way for that relationship to grow and deepen over time.

I begin with the way the means of grace help avoid misunderstandings. In Chapters II and III I presented two sets of misunderstandings which endanger the Christian life. With regard to the dangers of formalism and enthusiasm, each means of grace seems primarily concerned with avoiding one or the other. This is why the means of grace as a whole form a necessary context for the Christian life. To use only those means which hinder enthusiasm is to invite formalism; to participate only in those means which counter formalism is to encourage enthusiasm.

The means to the presence of God, discussed in Chapter IV, function to avoid formalism. Although they presuppose a degree of faith, they hinder formalism by enabling that faith to grow through encouraging an openness to God's presence.

On one hand they nurture faith through counteracting tendencies toward dissipation. Practices such as mutual accountability and self-critical awareness in the classes and bands, prayers of confession, fasting, watching, and self-denial are aimed at discovering and renouncing all that diverts attention from God and God's purposes in the world.

On the other hand, these means of grace nurture faith through focusing attention on God. Fellowship with God and others in the classes and bands, works of mercy, prayers of thanksgiving, petition, and intercession, the practice of the presence of God, and the taking up of one's cross are practices which direct attention to God and God's purposes in the world.

The means to the identity of God, discussed in Chapter V, function to avoid enthusiasm. They provide descriptive access to the character, activity, and promises of God through determinate narrative and imagery, thus giving "objective" content to the presence of God and thereby countering "subjective" projections of God into the experience. Through participation by faith in these means of grace, persons experience *who* God is as well as *that* God is. The means to identity not only enable one to know God, but to increase in the knowledge of God. It is the nature of narrative and imagery to render identity concretely, but in such a way that it cannot be fully "grasped" or exhaustively known. There is always more to the story and greater depth to the images. Thus, they invite continued participation, through which God is increasingly and experientially known.

The means of grace which render the identity of God are correspondingly descriptive of the Christian life. This is because the Christian life is fundamentally a recovery of the image of God, an imitation of Christ, a having of the mind of Christ, a loving as God loves. The means to identity include the Lord's Supper, scripture, preaching, the prayers of the church, and hymns.

It is essential to the Christian life that through these means of grace, the complete story and full range of imagery of God is experienced over time. For example, to reduce the Lord's Supper to remembrance of the fixed past without attending to God's promises, or to read only certain passages of scripture without considering the analogy of faith or the history of God, or to sing only a few hymns, is to distort the identity of God through a narrowed experience of God. Since the Christian affections are in response to and qualified by God as their object, the Christian life is correspondingly reduced and distorted through such a partial, impoverished rendering of God's identity.

Below is a chart listing which means of grace counter the dangers of formalism or enthusiasm. While the chart would be misleading if seen as limiting the effects of each means of grace to hindering only one of the two misunderstandings, it does show which misunderstanding each means of grace primarily counteracts.

The second set of misunderstandings includes despair, complacency, and presumption; each means of grace has resources to counter all three. If the dangers of formalism and enthusiasm necessitated the use of both the means to presence and identity, here the emphasis is on fully using each means of grace. Thus class meetings should include mutual accountability as well as fellowship; prayer should include thanksgiving and intercession as well as petition and confession; the Lord's Supper and searching the scriptures should include obedience as well as promise, self-examination as well as remembrance.

PATTERNS OF INTERACTION BETWEEN
THE MEANS OF GRACE

MISUNDERSTANDINGS AVOIDED:

FORMALISM

Disciplined Community
Extemporaneous Prayer
Fasting
General Means of Grace

ENTHUSIASM

The Lord's Supper
Scripture
Preaching
Prayers of the Church
Devotional Writings
Hymns

*NURTURE FAITH
(OPENNESS TO GOD'S
PRESENCE)*

DESCRIBE GOD'S IDENTITY

Despair is the absence of hope, and the consequent acceptance of sin as inescapable in this life. It is countered by the promise of new life experienced in scripture and the Lord's Supper, the present realization of new life and mutual love in the fellowship of the community, and the acknowledgment of God's present and promised gracious activity in prayers of thanksgiving. Through these experiences and practices the means of grace nurture Christian hope.

Complacency is related to despair, but because it lacks discontent, its acceptance of a minimal Christian life as normative is more thoroughgoing. It is thus more unconcerned than frustrated by sin. Complacency is hindered by the offering of ourselves to God in the Lord's Supper, obedience to God's commands in scripture, mutual accountability and discipline in the community, prayers of petition and intercession, the practice of the presence of God, and the taking up of one's cross. Through these experiences and practices the means of grace encourage active love.

Presumption is the claim that one has already reached an end point in the Christian life, either in terms of a relationship with God or in "possessing" a certain quality of life. It is avoided through the remembrance of Christ and Christ's continuing intercession for us in the Lord's Supper, prayers of thanksgiving for the grace upon which we depend, self-examination in light of scripture, mutual accountability and confession in the community, prayers of confession, fasting, watching, and self-denial. Through these experiences and practices the means of grace encourage critical reflection, nurture humility, and evoke repentance.

The chart on page 175 lists the resources within each means of grace by which despair, complacency, and presumption are countered. As with the previous chart, the listings under each misunderstanding are emphases rather than limitations.

Despair, complacency, and presumption all prevent growth in the Christian life, for they all assume that further growth is impossible and to desire it is contrary to Christianity. Wesley's optimism of grace and his dynamic vision of the Christian life necessitates the living of that life in the context of means of grace which avoid these hindrances to growth and encourage a progressively closer relationship with God.

In addition to avoiding misunderstandings, the means of grace enable and invite a distinctive relationship with God,

PATTERNS OF INTERACTION WITHIN EACH MEANS OF GRACE

MISUNDERSTANDINGS AVOIDED:

	DESPAIR	*COMPLACENCY*	*PRESUMPTION*
Disciplined Community	Fellowship of Love	Accountable Discipleship	Critical Reflection/ Mutual Confession
General Means of Grace		Practice of the Presence of God/Taking Up a Cross	Watching/Self-Denial
Prayer and Fasting	Thanksgiving and Petition	Intercession and Petition	Thanksgiving and Confession/Fasting
Lord's Supper	Means to/ Earnest of the Promised New Life	Our Self-Offering in Love	Remembrance of Christ's Offering for Us/Pledge of Life to Come
Scripture	Promise of New Life in Present	Obedience to Law of Love	Self-Examination

	HOPE	*ACTIVE LOVE*	*HUMILITY*

CHRISTIAN AFFECTIONS NURTURED

and provide a way for that relationship to grow and deepen over time. There are at least two modes of interaction involved in this.

The primary interrelationship is between the means to presence and the means to identity. A relationship requires the presence of an other who has a distinctive identity. The means to presence encourage faith which is open and attentive to God's presence; the means to identity provide descriptive and enacted access to who God is.

Because the Christian life is itself a specific patterning of human affections, it requires an ongoing experience of God as having a distinctive identity. God is the primary object of the Christian affections. The experience of the identity of God—as the one who loves in Christ—evokes, forms, and shapes the affections; without a continuing experience of God, the affections, divorced from their object, would become malformed or disappear. Thus identity and presence are not only necessary to a relationship with God, but are necessary to the affections which constitute the Christian life.

The relationship with God not only must continue, but also must grow; the means of grace encourage this through the use of narrative and imagery. Although Wesley himself was aware of scripture as an interconnected story and of the importance of the full range of biblical imagery, he offers no explicit account of their contribution to the Christian life. But as has been shown, it is characteristic of narrative and imagery to render the character and activity of a person in such a way that the person can be truly but not exhaustively known. Thus the means to identity enable a relationship through which God can be increasingly known over time, without ever reaching a point of knowledge in full.

To participate in the means of grace in faith is to experience the presence of God, and to increasingly come to know God. This unending growth in the relationship with God is not a limitation in the means of grace, to be later overcome in the Kingdom; rather it is a feature of any relationship. Wesley himself suggests this when he speaks of continued Christian growth in the Kingdom of God itself. What is true of any personal relationship is infinitely true of God: even "face to face," one can never exhaustively know God; one can only increasingly experience the depths of God's love and respond with ever-increasing love. This is what the means of grace enable in the present, as a foretaste of life in the Kingdom of God.

The second mode of interaction, which presupposes the first, results from the interrelation between the experience of God and the practice of the Christian life. We see this pattern in most of the means of grace. In the small communities there is a continual interaction between discipleship in the world and critical evaluation of that discipleship in community. In prayer there is the interrelation between intercession and confession. In the Lord's Supper there is the relationship between Christ's offering for us and our offering to serve Christ in the world. In searching the scriptures there is the promise of new life and the necessity of self-examination, interacting with the command to love one's neighbor.

There is a connection between God's presence and identity to us, and our own presence and identity as Christians in the world. As we have seen, our being affectively formed as Christians is fundamentally a response to God: our love for God and our neighbor is evoked by the experience of God's love for us. The means of grace not only enable us to experience that love, but provide the means and discipline to respond.

The Christian life, however, is not only an affective response, but an imitation of God as well. While our faith and hope are affections in response to but not in imitation of God, our humble, self-giving love is not only a response but a patterning of our lives after that of Christ. Here the reciprocity is between Christian practice and our knowledge of God, and between actual practice and the Christian life as a reflection of the life of God.

We cannot truly love unless we practice love in the world. Faith must issue in works, the affections are manifested in actions, the gift of holiness and happiness requires one to take up a cross. What it actually means to love as Christ loves, or to take up a cross, is related both to concrete situations in life and to one's knowledge and love of God. We learn what Christian love is through the practice of love over time and through the experience of God as love.

As we practice love, we come to more deeply understand

the meaning of God's love for us and the world. The meaning of words like "love" and "cross" take on specificity in concrete situations, and over time acquire a richness and depth as they are practiced in many situations. Thus practice deepens the experience of God's identity as love in the means of grace.

At the same time, our practice of love is continually examined and corrected in light of God's own identity and practice as revealed in the life and death of Jesus Christ. The means of grace, through rendering the identity of God and encouraging mutual accountability and self-critical awareness, enable us to strengthen our practice of love and deepen our sensitivity to human needs.

The practice of love enriches our understanding of God's love, and our experience of God's love deepens our practice of love. By this, we increasingly learn what it means to love as God loves, and increasingly become active expressions of that love in the world.

2. BAPTISM AND THE CHRISTIAN LIFE: AN EXCURSUS

Although Wesley clearly thought baptism was a means of grace, he consistently omitted it from his various lists and general discussions of means of grace. The most obvious reason for these omissions is practical: baptism was a onetime initiatory event, and thus had no further role to play in the ongoing life of the Christian. It is the Lord's Supper, not baptism, which preserves and develops the Christian life.[1]

This omission of baptism as an ongoing means of grace, together with Wesley's urging his baptized hearers to be born again, has led to a complex scholarly controversy concerning Wesley's beliefs. The debate has centered around two interrelated issues: does Wesley maintain, modify, or abandon his belief in the baptismal regeneration of infants, and is the content of infant and adult baptism the same? It is beyond the purpose of this study to analyze these issues at length. Rather,

I will briefly present two highly influential interpretations of Wesley, and then in contrast offer some suggestions of my own. I will show how we can better understand Wesley's position by considering the role of baptism within the larger context of means of grace and the Christian life.

Bernard Holland argues that, for Wesley, infant baptism is in many respects different from adult baptism or adult regeneration. First, while infants are always born again in baptism, adults are not. In addition to receiving forgiveness from original sins and being incorporated in the church, Wesley insists that "all who are baptized in their infancy are at the same time born again," while "it is sure all of riper years who are baptized are not at the same time born again."[2]

Second, the benefits received in infant baptism are invariably and immediately lost around the age of 9, through the commission of actual sin. "[Were] you devoted to God at eight years old" Wesley asks his adult readers and "all these years" since that time "devoting yourself to the devil?"[3] If so, you must be born again, no matter what once occurred in infant baptism. And adult regeneration, as we have seen, can occur through any of the means of grace.

Third, the content of infant and adult baptism is not the same. Although Wesley talks of infant regeneration, Holland believes this is new birth only in a restricted sense. Wesley, in his *Treatise on Baptism* (an abridgement and revision of a treatise written by his father), discusses the benefits of baptism in general, and then gives reasons for infant baptism in particular. Holland notes that while Wesley includes both "relative" benefits, such as forgiveness and incorporation into a covenant, with the "real" benefit of the infusion of a principle of grace (receiving the Holy Spirit) in his general discussion, he omits the "real" benefit from his argument for infant baptism. From this and other evidence, Holland concludes that only adult regeneration includes the reception of the Holy Spirit.[4]

In addition to this difference, Holland also argues that adult baptism is like all other means of grace in that it may convey prevenient, convincing, justifying, or sanctifying grace. A person may be reborn in adult baptism, but this is an occasional coincidence dependent on that person's degree of faith and present need. Thus regeneration, although signified by baptism, is in fact only sometimes connected with adult baptism. Infant baptism, in contrast, is always connected to the new birth, although it is a new birth in a more restricted sense than in adults.[5]

Ole Borgen strongly disagrees with Holland's conclusions. First, he denies that Wesley believed all adults had lost the benefits of their infant baptism. Rather, Wesley invites his readers to examine themselves as to whether or not they were now living as Christians. The grace of infant baptism can be lost, but only if "we quench the Holy Spirit of God by long-continued wickedness."[6] This is why Wesley was so concerned with the catechesis of children.[7]

Second, Borgen denies that Wesley saw any difference between the content of infant and adult baptism, or infant and adult regeneration. The reason infants are invariably born again is not that baptismal grace is irresistible for them, but, unlike adults, they are unable to resist it.[8] Infants, as in the case of adults, receive the Holy Spirit in regeneration; otherwise the Spirit could not subsequently be lost through long-continued wickedness.[9] Baptism is an initiatory sacrament for both infants and adults; thus it conveys to both grace only for forgiveness, regeneration, and related benefits. In this way, it is different from all other means of grace.[10] As Borgen argued concerning the Lord's Supper, the sovereign God may withhold grace at baptism.[11] Finally, those adults reborn through other means of grace should, if unbaptized, receive the water which signifies their condition,[12] although in an absolute sense baptism is not essential to salvation.[13]

Holland and Borgen offer two careful readings of Wesley with widely different conclusions. But they have in common a focus on infant baptism as the central question, and a discussion of baptism abstracted from the overall context of the means of grace and their patterns of interaction. In contrast, I will approach the issue of baptism from the standpoint of the Christian life and the means of grace.

The reason for this controversy over infant baptism is Wesley's concern with how actual lives were being lived in the present. He would present a description of those affections which constitute the life of a Christian, and then invite persons to examine themselves accordingly. In this context, the plea of infant baptism was not an affirmation of God's faithfulness, but an excuse to avoid confronting one's lack of faithfulness to God: "The question is not what you were made in baptism (do not evade!) but what you are now."[14]

This is a question addressed not to infants but to adults, to those who are able to respond to God's grace in an ongoing relationship. Wesley's normative model of the Christian life is the new born adult, not the baptized infant. This means adult regeneration is the place to begin an inquiry into Wesley's understanding of baptism.

The persons who responded to the Wesleyan message were largely not born again. In Wesley's terms, they had received convincing grace and responded with the faith of a servant, but were still seeking the promised new birth. These Wesley placed in a class, where the discipline and accountability would encourage them to use all the means of grace. In this context, a continuing relationship with God could be established, with a corresponding growth toward the new life. The new class members would learn through their own practice of prayer and love, and through experiencing the practice of others, how to live as Christians. The experience of new birth would come at God's own initiative, often after two or more years' participation in the class and other means of grace, but only to those who had begun a relationship with God through the means of grace.

This Wesleyan pattern of initiation into the Christian life has striking similarities to that of the early church. As with Wesley, adult initiation was the normative pattern. The early church placed those who had responded in faith to the gospel in a catechumenate, usually for a period of three years. The catechumens not only learned Christian practice, but experienced God through means of grace (except for the eucharist), which formed and shaped their affections.[15] During the Easter vigil, those ending this preparatory period received baptism, a powerful experience of moving from death to new life.

The parallel with the early church did not escape Wesley. Commenting on the initial establishment of a society, he adds that

> Upon reflection, I could not but observe, This is the very thing which was from the beginning of Christianity. . . . But as soon as any of these were so convinced of the truth as to forsake sin and seek the gospel salvation, they immediately joined them together, took account of their names, advised them to watch over each other, and met these . . . (catechumens, as they were then called) apart from the great congregation, that they might instruct, rebuke, exhort, and pray with them and for them, according to their several necessities.[16]

Because the Christian life is itself a specific patterning of human affections, it requires an ongoing experience of God as having a distinctive identity. God is the primary object of the Christian affections. The experience of the identity of God— as the one who loves in Christ—evokes, forms, and shapes the affections; without a continuing experience of God, the affections, divorced from their object, would become malformed or disappear. Thus identity and presence are not only necessary to a relationship with God, but are necessary to the affections which constitute the Christian life.

Besides the obvious fact that for Wesley the new birth occupies the place of adult baptism, the Wesleyan pattern differs from that of the early church in two ways. First, Wesley assumes that some form of small group meeting, apart from the larger congregation, is essential throughout the Christian life. Second, because most of those seeking the new birth had been baptized as infants, Wesley encouraged them to attend the Lord's Supper as a means of grace, through which the new birth may be experienced.

Given this pattern of initiation, what does baptism contribute to the Christian life? To answer this question, we begin by examining four categories of persons, classified according to whether they have been born again and whether they have received the sacrament of baptism.

First, Wesley encountered a number of unbaptized adults, mostly Quakers, who were not born again. In these instances it seems that both new birth and the witness of the Spirit normally accompanied the baptism:

> I baptized Hannah C—, late a Quaker. God as usual bore witness to his ordinance. A solemn awe spread over the whole congregation, and many could not refrain from tears.[17]

> In the evening I baptized a young woman, deeply convinced of sin. We all found the power of God was present to heal, and she herself felt what she had not words to express.[18]

> I baptized a gentlewoman at the Foundery; and the peace she immediately found was a fresh proof, that the outward sign, duly received, is always accompanied with inward grace.[19]

These examples substantiate Borgen's contention that adult baptism normatively is a means to new birth. When the adult is both unbaptized and seeking the new birth, baptism can occupy the same position in Wesley's pattern of initiation as it did in the early church. But the adults must be in a faith relationship with God, turning from sin and seeking new life; otherwise the baptism is not "duly received" and will not be a means of regenerating grace.[20]

Thus the degree of faith does have an effect on the function of baptism. While Holland goes too far in describing adult baptism as occasionally rather than normatively related to adult regeneration, it is clear that certain initiatory benefits of baptism may be received apart from the new birth:

> Of the adults I have known baptized lately, only one was
> at that time born again, in the full sense of the word; that
> is, found a thorough inward change, by the love of God
> filling her heart. Most of them were only born again in a
> lower sense; that is, received the remission of their sins.
> And some (as it has since too plainly appeared) neither
> in one sense nor the other.[21]

Here we see that some apparently were baptized without
having faith, some received justifying grace, and one received
the initial sanctifying grace of regeneration. The sacrament is
initiatory, but nonetheless operates within a relationship with
God in which God acts in accordance with the degree of faith
of the recipient.

This last passage, in which baptism has variable effects or
none at all, occurs in 1739, a number of months prior to the
founding of the first Methodist society with its attendant
discipline. The first three occur much later, long after
disciplined use of the means of grace became a feature of
Methodism. While Methodist practice was never up to
Wesley's ideal standard (e.g., the widespread neglect of
fasting), it is clear that his later candidates for baptism, due to
their participation in disciplined communities, were more like
catechumens than those baptized earlier.

A second category of persons hearing the Wesleyan message were those already born again but not baptized. Some of
these would be members of classes who experienced the new
birth through other means of grace; others would be non-
sacramental Christians such as Quakers. Baptism was not for
Wesley absolutely necessary to salvation; "If it were, every
Quaker must be damned, which I can in no wise believe."[22]
Yet he insists on baptism, even for the regenerate:

> (Peter) does not say, They have the baptism of the Spirit,
> therefore they do not need baptism with water, but just
> the contrary; If they have received the Spirit, then
> baptize them with water.[23]

Wesley's stated reason for baptizing those already born again is that Christ commands it. It may also be important in admitting one to church membership, and thus providing access to the Lord's Supper. Beyond this, the function of baptism is unclear, for one born again is at the same time forgiven, in a covenant with God, united with Christ, and an heir to the kingdom. Aside from membership in the church, there seems nothing left for baptism to convey which does not precede or come with new birth apart from baptism. We shall return to the question of the contribution of water baptism to the Christian life later in this section.

The third category—far and away the largest—includes those persons baptized as infants but not living the Christian life as adults. In all likelihood, these never had a degree of faith, and thus never responded to God's baptismal grace. Knowing only a formal religion, they lost the new life through a lack of participation in a full range of means of grace. Those who responded to the gospel were thus placed in classes, where faith could be nurtured and brought to the means of grace of the church. Through this participation, a relationship with God is maintained, and the promised new birth is sought.

The fourth category includes those baptized as infants who continue living the new life. Holland wrongly argues that Wesley denies this category as a theological possibility; rather Wesley seems to doubt it as an empirical reality. Borgen, on the other hand, imagines persons in this group were among those hearing Wesley and invited to examine their lives; if so, they would surely constitute only a tiny portion of the whole. While it may be true that the new life given in infant baptism may be lost through long-continued sin, the pervasive temptation to dissipation, unchecked by means of grace, virtually (though not absolutely) assures that the new life will be lost. Unless the child learns to use the faith given in new birth, through participation in the means of grace, no relationship with God develops, and the faith is subsequently lost.

This in turn sheds light on the relation of infant baptism to

Wesley's normative, adult description of the new life. The heart of the new life is the love of God and neighbor, in response to God's love for us. These affections are nurtured in an ongoing relationship with God, through the means of grace. To retain the gift of new life, as a child or as an adult, one must use the means of grace in faith.

Thus children need both opportunity and encouragement to participate in means of grace. For most baptized infants in Wesley's day, the opportunity was lacking to actively use the full range of means of grace. The absence of disciplined accountability and supportive fellowship led to the supplanting of the new life by formal religion. By providing a complete pattern of means of grace and the disciplined encouragement to use them, the Methodist movement, together with the church, enabled baptized infants to retain the new life through gradually learning to use the capacity for faith received in baptism.

"Baptism doth now save us," Wesley argued, "if we live answerable thereto; if we repent, believe, and obey the gospel."[24] Wesley undertook to encourage the children of Methodists to live answerable to their baptism, often through means specifically provided for children. As Borgen has perceptively noted, this included an insistence that children be instructed.[25] Wesley records that

> I met about an hundred children, who are catechized publicly twice a week. Thomas Walsh began this some months ago; the fruit of it appears already. What a pity that all our Preachers in every place have not the zeal and wisdom to follow his example.[26]

Wesley also considers instructing the children to be a part of each preacher's responsibility of family visitation.[27]

A similar concern is expressed in Wesley's instructions to godfathers and godmothers. The liturgy of the church expressly calls upon them to teach the child the meaning of the baptismal promise made on his or her behalf, and to insure the child hears sermons and learns the Creed, the Lord's Prayer, and the Ten Commandments. These are means to enable the child to "lead a godly and a Christian life,"[28] but are not guarantees. In the end, the child must live the new life given in baptism:

> You do not undertake that he shall renounce the devil and serve God; this the baptized himself undertakes. You do undertake to see that he be taught what things a Christian ought to know and believe.[29]

Wesley was concerned with more than traditional instruction. As we have seen, he prepared prayers especially for families and for children. Through this, he provided a means for children to be in relationship with God, experiencing and responding to the presence of the loving God. He also organized societies for children of ten members each, and urged his preachers to meet with them at least one hour per week.[30]

The child who has been born again in baptism and begins a relationship with God is, in Wesleyan terms, increasing in sanctification. But it would be a serious mistake to think that the practices of the catechumenate or the disciplined account-ability of the class meeting were, as activities prior to adult regeneration, irrelevant to baptized infants. A baptized child must learn to pray and to love as much as an adult seeking the new birth; the normativity of the adult pattern lies not in an absolute order but in the necessity of all its parts for every Christian. In the case of infants, a post-baptismal catechume-nate is essential to their continuation in the new life. This has serious implications for our current practice of confirmation.

We saw at the outset that baptism was for Wesley a onetime initiatory event. Holland argued that infant baptism was discontinuous with the adult Christian life, while Borgen insisted on their continuity. But in both cases, baptism, once completed, had no further role to play in the Christian life, and hence was never listed as an ongoing means of grace.

This does seem to be an accurate expression of what Wesley himself must have thought. Yet there are elements in Wesley's thought and practice which point toward a continuing significance for baptism in the Christian life. They invite theological reflection beyond that of Wesley himself, but do so within a Wesleyan framework of thought.

I begin by asking how baptism functioned for those recipients who had already experienced forgiveness and were born again. In traditional language, these had received the thing signified, and were now therefore being given the sign.

In discussing the Lord's Supper, it was argued that Wesley used the distinction between sign and grace to counter formalist misunderstandings of the sacrament; at the same time, to fail to see their sacramental unity would invite enthusiasm. The sign provides descriptive and enacted access to the identity of God, and thus gives distinctive shape to our understanding of who God is, and what God has done and is doing through the sacrament.

The sign-act of baptism has the same significance. The act of baptism with water, placed within its larger liturgical context, enables us to know the identity of God and the nature of the promised new life. God is experienced as the one who loves and who faithfully keeps promises. The new life is seen in terms of cleansing from sin, rising from death to life, the pouring out of the Holy Spirit, union with Christ, and other scriptural images in which we participate through the act of baptism.

Wesley's sensitivity to this may perhaps be indicated by his retention of the flood prayer in the baptismal liturgies prepared for Methodists in North America.[31] The prayer places baptism within the larger, interconnected story of God's saving activity through water, in the cases of Noah, the exodus through the Red Sea, and Jesus' own baptism in the Jordan River. Through the prayer, Christians remember the saving intention of God which is the foundation of baptism and new life.

The sign thus points to God's faithfulness to us. But of

paramount importance to the Christian life is what is meant by the faithfulness of God. When the sinner

> has been taught to say, 'I defy your new doctrine; I need not be born again. I was born again when I was baptized. What! Would you have me deny my baptism?'[32]

that person is using God's faithfulness as an excuse to avoid confronting his or her own lack of faithfulness to God. The act of God in baptism has taken on an irresistible or unchangeable quality which places no real value on human response. For Wesley, this was to misunderstand the content of the new life given in baptism, which consists of a loving response to God and one's neighbor.

The question for Wesley is never God's faithfulness, but our own. Wesley thus warns the sinner that

> You have already denied your baptism; and that in the most effectual manner. . . . For in your baptism you renounced the devil and all his works. Whenever therefore you give place to him again, whenever you do any of the works of the devil, then you deny your baptism.[33]

The sign of baptism, as Borgen notes, is an assurance or pledge of God's faithfulness, but does not insure our own;[34] baptism saves us now *if* we live answerable thereto. The remembrance of God's faithfulness and love does not make our response unnecessary, but should evoke a continuing response of love which is the heart of the new life.

For baptism to have continuing significance in the Christian life, there must be occasions in which persons reexperience God's faithfulness and renew their commitment to God. The Lord's Supper is of course one such occasion, in which Christ's offering for us is reexperienced and we in turn offer our lives to Christ. The annual services of covenant renewal, in which the remembrance of God's promises is combined with our own confession and recommitment, were others.[35]

The covenant renewal service consisted of a lengthy set of

"directions" followed by a covenant prayer, both drawn by Wesley from *Vindication of Godliness* by Richard Alleine.[36] Originally published by Wesley in the *Christian Library,* he later published the directions and prayer in a more usable pamphlet form entitled *Directions for Renewing our Covenant with God.*[37]

The covenant which is renewed in this service is the baptismal covenant.[38] This is made clear in the directions:

> There is a twofold covenanting with God, *In Profession, in Reality:* an entering our names, or an engaging our hearts: the former is done in Baptism, by all that are baptized, who by receiving the Seal of the Covenant, are visibly, or in Profession entered into it. . . .[39]

In baptism, God covenants with us; our response is twofold: we profess our faith and engage our hearts. The engagement of our hearts is likewise twofold: we choose to follow Christ (virtual covenant) and by solemn vow or promise we bind ourselves to Christ (formal covenant); the formal is a means to sustain the virtual.[40]

Wesley characteristically celebrated the eucharist after the covenant renewal service. Although he makes no explicit statement concerning their relationship, the covenantal imagery of the eucharist suggests their interconnectedness.[41] By itself, the eucharist invites covenant renewal, although not in the detailed and focussed manner of the renewal service.

The service of baptism was also an occasion to reexperience God's promise and renew our commitment. In two of the accounts of baptisms cited earlier, Wesley reports in one that a "solemn awe spread over the whole congregation," and in the other that "we all found the power of God was present to heal." Thus the entire community, and not just the one receiving baptism, participated in the baptismal event. Wesley's dislike of private baptism[42] probably indicates his commitment to baptism as a public act of worship, in which such communal participation is possible.

In these events the identity of God conveyed by the sign-act of baptism was intrinsic to the experienced presence of God. The God who is now baptizing is the God who has baptized each member of the congregation, and who is revealed afresh as the one who faithfully loves. Implicitly, one's own baptism is reexperienced in that of another, and one's own commitment in love is renewed.

3. THE PRESENCE OF GOD IN THE CHRISTIAN LIFE

Wesley urged the use of all the means of grace. In this he demonstrated a profound sense of how God's self-giving presence permeates the Christian community. Wesley recovered in the means of grace the rich understanding of sacramentality by the early church, before it was overlaid by attempts to more strictly delineate and enumerate the sacraments.

Within this diversity of means of grace the Christian life is enabled, formed, and shaped. Wesley never questions God's availability to us in the Christian life, but is concerned instead with our availability to God. To experience God, one must be open to God's presence, and this is encouraged by those means of grace which nurture an expectant, hopeful faith.

God is not experienced as an amorphous feeling but as a distinctive personal agent. Certain means of grace provide descriptive access to the character and identity of God through narrative, imagery, and metaphor. The Christian experience of God is thus for Wesley always given a determinate shape and pattern by God's identity.

This experience of God over time is fundamental to growth in the Christian life. As Christian affections are continually evoked, the heart is increasingly transformed. The affections are themselves constituted as responses to the distinctive identity of God. Such affections as gratitude, hope and humility take their particular form in relation to the character, history, and promises of God. To be characterized by such affections is to live the Christian life.

In presenting this understanding of the means of grace, Wesley rejects certain dichotomies which his opponents presupposed. Rational religion and the religion of the heart are not in Wesley's view mutually exclusive but mutually necessary; faith as a spiritual sense does not contradict natural senses but enables them to experience God in the means of grace and in the world. By maintaining necessary distinctions while avoiding sharp dualisms, Wesley sought to change the assumptions which had structured the eighteenth century debate.

Especially important is Wesley's critique of common understandings of immediacy and mediation. The formalists stressed mediation, and thus located grace automatically within the means of grace. But this made grace available at the expense of a relationship with the living, active, sovereign God. Ironically, this routinization of grace made God seem absent or distant, rather than present or near.

By denying mediation in order to emphasize immediacy, the enthusiasts sought to experience the living God. But without the means of grace, it became difficult to distinguish the experience of God from one's own self-generated feelings and desires.

It was Wesley's insight that, to faith, God is immediately present in the means of grace. To the person of faith, prayer becomes a conversation, scripture becomes the voice of God, and the Lord's Supper a meal with the risen Christ. Such faith must be nurtured in small communities in which each person is accountable to a common discipline. With this faith, immediate and mediated presence may become a single, unified experience of God.

Our experience of the presence and identity of God corresponds to the trinitarian activity of God. Wesley commonly describes justification as the gracious work Christ has done for us, and sanctification as the gracious work of the Holy Spirit in us. By making this distinction, Wesley is able to insist that sanctification is a present gift of God which transforms the heart.

But it would be a misunderstanding of Wesley to press this distinction too far. The work of the Spirit is itself christological: the Christian life is both a response to God's love for us in Christ and a having of the mind that was in Christ. While the Spirit is the agent of the new life it is Christ who determines the descriptive content and shape of that new life. The Holy Spirit is the active presence of God, but the crucified and risen Christ reveals the identity of the God who is present.

This trinitarian perspective illumines a contemporary controversy over the shape and emphases of Wesley's theology. Melvin Dieter sees the strength of the Wesleyan and holiness traditions in their emphasis on pneumatology. Drawing upon a discussion by Jurgen Moltmann, Dieter notes that Protestant orthodoxy understood history as divided into three kingdoms: the *regnum naturae,* the *regnum gratiae,* and the *regnum gloriae.* This has a trinitarian pattern, but the creative work of the Spirit is associated with the future kingdom of glory. Thus, the present activity of the Spirit in history is de-emphasized in favor of the past work of Christ.

In contrast, Wesleyan and holiness theology presuppose a four-way division of history, as does Moltmann: the kingdom of the Father, the kingdom of the Son, the kingdom of the Spirit, and the (triune) kingdom of glory. This emphasis on a present age of the Spirit enables them to hope for transformation by the Spirit in the present, within history.

Dieter is aware that Wesley's colleague, John Fletcher, explicitly proposed a similar scheme, to which Wesley gave a less than enthusiastic response. However, Dieter insists, such a view of history and eschatology is consistent with Wesley's own theology, and implicit in his understanding of sanctification.[1]

Donald Dayton considers Wesley's reservations to be highly significant. He argues that holiness preoccupation with pneumatology led to a separation of the work of the Spirit from the work of Christ, a loss of Wesley's christologically determined understanding of sanctification, and the eventual emergence of Pentecostalism. While recognizing a pneumatological tendency in Wesley's thought, Dayton believes Wesley held to the traditional Reformation pattern, in which the Holy Spirit administers the covenant or kingdom of Christ. To distinguish a separate age of the Spirit from the age of Christ is to divorce the church and the Christian life from its christological foundation.[2]

Dayton's historical analysis of how holiness pneumatology became divorced from Wesleyan Christology is compelling. At the same time, Dieter's emphasis on the present transforming activity of God is an authentically Wesleyan claim. In the categories of this dissertation, Dayton warns against enthusiasm and perfectionism, while Dieter targets formalism and antinomianism. Put positively, Dayton accents the need for christological identity and humble love; Dieter stresses pneumatological presence and expectant hope.

To speak of an age of the Spirit can be a helpful way of designating the transforming presence of God between the past and future Christ events, provided that it is understood as intrinsically connected to the life, death and resurrection of Christ, and to the coming kingdom. The work of the Spirit, then, is to transform present lives in accordance with and in response to their christological norm, and to realize in the present the eschatological life to come.

This present activity of God is best understood as a trinitarian unity of presence and identity. The Spirit is present not simply to create belief in the past and future salvific activity of God, but to transform the present in accordance with that past and future. The identity of the God who is present is revealed in the past and future of Jesus Christ, and it is the present experience of this identity which evokes, forms, and shapes the Christian life.

The experience of God's presence in and through means of grace is essentially related to our beliefs about God, based on our experience of God's identity, and to our accountability to a common discipline of active Christian practice. Today

theology is concerned with the relationship between orthodoxy (right doctrine) and orthopraxis (right practice). From
Wesley's perspective, these two cannot be discussed apart
from a consideration of how we experience the presence of
God in our lives.

Thus, as Theodore Runyon has noted, Wesley expands this
discussion by introducing a third element, which Runyon calls
"orthopathy" (right experience). For Runyon, orthopathy is an
epistemological category, referring to faith as a spiritual sense
given by way of a divine act of transformation.[3] In my own use
of the term, I will expand the definition to include as well the
resulting religious affections, rightly formed, shaped, and
ordered according to the identity of God who is their object.

The interrelationship of the means of grace indicates how
orthodoxy, orthopraxis, and orthopathy are mutually interdependent. From this perspective, orthodoxy and orthopraxis
serve both as means of expression and as contexts of growth
for orthopathy.

Orthopathy is expressed as love for God, in the form of
praise and gratitude. This expression of love is orthodoxy at
its more fundamental level: rightly ordered praise (*ortho
doxa*). Doctrine, or beliefs about God, are relevant insofar as
they enable the right praise of God, the praise of God for who
God is and what God has done—that is, for God's identity.

Orthopathy is also expressed as love for one's neighbor, in
the form of concrete works of love. This is orthopraxis, the
practice of Christian love in the world.

At the same time, orthodoxy is the theological and liturgical
context for orthopathy. Here orthodoxy refers not to doctrine in the narrow sense, but to the message of scripture, the
interpretations of tradition, and the enactment of the Lord's
Supper. The experience of God occurs and is understood
within the larger history of God's love, from creation to
eschaton. The affections are evoked and ordered in response
to the loving identity of God, and the resulting praxis is in
imitation of Christ and in service to God's larger purpose of
new creation.

Orthopraxis is the social and communal context for orthopathy. Through works of mercy in the world, love for one's
neighbor is actualized. In the class and band meetings, this
weekly praxis is evaluated and modified through critical
reflection in light of the identity of God. Such reflection
counteracts dissipation and uncovers hidden values, perceptions, and desires which prevent one from truly loving one's
neighbor. Critical reflection combined with praxis enables
Christians to learn increasingly what it means to love one's
neighbor in a world such as ours.

The means of grace enable both right praise and right
practice. But these are in turn the necessary expressions of
Christian affections which are formed and shaped in response
to the love of God for us in Christ. We cannot, in the end,
fully imitate that love. Rather, the presence of God through
the means of grace draws us into an everdeepening experience of God's love in Christ, evoking affections of awed
gratitude, expectant faith, confident hope, sincere humility,
and a love for God and neighbor which will continue to
increase throughout eternity.

Chapter Notes

ABBREVIATIONS

Notes   *Explanatory Notes upon the New Testament.*
(Reprinted 1981 by Baker Book House,
Grand Rapids, from an undated edition pub-
lished by The Wesleyan-Methodist Book-
Room, London.)

Works   *The Works of John Wesley,* ed. Frank Baker.
(Vols. 7, 11, 25, and 26 published by Oxford
University Press, New York, 1975–1983; the
remainder by Abingdon Press, Nashville, beginning in 1984.)

Works (TJ)   *The Works of the Rev. John Wesley, M.A.,* 14
vols., ed. Thomas Jackson. (Published by Ma-
son, London, 1829–1831; Reprinted by Baker
Book House, Grand Rapids, 1978.)

CHAPTER I: THE MEANS OF GRACE (pages 1–15)

1. "Minutes of Some Late Conversations Between the Rev. Mr. Wesleys and Others" (hereafter cited as "Doctrinal Minutes") (Aug.2, 1745), *Works* (TJ) VIII:286.

2. "Minutes of Several Conversations Between the Rev. Mr. Wesley and Others" (hereafter cited as "Large Minutes") (Q.48), *Works* (TJ) VIII:322–24; cf. Colin W. Williams, *John Wesley's Theology Today* (Nashville: Abingdon Press, 1960), pp. 132–39.

3. Ole E. Borgen, *John Wesley on the Sacraments* (Nashville: Abingdon Press, 1972), pp. 104–6.

4. "On Zeal" (ii/8–9), *Works* 3:314; cf. "On Working Out Our Own Salvation" (ii/4), *Works* 3:205–6; and "On Visiting the Sick" (i), *Works* 3:385.

5. Mt. 12:7, *Notes.*

6. "On Working Out Our Own Salvation" (ii/4), *Works* 3:205–6; "On Love," *Works* (TJ) VII:493–94; "The Nature, Design, and General Rules of the United Societies" (6), *Works* 9:72–73; "Doctrinal Minutes" (1745), *Works* (TJ) VIII:286; "Large Minutes" (Q.48), *Works* (TJ) VIII:323–24.

7. "John Wesley's Journal," (June 25–29, 1740), *Works* (TJ) I:278–80; "On Working Out Our Own Salvation" (ii/4), *Works* 3:205–6; "On Zeal" (ii/8), *Works* 3:314; "On Love," *Works* (TJ) VII:493–94; "General Rules" (6), *Works* 9:72–73; "Directions Given to the Band Societies" (iii), *Works* 9:79; "Doctrinal Minutes" (1745), *Works* (TJ) VIII:286; "Large Minutes" (Q.48,i), *Works* (TJ) VIII:322–23.

8. Eph. 6:18, *Notes.*

9. "General Rules" (4–5), *Works* 9:71–72; "Large Minutes" (Q.48,ii), *Works* (TJ) VIII:323; cf. Borgen, p. 105.

10. "The Character of a Methodist" (17–18), *Works* 9:41–42.

11. There have been only a few comprehensive studies of the means of grace in Wesley's theology and practice, and fewer still which describe their mutual interrelationship. Ole Borgen has a helpful chapter on the means of grace in general (*Sacraments,* pp. 94–121), and discusses the tension between enthusiasm and formalism. However, he does not show how the means of grace themselves provide a context within which these dangers are countered.

Much closer to my own argument is that of Howard Snyder in *The Radical Wesley* (Downers Grove, Ill.: Intervarsity Press, 1980). Snyder contends the Wesleyan movement had affinities with the radical reformation tradition, but instead of separating from the Church of England sought to renew it from within, as a pietist *ecclesiola in ecclesia.* This enabled Wesley to remain faithful to central sacramental and doctrinal traditions of Anglicanism while at the same time leading a renewal movement emphasizing discipline, accountability, voluntary association, and lay ministry. What Snyder has not done is show how the movement and the church are mutually necessary in terms of specific dangers to the Christian life (formalism and enthusiasm; despair, complacency, and presumption) or show the distinctive contributions of different means of grace to growth in the Christian life.

At the end of his essay on "John Wesley and the Means of Grace" (*The Drew Gateway*, 56:3, Spring, 1986), Kenneth J. Collins notes how the means of grace can be "undervalued or even repudiated" or "overvalued, considered as ends in themselves instead of means to a deeper piety" (p.30). In identifying these as the "two principle pitfalls in relating the means of grace to the Christian life," Collins describes the same dangers I identify as enthusiasm and formalism. However, he does not then show how the means of grace, through their pattern of interrelationship, counter these and other dangers to the Christian life.

David Trickett's excellent essay on "Spiritual Vision and Discipline in the Early Wesleyan Movement" (in *Christian Spirituality III*, ed. Louis Dupre, John Meyendorff, and Don E. Saliers, New York: Crossroads, 1989) is an especially good discussion of the Methodist societies, classes, and bands and their relation to instituted means of grace. While not framing his discussion in terms of dangers to be avoided, Trickett expresses well how means of grace provide a context for Christian growth and serve as means to a grace-initiated, cooperative relationship with God.

I have approached the means of grace somewhat differently than these in that I have argued for a pattern of relationship between and within means of grace and described the dynamics of that pattern. By seeing how means of grace enable us to attend to God's presence through active love and repentance, and convey God's identity through remembrance and promise, we come to understand not only Wesley's rich context for Christian growth, but gain a clearer perspective on the nature of that growth.

CHAPTER II: THE MEANS TO THE
CHRISTIAN LIFE

1. The Religion of the Heart (pages 16–29)

1. "Scriptural Christianity" (iv/1), *Works* 1:172–73.

2. *Ibid.* (iv/3), p. 174.

3. *Ibid.* (iv/7), p. 176.

4. *Ibid.* (iv/10), p. 179.

5. *Ibid.* (iv/7), p. 176.

6. "Journal," (Aug. 24, 1744), *Works* (TJ) I:250.

7. "Journal" (Nov. 25, 1739), *Works* (TJ) I:250; cf. *Works* 1:131–37; 2:51–52; 26:177, 200–201; *Works* (TJ) VII: 263.

8. "The Way to the Kingdom" (i/1–6), *Works* 1:218–21.

9. "The Almost Christian" (i/10–11), *Works* 1:136.

10. "Journal" (Nov. 25, 1744), *Works* (TJ) I:250; cf. *Works* 1:132–34.

11. "An Earnest Appeal to Men of Reason and Religion" (2), *Works* 11:45.

12. *Ibid.,* cf. *Works* 1:222; *Works* (TJ) VII:236, 269.

13. *Ibid.* (3–4), pp. 45–46; cf. *Works* (TJ) X:67–71; *Notes*, Philip. 1:10–11.

14. "The Way to the Kingdom" (i/12), *Works* 1:224; cf. *Works* 2:431; 3:97-100; *Works* (TJ) VII:267. Gregory Scott Clapper explores Wesley's understanding of the affections in detail in "John Wesley on Religious Affections: His Views on Experience and Emotion and Their Role in the Christian Life and Theology" (Ph.D. dissertation, Emory University, 1985; Metuchen, N.J.: Scarecrow Press, 1989).

15. "A Farther Appeal to Men of Reason and Religion," Part I (i/3), *Works* 11:106; cf. *Works* 1:121; 26:155; *Notes*, Eph. 2:8.

16. "Earnest Appeal" (9), *Works* 11:47–48; cf. pp. 107–8.

17. "Farther Appeal," I (i/3), *Works* 11:106; cf. p. 55; *Works* (TJ) VIII:363; X:73.

18. "Earnest Appeal," (29), *Works* 11:55.

19. "Farther Appeal," II (iii/21), *Works* 11:268.

20. "Original Sin" (ii/3), *Works* 2:177; cf. 1:119.

21. "The Way to the Kingdom" (ii/10), *Works* 1:230; cf. p. 120; 3:496–97; 26:157; *Works* (TJ) VIII:363; IX:103; X:73.

22. *Ibid.;* cf. *Works* (TJ) VII:326.

23. "The Scripture Way of Salvation" (ii/2), *Works* 2:161; cf. *Works* 1:121, 405; *Works* (TJ) VIII:363; X:73.

24. "Salvation by Faith" (i/4), *Works* 1:120.

25. "The Scripture Way of Salvation" (ii/1), *Works* 2:160–61; cf. 2:368–69; 3:492; 26:155; *Works* (TJ) X:73.

26. "Earnest Appeal" (7), *Works* 11:46–47; cf. 1:433–35; 2:177; *Works* (TJ) VII:349–54. Rex Matthews discusses this "transcendental epistemology" in detail in " 'Religion and Reason Joined': A Study in the Theology of John Wesley" (Th.D. dissertation, Harvard University, 1986).

27. In a book published after the completion of this manuscript, W. Stephen Gunter evaluates the criticism of Wesley by his contemporaries that he is an enthusiast and an antinomian. See *The Limits of "Love Divine"* (Nashville: Abingdon Press, 1989).

28. "Earnest Appeal" (31), p. 56; cf. *Works* 2:587–600.

29. "Farther Appeal" I (v/27), *Works* 11:170.

30. "The Nature of Enthusiasm" (12), *Works* 2:50.

31. *Ibid.,* (13–32), p. 50–58.

32. "An Answer to the Rev. Mr. Church's Remarks" (iii/6), *Works* (TJ) VIII:408; cf. IX:103.

33. "Farther Appeal," I (v/2), *Works* 11:140; cf. p. 108.

34. "Farther Appeal," II (iii/9), *Works* 11:258–59.

35. "On Faith" (i/10–12), *Works* 3:497–98.

36. "Original Sin" (iii/1), *Works* 2:182–83.

37. "On Perfection" (ii/9), *Works* 3:79; cf. *Works* (TJ) VII:347.

38. "On Working Out Our Own Salvation" (ii/1), *Works* 3:203–4.

39. *Ibid.* (iii/4), p. 207; cf. *Works* 3:481–84.

40. *Ibid.*

41. "The Scripture Way of Salvation" (i/2), *Works* 2: 156–57.

42. "The Great Privilege of Those That are Born of God" (i/6), *Works* 1:434.

43. *Ibid.* (i/7).

44. "On Faith" (i/10–11), *Works* 3:497.

2. Against Formalism: The Faith That *Works* by Love (pages 29–35)

1. "Farther Appeal" I (iii/4), *Works* 11:121.

2. *Ibid.*, pp. 122–23.

3. *Ibid.*

4. *Ibid.*, p. 122.

5. *Ibid.;* cf. *Works* 1:379, 381–82; *Works* (TJ) X:365–66.

6. "Letter to John Smith" (June 25, 1746) (8), *Works* 26:201.

7. "Farther Appeal" III (i/2), *Works* 11: 273.

8. "On the Discoveries of Faith" (4), *Works* (TJ) VII: 232.

9. "The Marks of the New Birth" (iv/5), *Works* 1:430.

10. "Farther Appeal" II (iii/5), *Works* 11:254–55; cf. *Works* (TJ) X:187.

11. "Letter to Miss Bishop" (October 18, 1778), *Works* (TJ) XIII:36.

12. "Farther Appeal" II (iii/7), *Works* 11:256–7.

13. *Ibid.* (iii/6), p. 256.

14. *Ibid.* (iii/10), p. 259.

15. *Ibid.*

16. "On Dissipation" (12), *Works* 3:120; cf. *Works* 3: 523–24; *Works* (TJ) X:74; XI:524–26.

17. "Walking by Sight and Walking by Faith" (20), *Works* 4:58.

18. "On Dissipation" (6–8), *Works* 3:118–19; cf. *Works* 3: 103–14.

19. *Ibid.* (8), p. 119.

20. *Ibid.* (10), p. 120; cf. *Works* 1:441.

21. *Ibid.* (14), p. 121.

22. *Ibid.* (16), p. 122; cf. *Works* 1:442; 3:204–5.

23. *Ibid.* (19), pp. 123–24.

24. "Farther Appeal" I (iii/4), *Works* 11:122.

25. "The Means of Grace" (v/2), *Works* 1:394–95.

26. "An Answer to the Rev. Mr. Church's Remarks" (iii/1), *Works* (TJ) VIII:404; "Journal" (June 27, 1740), *Works* (TJ) I:279; cf. *Works* 1:381; *Works* (TJ) X:149.

27. "On Dissipation" (17), *Works* 3:122–23.

28. *Ibid.* (19), p. 123.

29. *Ibid.* (20), p. 124.

30. "A Letter to a Person Lately Joined with the People Called Quakers" (11), *Works* (TJ) X:182–83.

31. "The Means of Grace" (i/4), *Works* 1:379; cf. pp. 381–82.

3. Against Enthusiasm: The Traditional Means of Grace (pages 36–49)

1. "Journal" (Dec. 31, 1739), *Works* (TJ) I:257–58; cf. pp. 275–76, 328–29; *Works* 26:56–57; Gunter, *Limits,* pp. 83–103.

2. *Ibid.,* pp. 256–57; cf. pp. 275, 328.

3. *Ibid.* (June 22, 1740), p. 276.

4. *Ibid.* (Sept. 3, 1741), p. 330; cf.p. 307; *Works* 1: 532.

5. For example see "Journal," *Works* (TJ) I:247, 248, 255.

6. "Farther Appeal" I (v/28), *Works* 11:171–72; cf. *Notes,* Acts 10:38.

7. "The Means of Grace" (iv/3), *Works* 1:391.

8. "Journal" (Sept. 3, 1741), *Works* (TJ) I:328; cf. *Works* 1:390.

9. *Ibid.,* p. 329; cf. p. 247.

10. *Ibid.* (May 1, 1741), p. 307; cf. *Works* (TJ) XI: 431.

11. "The Means of Grace" (iv/3), *Works* 1:391.

12. *Ibid.* (v/4), p. 396.

13. *Ibid.* (iv/1), pp. 390–91.

14. "Journal" (Sept. 3, 1741), *Works* (TJ) I:328.

15. *Ibid.* (June 29, 1740), p. 280.

16. *Ibid.* (June 15, 1741), p. 315; cf. *Works* 3:505. Wesley misunderstood Luther, reading him in light of his controversy with the Moravians See Jerry L. Walls, "John Wesley's Critique of Martin Luther," *Methodist History,* 30:1 (October, 1981), pp. 29–41.

17. *Ibid.* (Sept. 3, 1741), pp. 330–31; cf. pp. 334–35; *Works* 26:57.

18. "The Means of Grace" (iv/6), *Works* 1:393.

19. "Journal" (Nov. 15, 1739), *Works* (TJ) I:249.

20. "A Plain Account of Christian Perfection" (19), *Works* (TJ) XI:402–3; cf. pp. 383, 429; VIII:364; XIV:328.

21. "The Great Privilege of Those That are Born of God" (i/8), *Works* 1:434; cf. p. 442.

22. *Ibid.* (iii/3), p.442; cf. *Works* 3:206–9.

23. "On Working Out Our Own Salvation" (ii/4), *Works* 3:205.

24. "Large Minutes" (Q. 34), *Works* (TJ) VIII:316.

25. "The Nature of Enthusiasm" (14), *Works* 2:51.

26. For examples see "Journal," *Works* (TJ) I:172, 307.

27. "The Nature of Enthusiasm" (19), *Works* 2:53.

28. *Ibid.* (19–21), pp. 53–54; cf. *Works* 2:515.

29. *Ibid.* (21), p. 54; cf. *Works* (TJ) VIII:284.

30. *Ibid.* (22–25), pp. 54–55; cf. *Works* (TJ) X:178, 181; *Notes,* Acts 18:5, I Jn. 4:1.

31. *Ibid.* (23–24), pp. 54–55.

32. I Thes. 2:17, *Notes.*

33. "The Nature of Enthusiasm" (27), *Works* 2:56.

34. *Ibid.* (39), pp. 59–60; cf. *Works* 11:418; *Notes,* Mt. 3:16, I Tim. 4:13.

35. "Large Minutes" (Q. 34), *Works* (TJ) VIII:316.

36. "A Plain Account of Christian Perfection" (Q. 33), *Works* (TJ) XI:429.

37. "The Means of Grace" (v/4), *Works* 1:396.

38. *Ibid.* (iii), pp. 384–90; cf. *Works* 3:428–33; *Works* (TJ) I:248, 278–80.

CHAPTER III: THE ENDS OF THE CHRISTIAN LIFE

1. The Heart Perfected in Love (pages 50–62)

1. Timothy L. Smith, "George Whitefield and Wesleyan Perfectionism," *Wesleyan Theological Journal,* 19:1 (Spring, 1984), p. 64.

2. *Ibid.,* p. 65.

3. *Ibid.,* p. 66.

4. *Ibid.,* p. 69.

5. *Ibid.,* pp. 70–71.

6. *Ibid.,* p. 71.

7. *Ibid.,* p. 72.

8. *Ibid.*

9. Albert C. Outler, "Introduction to Part Three," in Outler, ed., *John Wesley,* (New York: Oxford University Press, 1964), p. 350.

10. Smith, "Whitefield," pp.71–72; cf. *Works* (TJ), XI:481–82.   See also Gunter, *Limits,* pp. 227–266.

11. Albert C. Outler, "Editor's Introduction to the Menace of Antinomianism," in *John Wesley*, p. 377; cf. *Works* (TJ) XI:431.

12. "Journal," *Works* (TJ) I:308, 315–16, 326–27, 330–31, 333–34; cf. X:201–4.

13. "A Short History of Methodism" (12), *Works* (TJ) VIII:349–50.

14. "The Lord Our Righteousness" (ii/19), *Works* 1:462; cf. *Works* (TJ) X:366–69; Gunter, *Limits*, pp. 104–117.

15. *Ibid.* (ii/20), pp. 463–65; "Thoughts on the Imputed Righteousness of Christ" (13–14), *Works* (TJ) X:315; "Some Remarks on Mr. Hill's 'Farrago Double–Distilled' " (iii/27), *Works* (TJ) X:430; cf. *Works* (TJ) X:318, 328–35.

16. "The Lord Our Righteousness" (ii/17–18), *Works* 1:46–162; "Predestination Calmly Considered" (90), *Works* (TJ) X:258–59; "A Dialogue Between an Antinomian and His Friend," *Works* (TJ) X:272–75.

17. "A Second Dialogue Between an Antinomian and His Friend," *Works* (TJ) X:278.

18. "A Dialogue," pp. 266–67.

19. John Deschner, *Wesley's Christology: An Interpretation* (Dallas: Southern Methodist University Press, 1960), pp. 73, 81.

20. "A Dialogue," pp. 272–76.

21. "The Lord Our Righteousness" (ii/12–13), *Works* 1:458–59; cf. *Works* (TJ) VIII:284–85; X:254.

22. Theodore Runyon, "Introduction: Wesley and the Theologies of Liberation," in Runyon, ed., *Sanctification and Liberation* (Nashville: Abingdon Press, 1981), p. 27.

23. Clarence Luther Bence, "John Wesley's Teleological Hermeneutic" (Ph.D. dissertation, Emory University, 1981), p. 37.

24. "Journal" (Sept. 13, 1739), *Works* I:225.

25. "Upon our Lord's Sermon on the Mount, II" (ii/6), *Works* 1:498.

26. Bence, "Teleological," p. 38; cf. Runyon "Liberation," p. 28.

27. Albert C. Outler, "Introduction," in *Works* 1:75.

28. "The General Spread of the Gospel" (11), *Works* 2:489.

29. Deschner, *Christology*, pp. 154–57; cf. *Works* (TJ) X:386.

30. "Thoughts on the Imputed Righteousness of Christ" (14), *Works* (TJ) X:315.

31. Deschner, *Christology*, p. 154.

32. *Ibid.,* p. 105.

33. *Ibid.,* pp. 27, 61.

34. *Ibid.,* p. 38.

35. *Ibid.,* p. 105.

36. *Ibid.,* p. 106.

37. *Ibid.,* p. 107.

38. *Ibid.,* pp. 181–83.

39 "On Working Out Our Own Salvation" (iii/7), *Works* 3:208.

40. "Christian Perfection" (ii/24), *Works* 2:118. This "unfinished" and "ongoing" aspect of Wesley's Christology has certain affinities with that of Jurgen Moltmann. For both, the work of Christ continues in the present through the power of the Spirit. In addition, Wesley's linkage of eschatology with the present work of the Spirit, which will be discussed in section 2, is similar to Moltmann's approach. In the future, I plan to give full attention to these doctrinal interrelationships in Wesley and in the process to further compare his theology with that of Moltmann.

41. "On Working Out Our Own Salvation" (2), *Works* 3:200.

42. "Christian Perfection (iii/1), *Works* 2:105.

43. "A Plain Account of Christian Perfection" (27), *Works* (TJ) XI:444; cf. *Works* 3:74–75; *Works* (TJ) I:225; III:369.

44. *Ibid.*

45. See, for examples, *Works* 2:491; 3:96–97, 201; *Works* (TJ) X:364, 369; XI:384.

46. J. Blake Neff, "John Wesley and John Fletcher on Entire Sanctification: A Metaphoric Cluster Analysis" (Ph.D. dissertation, Bowling Green State University,1982).

47. Donald W. Dayton has shown the significance of such a shift from a christological to pneumatological language, with an attendant increase in the language of power, for the nineteenth century Holiness movement. Dayton argues that this shift in language sowed the seeds for the Pentecostal movement, and shifted the focus of the Holiness movement from growth in love to an experience of power. See his *Theological Roots of Pentecostalism* (Grand Rapids: Zondervan, 1987; Metuchen, N.J.: Scarecrow Press, 1987) for a detailed account. Shorter versions of his argument can be found in "Asa Mahan and the Development of American Holiness Theology," *Wesleyan Theological Journal,* 9 (Spring, 1974) pp. 60–69, and "From Christian Perfection to the 'Baptism of the Holy Ghost,'" in *Aspects of Pentecostal-Charismatic Origins,* Vinson Synan, ed., (Plainfield, N.J.: Logos International, 1975) pp. 39–54.

48. "On Perfection" (i/5), *Works* 3:74.

49. Deschner, *Christology,* pp. 59–60.

50. "A Letter to the Reverend Dr. Conyers Middleton" (vi/ii/1–5), *Works* (TJ) X:72–73.

2. Against Antinomianism: The Promise of New Creation (pages 62–78)

1. Wesley's opposition to predestination was fixed at an early age. In a letter to his mother in 1725 he argued that it was inconsistent with divine justice and mercy, "a contradiction of the

210 The Presence of God in the Christian Life

clearest ideas we have of the divine nature and perfections." See his
"Letter to Mrs. Susanna Wesley" (July 29, 1725), *Works* 25:175.

2. "Predestination Calmly Considered" (86), *Works* (TJ) X:256.

3. *Ibid.* (88) p. 258.

4. "The Question, 'What is an Arminian?' Answered" (10),
Works (TJ) X:360.

5. "Thoughts Upon God's Sovereignty," *Works* (TJ) X:362; cf.
Works 2:417–18, 488–89; *Works* (TJ) X:233–34, 298, 372–74.

6. "Some Remarks on 'A Defence of the Preface to the Ed-
inburgh Edition of Aspasio Vindicated' " (2), *Works* (TJ) X:348.

7. "Thoughts Upon Necessity" (iii/1), *Works* (TJ) X:463; cf.
Works (TJ) X:260–66, 372–74, 459.

8. "Thoughts Upon God's Sovereignty," *Works* (TJ) X:361.

9. *Ibid.,* p. 362; cf. *Works* (TJ) X:220–21, 235.

10. *Ibid.,* p. 363.

11. "Predestination Calmly Considered" (49), *Works* (TJ) X:231.

12. "Thoughts Upon Necessity" (iv/5), *Works* (TJ) X:474.

13. "On the Omnipresence of God" (ii/1), *Works* (TJ) VII:240.

14. "Predestination Calmly Considered" (23), *Works* (TJ) X:217.

15. I Jn. 4:8, *Notes.*

16. "Predestination Calmly Considered" (42), *Works* (TJ) X:227;
cf. pp. 234–35.

17. *Ibid.* (59), p. 238.

18. "Serious Thoughts Upon the Perseverance of the Saints"
(14), *Works* (TJ) X:290.

19. *Ibid.* (15), p. 290; cf. *Works* (TJ) X:238–39.

20. "A Letter to the Reverend Dr. Conyers Middleton" (vi/5), *Works* (TJ) X:68.

21. "A Dialogue Between a Predestinarian and His Friend," *Works* (TJ) X:260; cf. *Works* (TJ) X:459.

22. "Predestination Calmly Considered" (37), *Works* (TJ) X:223.

23. "On the Wedding Garment" (10), *Works* 4:144.

24. Bence, "Teleological," p. 226.

25. "On Predestination" (4), *Works* 2:416.

26. *Ibid.* (11), p. 419.

27. *Ibid.* (15), p. 420.

28. "On Eternity" (4), *Works* 2:360.

29. "On Predestination" (5), *Works* 2:416–17.

30. Harold Lindstrom, *Wesley and Sanctification* (Nashville: Abingdon Press, 1946), pp. 99, 172.

31. *Ibid.,* p. 174.

32. Deschner, *Christology,* p. 138.

33. *Ibid.,* pp. 19–23.

34. *Ibid.,* p. 9.

35. Theodore Runyon, "What Is Methodism's Theological Contribution Today?" in Runyon, ed., *Wesleyan Theology Today* (Nashville: Kingswood Books, 1985), p. 11; cf. Bence, "Teleological," pp. 245–47.

36. Theodore Runyon, "System and Method in Wesley's Theology," n.d.: unpublished paper read at the American Academy of Religion, New York, 1982, p. 1; cf. Runyon, "Contribution," p. 8–9; Bence, "Teleological," p. 20.

37. Runyon, "Liberation," pp. 10–11; cf. Bence, "Teleological," pp. 164–171; Williams, *Today*, p. 194.

38. Mt. 3:2, *Notes;* cf. *Works* 1:224–25, 481; 2:111; *Works* (TJ) VII:267; XII:388.

39. II Cor. 12:4, *Notes;* cf. Lk. 23:43; *Works* (TJ) VII:332; XIII:138.

40. II Cor. 1:22, *Notes.*

41. Rom. 5:5, *Notes.*

42. "Doctrinal Minutes" (June 25, 1744), *Works* (TJ) VIII:276.

43. "On Eternity" (16), *Works* 2:367–68; cf. *Works* 11:73.

44. *Ibid.* (17), pp. 368–69.

45. "The New Creation" (18), *Works* 2:510; cf. pp. 469–70, 488.

46. Deschner, *Christology,* pp. 127–29; Bence, "Teleological," p. 234; cf. *Notes,* Mt. 5:3, Lk. 11:52, Jn. 3:3, James 1:17, I Jn. 5:11.

47. "Upon Our Lord's Sermon on the Mount, VI" (iii/8), *Works,* 1:581–82.

48. "The Scripture Way of Salvation" (iii/14), *Works* 2:167; cf. p. 160.

49. "The Repentance of Believers" (i/20), *Works* 1:346–47; cf. *Works* (TJ) VIII:329.

50. "A Plain Account of Christian Perfection" (26), *Works* (TJ) XI:442.

51. Runyon, "System," p. 3; cf. Runyon, "Liberation," p. 10.

52. *Ibid.,* p. 4; Runyon, "Contribution," pp. 10–11; Bence, "Teleological," pp. 192 ff.

53. Mt. 3:2, *Notes.*

54. "The General Spread of the Gospel" (20), *Works* 2:494–95; cf. pp. 454–55; Runyon, "System," pp. 10–11.

55. "The Mystery of Iniquity" (27), *Works* 2:462–63.

56. "The General Deliverance" (iii/3), *Works* 2:446; "The New Creation" (16), *Works* 2:508.

57. Runyon, "System," p. 2.

58. "The General Deliverance" (iii/1), *Works* 2:445.

59. "On Eternity" (7), *Works* 2:361–63; "The New Creation" (10), *Works* 2:504.

60. Bence, "Teleological," p. 229.

61. "Farther Appeal" I (i/3), *Works* 11:106.

62. "On the Fall of Man" (ii/10), *Works* 2:411–12; cf. *Notes,* Rom. 5:20.

63. Bence, "Teleological," pp. 5–6, 79–81.

64. *Ibid.,* p. 89; cf. *Works* 2:482.

65. "God's Love to Fallen Man" (ii/15), *Works* 2:434.

66. *Ibid.* (4), p. 424.

67. *Ibid.* (i/1), pp. 425–26.

68. "On the Fall of Man" (ii/10), *Works* 2:411.

69. "God's Love to Fallen Man" (i/2–4), *Works* 2:426–27.

70. *Ibid.* (i/5), p. 428.

71. *Ibid.* (i/6–9), pp. 428–31.

72. Bence, "Teleological," pp. 19–20; cf. pp. 3–4, 106, 270.

73. *Ibid.,* p. 7.

74. *Ibid.*, pp. 7, 15, 103, 106.

75. "Doctrinal Minutes" (Aug. 2, 1745), *Works* (TJ), VIII:286.

76. "Satan's Devices" (i/3), *Works* 2:142.

77. "Large Minutes" (Q. 56), *Works* (TJ), VIII:329.

78. Runyon, "Liberation," p.10.

79. "The Circumcision of the Heart" (i/9), *Works* 1:406.

80. "Christian Perfection" (i/9), *Works* 2:104–5; cf. *Works* 3:204; *Works* (TJ), XI:402, 426, 451; *Notes,* Lk. 2:52, I Pet. 1:22.

81. "On Faith" (Hebrews 11:1) (6), *Works* 4:192; and (11), 4:195–7.

82. "A Plain Account of Christian Perfection" (19), *Works* (TJ), XI:402; and (25), XI:426.

83. "On Faith" (Hebrews 11:6) (ii/5), *Works* 3:501.

3. Against Perfectionism: A Continual Reliance on Christ (pages 78–91)

1. Stanley Ayling, *John Wesley* (Cleveland: Collins, 1979), p. 134. Ayling implies Maxfield was the first of Wesley's lay preachers. Gunter, however, notes that two or three others served as lay preachers for Wesley prior to Maxfield, but Maxfield was the first Lay Assistant or "Son in the Gospel" who remained with him for a lengthy period of time (*Limits,* pp.162–163).

2. *Ibid.*, p. 210.

3. *Ibid.*, pp. 210–11; cf. *Works* (TJ), III:125; VIII:350.

4. "Letter to Charles Wesley" (Jan. 5, 1762), *Works* (TJ), XII:122.

5. "Journal" (April 23, 1763), *Works* (TJ) III:130–32.

6. *Ibid.* (Jan. 1, 1763), p. 125.

7. *Ibid.* (Aug. 21, 1762), p. 111; (Jan. 7, 1763), p. 125; (Jan. 17, 1763), p. 126–28.

8. For example, "Some Remarks on Mr. Hill's 'Review of All the Doctrines Taught by Mr. John Wesley' " (28), *Works* (TJ) X:409; "Some Remarks on Mr. Hill's 'Farrago Double-Distilled' " (19), *Works* (TJ) X:423–24; cf. Gunter, *Limits,* pp. 202–226.

9. "Journal" (Oct. 29, 1762), *Works* (TJ) III:119–20.

10. cf., *Ibid.* (Feb. 4, 1763), p. 127.

11. cf., *Ibid.* (Apr. 15, 1765), p. 207.

12. cf., *Ibid.* (Aug. 27, 1768), p.341.

13. "Letter to Miss Bolton" (Dec. 5, 1772), *Works* (TJ) XII:481.

14. Bence, "Teleological," pp. 252–60.

15. *Ibid.,* p. 7; cf. pp. 20, 254.

16. "The End of Christ's Coming" (iii/3), *Works* 2:482; cf. pp. 508–10.

17. "A Plain Account of Christian Perfection" (15), *Works* (TJ) XI:383; cf. *Works* (TJ) VIII:364.

18. *Ibid.* (13), pp. 379–80.

19. "Christian Perfection" (i/1), *Works* 2:100–101; cf. *Works* (TJ) XI:374, 396, 442.

20. "On Perfection" (i/1), *Works* 3:72.

21. "A Plain Account of Christian Perfection" (25), *Works* (TJ) XI:419.

22. *Ibid.,* p. 417; cf. *Works* 3:73–74; *Works* (TJ) X:327; XI:394–95; XII:257.

23. *Ibid.* (19), p. 395.

24. *Ibid.*, p. 396.

25. *Ibid.*, pp. 396–97.

26. Bence, "Teleological," p. 184.

27. Albert L. Truesdale, "Christian Holiness and the Problem of Systemic Evil," *Wesleyan Theological Journal,* 19:1 (Spring, 1984), pp. 53–54.

28. William Hasker, "Holiness and Systemic Evil: A Response to Albert Truesdale," *Wesleyan Theological Journal,* 19:1 (Spring, 1984), p. 62.

29. "Christian Perfection" (i/8), *Works* 2:104; cf. *Works* (TJ) XI:374, 419.

30. "A Plain Account of Christian Perfection" (25), *Works* (TJ) XI:427.

31. *Ibid.*, pp. 429–31.

32. *Ibid.*, p. 428.

33. *Ibid.*, pp. 427–28.

34. *Ibid.* (19), p. 395.

35. *Ibid.*, pp. 395–96.

36. *Ibid.* (25), p. 417.

37. *Ibid.*

38. *Ibid.* (19), p. 396; cf. pp. 417–19.

39. *Ibid.* (25), p. 418.

40. *Ibid.* (19), p. 395; (25), p. 419; cf. *Works* (TJ) X:327.

41. *Ibid.* (19), p. 395.

42. "The Repentance of Believers" (i/1), *Works* 1:336.

43. *Ibid.* (i/16), pp. 344–45; cf. *Works* 1:240.

44. "The Scripture Way of Salvation" (iii/6), *Works* 2:164–65.

45. "The Repentance of Believers" (i/17), *Works* 1:345.

46. *Ibid.* (i/2–10), pp. 336–41; cf. *Works* 1:239, 245–46.

47. "The Scripture Way of Salvation" (iii/6), *Works* 2:164–65.

48. "The First Fruits of the Spirit" (iii/2), *Works* 1:244.

49. "The Repentance of Believers" (i/14), *Works* 1:343–44; cf. *Works* 2:215.

50. "The Wilderness State" (iii/5), *Works* 2:216–17.

51. "The Repentance of Believers" (i/11–13), *Works* 1:341–42; cf. pp. 240–41; *Works* 2:165–66.

CHAPTER IV: THE MEANS TO THE PRESENCE OF GOD

1. Remaining in the Church: *Ecclesiola in Ecclesia* (pages 92–95)

1. "Large Minutes" (Q.3), *Works* (TJ) VIII:299; cf. *Works* 3:511.

2. "Thoughts Upon a Late Phenomenon" (7), *Works* (TJ) XIII:266.

3. "On Schism" (10–11), *Works* 3:64.

4. *Ibid.* (17), pp. 66–67

5. *Ibid.* (11), p. 64.

6. "Reasons Against a Separation From the Church of England" (3), *Works* 9:338; cf. *Works* 3:477–78.

7. "Large Minutes" (Q.45), *Works* (TJ) VIII:321.

8. "On God's Vineyard" (7), *Works* 3:511.

9. "Large Minutes" (Q.45), *Works* (TJ) VIII:321–22.

10. "Reasons Against a Separation" (3), *Works* 9:339; cf. *Works* (TJ) VIII:442.

11. "A Plain Account of the People Called Methodist" (v), *Works* 9:265–6.

12. David Lowes Watson, *The Early Methodist Class Meeting* (Nashville: Discipleship Resources, 1985), pp. 126–27; cf. 6–7.

13. *Ibid.*, p. 128.

2. Discipline in Community: Classes and Bands (pages 95–116)

1. "A Plain Account of the People Called Methodist" (i/4–5), *Works* 9:255–6.

2. *Ibid.* (i/7).

3. *Ibid.* (i/9), pp. 257–8.

4. *Ibid.* (i/10), p. 258.

5. Watson, *Class Meeting,* pp. 107–08, 122, 151–52.

6. "A Plain Account of the People Called Methodist" (ii/1–2), *Works* 9:260. The society meetings became occasions for preaching, teaching, and hymn singing. David Michael Henderson, in "John Wesley's Instructional Groups" (Ph.D. dissertation, Indiana University, 1980), sees their function as providing doctrinal information and motivation; through "cognitive instruction it was the educational channel by which the tenets of Methodism were presented to the target population"(p. 105). I generally agree, but am cautious about the cognitive language. Henderson is himself aware that "impassioned preaching and fervent singing" provide an "affective dimension" to instruction; the "major aim," however, "was to present scriptural truth and have it clearly understood"(p.

129). Henderson distinguishes between cognitive and affective, passion and clear understanding in a way that I do not find helpful. Often passion is essential and intrinsic to the clear understanding of a teaching, such as to love God or to love our neighbor.

7. *Ibid.* (ii/3–4), pp. 260–1; cf.528–9; *Works* (TJ) I:357, 364.

8. "On God's Vineyard" (iii/1), *Works* 3:511–12.

9. "General Rules of the United Societies," *Works* 9:69–73. Thus I agree with David Henderson that the central function of the class meeting was nurture and growth by way of modifying outward behavior ("Instructional," pp. 134–135).

10. William B. Lewis, "The Methodist Class Meeting: Its Conduct and Nature," in Samuel Emerick, ed., *Spiritual Renewal for Methodism* (Nashville: Methodist Evangelistic Materials, 1958), pp. 24–25.

11. "A Plain Account of the People Called Methodist" (ii/6–7), *Works* 9:261–2.

12. *Ibid.* (ii/8), p. 262.

13. *Ibid.* (ii/5), p. 261; cf. p. 70.

14. Watson, *Class Meeting,* p. 97.

15. *Ibid.,* p. 115.

16. "Large Minutes" (Q.11), *Works* (TJ) VIII:301.

17. Watson, *Class Meeting,* p. 109.

18. "A Plain Account of the People Called Methodist" (vi/1), *Works* 9:266.

19. *Ibid.* (vi/2), p. 266–7.

20. *Ibid.* (vi/3), p. 267.

21. Watson, *Class Meeting,* pp. 83, 95.

22. "Rules of the Band-Societies," *Works* 9:77; cf. 267, 529. Henderson describes the bands as facilitating "affective re-direction" ("Instructional," p. 163). This is an apt description. But on the same page he comments "It could be said metaphorically that the society aimed for the head, the class meeting for the hands, and the band for the heart." Again, I am uneasy with too sharp a distinction between reason, action, and affections, seeing them instead as essentially interrelated. In a fundamental sense, *all* of Wesley's groups were aimed at the heart.

23. "Directions Given to the Band-Societies," *Works* 9:79.

24. "A Plain Account of the People Called Methodist" (vi/6), *Works* 9:268.

25. *Ibid.* (vii/1–2), pp. 268–9.

26. *Ibid.* (viii/1), p. 269.

27. *Ibid.* (viii/2), pp. 269–70.

28. *Ibid.* (viii/3), p. 270. In the text in Albert Outler's *John Wesley* (p. 144), this passage continues with the words "till we can have all things common."

29. *Ibid.* (viii/4). I agree with Henderson that the group experience in the Select Society provided "a standard of excellence for all other groups within the system" ("Instructional," p. 181). However, while the Select Societies consisted of the Methodist leadership, I am not convinced that their central purpose was leadership training (*Ibid.*, p. 179).

30. "The Mystery of Iniquity" (10), *Works* 2:455; cf. p. 494.

31. "General Rules," *Works* 9:69–73.

32. *Ibid.* (1,4), pp. 69–70; cf. p. 256–7.

33. "Upon Our Lord's Sermon on the Mount, XI" (iii/5–6), *Works* 1:673–74.

34. "General Rules," *Works* 9:73.

35. "A Plain Account of the People Called Methodist" (iv/3), *Works* 9:265; cf. p. 307; *Works* 3:512.

36. "Journal" (Mar. 9–11, 1747), *Works* (TJ) II:48; cf. VIII:279.

37. "General Rules" (4), *Works* 9:70.

38. *Ibid.,* pp.70–1; cf. p.79; *Works* (TJ) VIII:302.

39. *Ibid.,* pp. 71–2; cf. 79; *Works* 1:528.

40. *Ibid.,* pp. 71; cf. 79.

41. Albert Outler, in *Works* 1:617, note 42; 2:263–65.

42. "Upon Our Lord's Sermon on the Mount, VIII" (22), *Works* 1:626; cf. pp. 528, 548; 2:263–80; 3:227–46, 518–30; *Works* (TJ) VII:355–62.

43. *Ibid.* (18–21), pp.623–26.

44. *Ibid.* (26), p. 629.

45. "Large Minutes" (Q.13), *Works* (TJ) VIII:302.

46. "Rules of the Band-Societies," *Works* 9:78.

47. Watson, *Class Meeting,* p. 116.

48. Howard Snyder, "John Wesley: Hope in Action," *The Other Side,* 74 (November, 1977), p. 53.

49. "Upon Our Lord's Sermon on the Mount, III" (iii/6), *Works* 1:525.

50. *Ibid.* (iii/8), p. 526.

51. "General Rules" (5), *Works* 9:72.

52. *Ibid.* (4), p. 71.

53. "The Repentance of Believers" (i/11), *Works* 1:341–42; cf. *Works* (TJ) VIII:323.

54. Albert Outler, "An Introductory Comment" to "The Cure of Evil-Speaking," *Works* 2:251.

55. "The Cure of Evil-Speaking" (4), *Works* 2:253–54.

56. *Ibid.* (3), p. 253.

57. *Ibid.* (i/1–2), pp. 255–56.

58. "Upon Our Lord's Sermon on the Mount, III" (ii/4), *Works* 1:518; cf. p. 534.

59. "Upon Our Lord's Sermon on the Mount, IV" (4), *Works* 1:533.

60. "Upon Our Lord's Sermon on the Mount, VI" (i/1), *Works* 1:573; cf. pp. 519–20; 3:389–92; *Works* (TJ) VIII:271.

61. "On Visiting the Sick" (i/3), *Works* 3:387–88.

62. "Directions Given to the Band-Societies" (ii/3), *Works* 9:79; cf. p. 72.

63. "Thoughts Upon Methodism" (9), *Works* 9:529.

64. *Ibid.* (11), p. 530.

65. "Directions" (ii/1), *Works* 9:79.

66. "Upon Our Lord's Sermon on the Mount, IV" (i/6), *Works* 1:536.

67. *Ibid.* (i/3), p. 534.

68. "Letter From Thomas Willis" (Nov. 13, 1744), *Works* 26:116.

69. *Ibid.*

70. *Ibid.*, pp. 117–118.

71. *Ibid.*, p. 118.

3. Prayer and Fasting (pages 116–122)

1. "Letter to Miss March" (Mar. 29, 1760), *The Letters of the Rev. John Wesley, A.M.,* ed. John Telford (London: The Epworth Press, 1931), 4:90.

2. "The Character of a Methodist" (8), *Works* 9:37; cf. *Notes,* Eph. 6:18.

3. I Thes. 5:16, *Notes.*

4. "The Means of Grace" (iii/6), *Works* 1:386.

5. *Ibid.* (v/1), p. 394.

6. *Ibid.* (iii/2), p. 385.

7. "Upon Our Lord's Sermon on the Mount, VI" (ii/1), *Works* 1:575.

8. "Letter to Miss Bishop" (Sept. 19, 1773), *Works* (TJ) XIII:25.

9. "The Means of Grace" (iii/1–3), *Works* 1:384–85; cf. p. 659; *Works* (TJ) I:278–79; XIII:32.

10. "Upon Our Lord's Sermon on the Mount, VI" (ii/5), *Works* 1:577.

11. Mt. 6:8, *Notes.*

12. "Upon Our Lord's Sermon on the Mount, X" (18), *Works* 1:659.

13. "The Wilderness State" (ii/4), *Works* 2:209.

14. I Thes. 5:16, *Notes;* cf. Philip. 4:6; *Works* (TJ) VIII:342.

15. "The More Excellent Way" (ii), *Works* 3:267–68.

16. Steve Harper, *Devotional Life in the Wesleyan Tradition* (Nashville: The Upper Room, 1983), p.20.

17. "Large Minutes" (Q.34), *Works* (TJ) VIII:316; cf. VII:288–89; XI:323; XIII:19.

18. *Ibid.;* cf. *Works* (TJ) VII:288.

19. "Upon Our Lord's Sermon on the Mount, VII" (i/1–5), *Works* 1:594–96.

20. *Ibid.* (ii), pp. 597–604.

21. *Ibid.* (ii/6), p. 600.

22. *Ibid.* (ii/1–2), pp. 597–98.

23. *Ibid.* (ii/4), pp. 599–600.

4. The General Means of Grace (pages 122–126)

1. "General Rules" (4–5), *Works* 9:70–72.

2. "Large Minutes" (Q.48), *Works* (TJ) VIII:323.

3. *Ibid.,* p. 324.

4. II Tim. 4:5, *Notes.*

5. "Large Minutes" (Q.48), *Works* (TJ), VIII:323; cf. XI:427–28.

6. Eph. 6:18, *Notes.*

7. "Large Minutes" (Q.48), *Works* (TJ) VIII:324.

8. "Self–Denial" (2), *Works* 2:238–39.

9. *Ibid.* (i/6), p. 243; cf. *Works* (TJ) VIII:323–24; XIV:271; *Notes,* Mk. 8:34; II Pet. 1:6.

10. "Causes of the Inefficacy of Christianity" (16), *Works* 4:95; cf. p. 94.

11. "On Riches" (9), *Works* 3:527.

12. "Self-Denial" (i/7), *Works* 2:243; cf. *Works* (TJ) VIII:324; XIII:29; *Notes,* Mk. 8:34.

13. *Ibid.* (i/11), p. 244.

14. "Letter to Miss Bishop" (June 7, 1744), *Works* (TJ) XIII:28–29.

15. "Self-Denial" (ii/2–5), *Works* 2:246–47.

CHAPTER V: THE MEANS TO THE IDENTITY OF GOD

1. Renewing the Church: Experienced Identity (pages 127–130)

1. "Upon Our Lord's Sermon on the Mount, IV" (iii/6), *Works* 1:545.

2. "Letter to Miss Bishop" (Feb. 16, 1771), *Works* (TJ) XIII:20.

3. "Upon Our Lord's Sermon on the Mount, III" (i/8), *Works* 1:514.

4. "The Spirit of Bondage and of Adoption" (iii/3), *Works* 1:261.

2. The Lord's Supper (pages 130–148)

1. "Hymns on the Lord's Supper," Hymn 42, in J. Ernest Rattenbury, *The Eucharistic Hymns of John and Charles Wesley* (London: The Epworth Press, 1948) (hereafter cited as Rattenbury), p. 208; cf. Hymn 54; "The Christian Sacrament and Sacrifice, Extracted from Dr. Brevint" (iv/6), in Rattenbury, p. 183.

2. Borgen, *Sacraments,* p. 51.

3. *Ibid.,* p. 53.

4. *Ibid.,* p. 57.

5. Hymn 57, Rattenbury, p. 213; cf. Hymn 71.

6. Borgen, *Sacraments,* p. 69; cf. p. 54.

7. *Ibid.,* p. 74.

8. Hymn 58, Rattenbury, p. 213; cf. Hymns 11, 60, 77, 80, 82, 86.

9. Borgen, *Sacraments,* p. 75.

10. *Ibid.,* p. 211.

11. "Brevint" (i/1), Rattenbury, p. 176.

12. Hymn 18, Rattenbury, p. 200; cf. Hymns 4, 5, 21, 22.

13. Hymn 37, Rattenbury, p. 207; cf. Hymns 38, 46, 74, 75, 76; Borgen, *Sacraments,* pp. 191–92.

14. Hymn 83, Rattenbury, p. 220.

15. Hymn 49, Rattenbury, p. 210; cf. Hymns 47, 48, 50, 51.

16. Hymn 40, Rattenbury, p. 208.

17. Borgen, *Sacraments,* p. 212; cf. pp. 202–03.

18. Hymn 62, Rattenbury, p. 215.

19. "The Means of Grace" (v/4), *Works* 1:395. In his sermon "The Duty of Constant Communion" (ii/19) Wesley asks, "But suppose a man has often been at the sacrament, and yet received no benefit. Was it not his own fault? Either he was not rightly prepared, willing to receive all the promises of God; or he did not receive it aright, trusting in God. Only see that you are duly prepared for it, and the oftener you come to the Lord's table the greater benefit you will find there" (*Works* 3:438).

20. *Ibid.* (ii/1), p. 381.

21. "Brevint" (i/1), Rattenbury, p. 176.

22. *Ibid.* (ii/1), p. 176.

23. *Ibid.* (ii/8), p. 178.

24. Hymn 94, Rattenbury, p. 225.

25. Hymn 111, Rattenbury, p. 236.

26. "Brevint" (iv/5), Rattenbury, p. 183; cf. pp. 181–82.

27. *Ibid.* (iv/7).

28. *Ibid.*

29. *Ibid.* (iv/5).

30. Hymn 30, Rattenbury, p. 205; cf. Hymns 57, 58, 64.

31. Borgen, *Sacraments,* p. 88.

32. "Brevint" (ii/5), Rattenbury, p. 177; cf. (ii/2).

33. *Ibid.* (ii/4); cf. (ii/3).

34. Hymn 8, Rattenbury, p. 197; cf. Hymns 3, 5, 16, 22, 25, 33, 74.

35. Hymn 16, Rattenbury, p. 200.

36. "Brevint" (ii/7), Rattenbury, p. 178; cf. (ii/9).

37. Borgen, *Sacraments,* p. 91.

38. Hymn 18, Rattenbury, p. 200; cf. Hymn 21.

39. Hymn 23, Rattenbury, p. 202; cf. Hymn 6; *Notes,* I Cor. 11:24.

40. "Brevint" (ii/8), Rattenbury, p. 178.

41. Hymn 45, Rattenbury, p. 209; cf. Hymns 5, 6, 18, 21, 24.

42. "Brevint" (v/4), Rattenbury, p. 185; cf. (v/7); *Notes,* Mt. 26:26.

43. *Ibid.*

44. *Ibid.* (v/1).

45. Borgen, *Sacraments,* p. 219.

46. Hymn 93, Rattenbury, p. 225; cf. Hymns 99, 111, 112, 114.

47. Hymn 101, Rattenbury, p. 227; cf. Hymn 103.

48. Hymn 96:1, 3, Rattenbury, p. 225; cf. Hymns 94, 101, 103, 158, 164.

49. Hymn 40:1, Rattenbury, p. 208.

50. Hymn 106, Rattenbury, p. 228.

51. "Brevint" (i/1), Rattenbury, p. 176.

52. *Ibid.* (vi/2), p. 187; cf. *Notes,* I Cor. 11:26.

53. Hymn 120, Rattenbury, p. 233; cf. Hymns 116, 119, 121–126.

54. Hymn 117, Rattenbury, p. 222; cf. Hymns 118, 140.

55. "Brevint" (vii/1), Rattenbury, p. 188; cf. Hymns 128, 131, 136, 147.

56. *Ibid.* (vii/10), p. 190; cf. (vii/8).

57. *Ibid.* (vii/5), p. 189.

58. Hymn 130, Rattenbury, p. 236; cf. Hymns 128, 142.

59. "Brevint" (vii/5), Rattenbury, p. 189; cf. Hymns 131, 132, 143, 146, 149, 154.

60. *Ibid.* (vii/4), p. 188; cf. (vii/3).

61. Hymn 133, Rattenbury, p. 238; cf. Hymns 151, 152; "Brevint" (vii/7).

62. *Ibid.*

63. *Ibid.*

64. "Brevint" (viii), Rattenbury, pp. 192–93.

65. Hymn 155, Rattenbury, p. 244; cf. Hymns 153, 157.

66. Albert Outler, comments in footnote 9, "The Duty of Constant Communion," *Works* 3:431.

67. "The Duty of Constant Communion" (ii/1) *Works* 3:431.

3. Searching the Scriptures (pages 148–159)

1. "Preface, Sermons on Several Occasions" (5), *Works* 1:105.

2. Albert Outler, "Introduction," *Works* 1:57.

3. Albert Outler, "The Wesleyan Quadrilateral in Wesley," *Wesleyan Theological Journal*, 20:1 (Spring, 1985), p. 9; cf. Donald Dayton, "The Use of Scripture in the Wesleyan Tradition," in Robert K. Johnston, ed., *The Use of the Bible in Theology* (Atlanta: John Knox Press, 1985), pp. 135–36.

4. Gerald R. Cragg, "Introduction" to "A Farther Appeal to Men of Reason and Religion," *Works* 11:100.

5. Outler, "Introduction," *Works* 1:57.

6. Col. 3:16, *Notes.*

7. *Ibid.*

8. Dayton, "The Use of Scripture," in Johnston, p. 131.

9. *Ibid.*, p. 133.

10. "Journal" (June 26, 1740), *Works* (TJ) I:279.

11. "The Means of Grace" (iii/8), *Works* 1:388: cf. *Notes,* II Tim. 3:16.

12. *Ibid.* (iii/7), p. 387; cf. *Works* (TJ) VIII:323.

13. Borgen, *Sacraments,* pp. 116–17.

14. "Large Minutes" (Q.48), *Works* (TJ) VIII:323.

15. "Preface, Notes on the Old Testament," (18), *Works* (TJ) XIV:253.

16. *Ibid.*

17. *Ibid.;* cf. XIV:247; Rom. 12:16, *Notes;* Outler, "Introduction," *Works* 1:1, 57; Outler, "Quadrilateral," pp. 12–13.

18. "Preface, Sermons on Several Occasions" (5), *Works* 1:106.

19. "Preface, Notes on the Old Testament," (18), *Works* (TJ) XIV:253.

20. "Preface, Sermons on Several Occasions" (5), *Works* 1:106.

21. "Preface, Notes on the Old Testament," (17), *Works* (TJ) XIV:252.

22. *Ibid.* (18), p. 253.

23. *Ibid.*

24. Outler, "Quadrilateral," p. 12; cf. *Notes,* Rom. 12:16.

25. "A Letter to the Reverend Doctor Conyers Middleton Occasioned by His Late 'Free Inquiry' " (vi/II/1), *Works* (TJ) X:72.

26. "On Laying the Foundation of the New Chapel" (ii/2), *Works* 3:585.

27. "Letter to Middleton" (vi/II/2), *Works* (TJ) X:72.

28. *Ibid.* (vi/II/3).

29. "Journal" (June 4, 1738), *Works* (TJ) I:105–06; cf. p. 103.

30. "On Divine Providence" (4), *Works* 2:536.

31. "The End of Christ's Coming" (iii/5), *Works* 2:483; cf. p. 536.

The "analogy of faith" is a theological development of Romans 12:6, where Paul says one should prophesy "in proportion to" one's faith or "according to the analogy of faith." Its basic theological meaning is hermeneutical: an obscure text "may be illumined by other texts of scripture whose meaning is clear." Augustine extended the principle further, arguing that any interpretation of scripture which is contrary to the universally accepted rule of faith as summarized in the Apostles' Creed must be questioned (Bruce A. Demarest, "Analogy of Faith," in Walter A. Elwell, ed., *Evangelical Dictionary of Theology,* Grand Rapids: Baker Book House, 1984).

Wesley interprets Paul's injunction to prophesy according to the analogy of faith as "according to the general tenor" of scripture; "according to that grand scheme of doctrine which is delivered therein, touching original sin, justification by faith, and present, inward salvation. There is a wonderful analogy between all these; and a close connexion between the chief heads of that faith 'which was once delivered to the saints.' Every article therefore concerning which there is any question should be determined by this rule; every doubtful scripture interpreted according to the grand truths which run through the whole" (Romans 12:6, *Notes*).

32. "Letter to Middleton" (vi/II/3–4), *Works* (TJ) X:72–73; cf. Outler, "Introduction," *Works* 1:58; Timothy L. Smith, "John Wesley and the Wholeness of Scripture," *Interpretation,* 39:3 (July, 1985), pp. 253, 255.

33. *Ibid.* (vi/II/5), p. 73.

34. Outler, "Quadrilateral," pp. 12–13.

35. Smith, "Wholeness," p.262.

36. "Large Minutes" (Q.48), *Works* (TJ) VIII:323.

37. *Ibid.* (Q.36), p. 317.

38. "Doctrinal Minutes" (Aug. 2, 1745, Q.15), *Works* (TJ) VIII:283–84; "The Means of Grace" (v/1–2), *Works* 1:394; cf. *Works* 11:122–23.

39. "Letter to Miss Bishop" (Oct. 18, 1778), *Works* (TJ) XIII:36; cf. p. 230.

40. "Letter to Charles Wesley" (Nov. 4, 1772), *Works* (TJ) XII:140.

41. "Large Minutes" (Q.38), *Works* (TJ) VIII:318.

42. *Ibid.;* cf. p. 284; *Works* 2:25, 37–38.

43. "Letter on Preaching Christ," *Works* (TJ) XI:491.

44. "A Blow at the Root" (10), *Works* (TJ) X:369.

45. "Doctrinal Minutes" (June 17, 1747, Q.16), *Works* (TJ) VIII:297.

46. "Letter on Preaching Christ," *Works* (TJ) XI:487.

4. Tradition, Prayers, and Hymns (pages 159–167)

1. "Preface, A Christian Library," (9), *Works* (TJ) XIV:222.

2. *Ibid.* (10).

3. *Ibid.* (9).

4. *Ibid.;* cf. *Works* (TJ) X:381–82, 418–22.

5. Robert C. Monk, *John Wesley: His Puritan Heritage* (Nashville: Abingdon Press, 1966), pp. 245–46, 255–64.

6. "Large Minutes" (Q.29), *Works* (TJ) VIII:314.

7. "Journal" (May 13, 1754), *Works* (TJ) II:312.

8. "Reasons Against a Separation from the Church of England" (3), *Works* 9:339; cf. *Works* (TJ) XIII:36.

9. James F. White, "Introduction," in *John Wesley's Sunday Service of the Methodists in North America* (Nashville: The United Methodist Publishing House, 1984).

10. "Preface, The Sunday Service of the Methodists in North America," *Works* (TJ) XIV:304.

11. *Ibid.*

12. White, "Introduction," in *Sunday Service,* p. 18.

13. *Ibid.,* summarizing the conclusions of William N. Wade, "A History of Public Worship in the Methodist Episcopal Church and Methodist Episcopal Church, South from 1784 to 1905" (Ph.D. dissertation, University of Notre Dame, 1981), pp. 52–76.

14. *Ibid.,* pp. 18–19.

15. *Ibid.,* p. 26.

16. Frederick C. Gill, ed., *John Wesley's Prayers* (London: The Epworth Press, 1951), pp. 10–11; cf. *Works* (TJ) XI:203–37.

17. *Ibid.,* p. 12; cf. *Works* (TJ) XI:237–72.

18. *Ibid.,* pp. 12–13.

19. "Preface, A Collection of Hymns for the Use of the People called Methodists" (4), *Works* 7:73–74.

20. *Ibid.* (5), p. 74.

21. "Letter to Miss Bishop" (Apr. 17, 1776), *Works* (TJ) XIII:30.

22. "Preface, A Collection of Hymns" (8), *Works* 7:75.

23. "The Contents, A Collection of Hymns," *Works* 7:77–78.

24. "Preface, A Collection of Hymns," *Works* (4) 7:74.

25. Craig B. Gallaway, "The Presence of Christ With the Worshipping Community: A Study in the Hymns of John and Charles Wesley" (Ph.D. dissertation, Emory University, 1988). Gallaway argues that the hymns contain a full range of christological imagery (the *totus Christus*) which are embedded in the different elements of Wesley's soteriology. Remembrance and hope in worship is given shape by the identity of Christ and is a response to the presence of Christ. He has thus discovered in the hymns a pattern of identity and presence much like that which I am presenting for the means of grace as a whole.

26. Hymn 184:1, *Works* 7:311.

27. Hymn 374:1, *Works* 7:545.

28. Hymn 6:1, *Works* 7:86.

29. Hymn 27:1, *Works* 7:114.

30. *Ibid.*, 27:3.

CHAPTER VI: THE MEANS OF GRACE AND THE CHRISTIAN LIFE

2. Baptism and the Christian Life: An Excursus (pages 178–191)

1. Borgen, *Sacraments,* pp. 122, 176.

2. "The New Birth" (iv/2), *Works* 2:197; cf. Bernard Holland, *Baptism in Early Methodism* (London: Epworth Press, 1970), pp. 63, 66, 73.

3. *Ibid.* (iv/4), p. 199; cf. Holland, *Baptism,* pp. 71, 73.

4. Holland, *Baptism,* pp. 56–59.

5. *Ibid.,* p. 73.

6. "A Treatise on Baptism" (ii/4), *Works* (TJ) X:192; cf. Borgen, *Sacraments,* pp. 157–59, 173, 176, 179–81.

7. Borgen, *Sacraments,* p. 167.

8. *Ibid.,* p. 166.

9. *Ibid.,* p. 180.

10. *Ibid.,* pp. 155, 159, 169.

11. *Ibid.,* p. 128.

12. *Ibid.,* p. 159.

13. *Ibid.,* p. 128.; cf. *Works* 26:425.

14. "The Marks of the New Birth" (iv/2), *Works* 1:428.

15. John Berntsen, "Christian Affections and the Catechumenate," *Worship,* 50 (1978), pp. 194–210.

16. "A Plain Account of the People Called Methodist" (i/10), *Works* 9:258.

17. "Journal" (Oct. 16, 1756), *Works* (TJ) II:387.

18. *Ibid.* (Oct. 1, 1758), p. 459.

19. *Ibid.* (Feb. 5, 1760), p. 523; cf. Hymns 464, 465, *Works* 7:646–48.

20. "A Farther Appeal to Men of Reason and Religion," I (i/5), *Works* 11:107; "The New Birth" (iv/2), *Works* 2:197.

21. "Journal" (Feb. 25, 1739), *Works* (TJ) I:172.

22. "Letter to the Revd. Gilbert Boyce" (May 22, 1750), *Works* 26:425.

23. Acts 10:47, *Notes;* cf. "Journal" (Apr. 15, 1745), *Works* (TJ) I:490.

24. "A Treatise on Baptism" (ii/5), *Works* (TJ) X:192.

25. Borgen, *Sacraments,* p. 167. For a thorough discussion of these issues see David I. Naglee, *From Font to Faith: John Wesley on Infant Baptism and the Nurture of Children* (New York: Peter Lang, 1987).

26. "Journal" (Apr. 11, 1756), *Works* (TJ), II:360–61.

27. "Large Minutes" (Q.13), *Works* (TJ) VIII:305.

28. "Serious Thoughts Concerning Godfathers and Godmothers" (7), *Works* (TJ) X:508; cf. XIII:476.

29. *Ibid.* (8).

30. "Large Minutes" (Q.33), *Works* (TJ) VIII:316.

31. White, "Introduction," in *Sunday Service*, p. 29.

32. "The New Birth" (iv/4), *Works* 2:199.

33. *Ibid.*, p. 200.

34. Borgen, *Sacraments*, pp. 220–21.

35. See, for example, "Journal," *Works* (TJ), II:80, 338–39, 346, 361, 396–397, 438–39, 454, 525.

36. David Tripp, *The Renewal of the Covenant in the Methodist Tradition* (London: Epworth Press, 1969), p. 2.

37. *Ibid.*, p. 56.

38. *Ibid.*, p. 153.

39. "Directions for Renewing Our Covenant with God" (v), in Tripp, *Renewal*, p. 184.

40. *Ibid.*

41. Tripp, *Renewal*, p. 112.

42. White, "Introduction," *Sunday Service*, p. 29.

3. The Presence of God in the Christian Life (pages 191–196)

1. Melvin E. Dieter, "The Development of Holiness Theology in Nineteenth Century America," *Wesleyan Theological Journal*, 20:1 (Spring, 1985), pp. 61–77.

2. Donald W. Dayton, "Pneumatological Issues in the Holiness Movement," in Theodore Stylianopoulos and Mark Heim, eds.,

Spirit of Truth: Ecumenical Perspectives on the Holy Spirit (Brookline, Mass.: Holy Cross Orthodox Press, 1986), pp. 131–157. A detailed discussion is found in his *Theological Roots of Pentecostalism* (Grand Rapids: Zondervan, 1987; Metuchen, N.J.: Scarecrow Press, 1987).

3. Theodore Runyon, "A New Look at 'Experience,'" *Drew Gateway* (Fall, 1987), pp. 44–55.

Selected Bibliography

I. PRIMARY SOURCES

Explanatory Notes upon the New Testament (Grand Rapids: Book House, 1981). Reprinted from an undated edition published by the Wesleyan-Methodist Book-Room, London.

Gill, Frederick C., ed. *John Wesley's Prayers* (London: The Epworth Press, 1951).

John Wesley's Sunday Service of the Methodists in North America (Nashville: United Methodist Publishing House, 1984), with an introduction by James F. White.

The Letters of the Rev. John Wesley, M.A., ed. John Telford (London: The Epworth Press, 1931).

Outler, Albert, ed. *John Wesley* (New York: Oxford University Press, 1964).

Rattenbury, J. Ernest, *The Eucharistic Hymns of John and Charles Wesley* (London: The Epworth Press, 1948).

The Works of John Wesley, gen. ed. Frank Baker.

Published by Abingdon Press, Nashville:
Vol. 1: Sermons I (1984, ed. Albert C. Outler).
Vol. 2: Sermons II (1985, ed. Albert C. Outler).
Vol. 3: Sermons III (1986, ed. Albert C. Outler).
Vol. 4: Sermons IV (1987, ed. Albert C. Outler).
Vol. 9: The Methodist Societies (1989, ed. Rupert E. Davies).
Vol. 18: Journals and Diaries I (1988, ed. W. Reginald Ward and Richard P. Heitzenrater).

Published by Oxford University Press, New York:
Vol. 7: A Collection of Hymns (1983, ed. Franz Hilderbrandt and Oliver A. Beckerlegge with the assistance of James Dale).

Vol. 11: The Appeals to Men of Reason and Religion (1975, ed. Gerald R. Cragg).

Vol. 25: Letters I (1980, ed. Frank Baker).

Vol. 26: Letters II (1982, ed. Frank Baker).

The Works of the Rev. John Wesley, M.A., ed. Thomas Jackson, 14 vols. (London: Mason, 1829–1831; reprinted by Baker Book House, Grand Rapids, 1978).

II. SECONDARY SOURCES: BOOKS AND DISSERTATIONS

Ayling, Stanley. *John Wesley* (Cleveland: Collins, 1979).

Bence, Clarence Luther. "John Wesley's Teleological Hermeneutic" (Ph.D. dissertation, Emory University, 1981).

Borgen, Ole E. *John Wesley on the Sacraments* (Nashville: Abingdon Press, 1972).

Clapper, Gregory Scott. "John Wesley on Religious Affections: His Views on Experience and Emotion and Their Role in the Christian Life and Theology" (Ph.D. dissertation, Emory University, 1985; Metuchen, NJ: Scarecrow Press, 1989).

Dayton, Donald W. *Theological Roots of Pentecostalism* (Grand Rapids: Zondervan, 1987; Metuchen, NJ: Scarecrow Press, 1987).

Deschner, John. *Wesley's Christology: An Interpretation* (Dallas: Southern Methodist University Press, 1960).

Emerick, Samuel, ed. *Spiritual Renewal for Methodism* (Nashville: Methodist Evangelistic Materials, 1958).

Gallaway, Craig B. "The Presence of Christ With the Worshipping Community: A Study in the Hymns of John and Charles Wesley" (Ph.D. dissertation, Emory University, 1988).

Gunter, W. Stephen. *The Limits of "Love Divine"* (Nashville: Abingdon Press, 1989).

Harper, Steve. *Devotional Life in the Wesleyan Tradition* (Nashville: The Upper Room, 1983).

Henderson, David Michael. "John Wesley's Instructional Groups" (Ph.D. dissertation, Indiana University, 1980).

Holland, Bernard. *Baptism in Early Methodism* (London: The Epworth Press, 1970).

Lindstrom, Harold. *Wesley and Sanctification* (Nashville: Abingdon Press, 1946).

Matthews, Rex Dale. " 'Religion and Reason Joined': A Study in the Theology of John Wesley" (Th.D. dissertation, Harvard University, 1986).

Monk, Robert C. *John Wesley: His Puritan Heritage* (Nashville: Abingdon Press, 1966).

Naglee, David I. *From Font to Faith: John Wesley on Infant Baptism and the Nurture of Children* (New York: Peter Lang, 1987).

Neff, J. Blake. "John Wesley and John Fletcher on Entire Sanctification: A Metaphoric Cluster Analysis" (Ph.D. dissertation, Bowling Green State University, 1982).

Rowe, Kenneth E., ed. *The Place of Wesley in the Christian Tradition* (Metuchen, NJ: Scarecrow Press, 1976).

Runyon, Theodore, ed. *Sanctification and Liberation* (Nashville: Abingdon Press, 1981).

————, ed. *Wesleyan Theology Today* (Nashville: Kingswood Books, 1985).

Snyder, Howard A. *The Radical Wesley* (Downers Grove, IL: Intervarsity Press, 1980).

Tripp, David. *The Renewal of the Covenant in the Methodist Tradition* (London: The Epworth Press, 1969).

Watson, David Lowes. *The Early Methodist Class Meeting* (Nashville: Discipleship Resources, 1985).

Williams, Colin. *John Wesley's Theology Today* (Nashville: Abingdon Press, 1960).

III. SECONDARY SOURCES: ARTICLES AND ESSAYS

Berntsen, John. "Christian Affections and the Catechumenate." *Worship* 50 (1978), 194–210.

Collins, Kenneth J. "John Wesley and the Means of Grace." *The Drew Gateway* 56:3 (Spring, 1986) 26–33.

Dayton, Donald. "Asa Mahan and the Development of American Holiness Theology." *Wesleyan Theological Journal* 9 (Spring, 1974) 60–69.

―――. "From Christian Perfection to the 'Baptism of the Holy Ghost.'" In *Aspects of Pentecostal–Charismatic Origins,* Vinson Synan, ed. (Plainfield, NJ: Logos International, 1975) 39–54.

―――. "Pneumatological Issues in the Holiness Movement." In *Spirit of Truth: Ecumenical Perspectives on the Holy Spirit,* Theodore Stylianopoulos and Mark Heim, eds. (Brookline, MA: Holy Cross Orthodox Press, 1986) 131–157.

―――. "The Use of Scripture in the Wesleyan Tradition." In *The Use of the Bible in Theology: Evangelical Options,* Robert K. Johnston, ed. (Atlanta: John Knox, 1985).

Demarest, Bruce A. "Analogy of Faith." In *Evangelical Dictionary of Theology,* Walter A. Elwell, ed. (Grand Rapids: Baker Book House, 1984).

Dieter, Melvin E. "The Development of Holiness Theology in Nineteenth Century America." *Wesleyan Theological Journal* 20:1 (Spring, 1985) 61–77.

Hasker, William. "Holiness and Systemic Evil: A Response to Albert Truesdale." *Wesleyan Theological Journal* 19:1 (Spring, 1984) 60–62.

Matthews, Rex. "Reason, Faith, and Experience in the Thought of John Wesley." Unpublished (1982).

―――. "With the Eyes of Faith: Spiritual Experience and the Knowledge of God in the Theology of John Wesley." In *Wesleyan*

Theology Today, Theodore Runyon, ed. (Nashville: Kingswood Books, 1985).

Outler, Albert. "The Wesleyan Quadrilateral in Wesley." *Wesleyan Theological Journal* 20:1 (Spring, 1985) 7–18.

Runyon, Theodore. "A New Look at 'Experience.' " *The Drew Gateway* (Fall, 1987) 44–55.

———. "System and Method in Wesley's Theology." Unpublished paper read at the American Academy of Religion, New York, 1982.

Smith, Timothy L. "George Whitefield and Wesleyan Perfectionism." *Wesleyan Theological Journal* 19:1 (Spring, 1984) 63–85.

———. "John Wesley and the Wholeness of Scripture." *Interpretation* 39:3 (July, 1985) 246–62.

Snyder, Howard. "John Wesley: Hope in Action." *The Other Side* 74 (November, 1977) 52–55.

Trickett, David. "Spiritual Vision and Discipline in the Early Wesleyan Movement." In *Christian Sprituality III*, Louis Dupre, John Meyendorff, and Don E. Saliers, eds. (New York: Crossroads, 1989).

Truesdale, Albert L. "Christian Holiness and the Problem of Systemic Evil." *Wesleyan Theological Journal* 19:1 (Spring, 1984) 39–59.

Walls, Jerry L. "John Wesley's Critique of Martin Luther." *Methodist History* 30:1 (October, 1981) 29–41.

Index

About the Author

Henry H. Knight III (B.A., Emory University; M.Div., Candler School of Theology; Ph.D., Emory University, Atlanta, GA) is Adjunct Lecturer at the Candler School of Theology, where he teaches Methodist Studies and Systematic Theology. In addition, he teaches Wesleyan theology and Methodist history in the United Methodist Course of Study School at Candler and in the Appalachian Lay Pastors School. Dr. Knight has served as a pastor in the United Methodist Church and continues to serve as a part-time associate pastor. He has published several articles on Wesley's theology in professional journals.